THE SENSIBLE SPIRIT

THE SENSIBLE SPIRIT

WALTER PATER AND THE MODERNIST PARADIGM

───

BY

F. C. McGRATH

UNIVERSITY PRESSES OF FLORIDA

UNIVERSITY OF SOUTH FLORIDA PRESS / TAMPA

University Presses of Florida
University of South Florida Press
© 1986 by the Board of Regents of the State of Florida
Printed in the U.S.A. on acid-free paper ∞

Library of Congress Cataloging-in-Publication Data

McGrath, F. C. (Francis Charles)
    The sensible spirit.

    Bibliography: p.
    Includes index.
    1. Pater, Walter, 1839–1894—Philosophy.
2. Philosophy in literature.   3. Modernism (Literature)
4. Empiricism.   5. Idealism.   I. Title.
PR5138.P5M34   1986   824'.8   85-29503
ISBN 0-8130-0829-8

UNIVERSITY PRESSES OF FLORIDA is the central agency for scholarly publishing of the State of Florida's university system, producing books selected for publication by the faculty editorial committees of Florida's nine public universities: Florida A&M University (Tallahassee), Florida Atlantic University (Boca Raton), Florida International University (Miami), Florida State University (Tallahassee), University of Central Florida (Orlando), University of Florida (Gainesville), University of North Florida (Jacksonville), University of South Florida (Tampa), University of West Florida (Pensacola).

ORDERS for books published by all member presses of University Presses of Florida should be addressed to University Presses of Florida, 15 NW 15th Street, Gainesville, FL 32603.

FOR

BARBARA

CONTENTS

ACKNOWLEDGMENTS

CONTRARY TO popular opinion, scholarly books are not produced by solitary researchers. They require as much cooperative effort as any corporate enterprise. An author can do little without the collective knowledge, advice, and assistance of other people and institutions. While many may believe that publishing a book inflates the individual ego, an author actually has more reason to be humble than to be proud.

My own debts begin with the many scholars who have preceded me and whose work has provided the foundations on which I have built. In addition to these past scholars of Pater and of Modernism, this book has benefited substantially from the generous criticism, counsel, and encouragement of scholars and colleagues who read my typescript or portions of it at various stages. They include David J. DeLaura, Nancy Gish, Billie A. Inman, A. Walton Litz, Timothy P. Martin, Gerald Monsman, Morse Peckham, Elton Smith, and Lisa Zeidner. I am especially grateful to David DeLaura for his many years of encouragement and support.

I also wish to thank my colleague John Berkey for his friendship and for his support, moral and otherwise.

The Rutgers University Faculty Academic Study Program provided me with a semester's leave in the spring of 1981 that enabled me to write a first draft of this book, and the Rutgers Research Council also provided financial support through grants in 1981 and in 1983.

ACKNOWLEDGMENTS

Permission has been granted by the *James Joyce Quarterly* to reprint the portion of my concluding chapter that appeared in the Spring 1986 issue of that journal.

I am also obliged to Thomas Noonan and his staff of the Houghton Library at Harvard University for permission to read Pater's unpublished manuscripts. I have quoted from them by permission of the Houghton Library.

For assistance in the preparation of my typescript I am grateful to Barbara Groark, Ida Levin, Anna Lorang, Rita Lorang, Betty Musetto, and Phyllis Ostroff. Jennifer Steves also provided resources that facilitated the production of the typescript.

I reserve my deepest gratitude for my wife, Barbara. She provided me with the tolerance, love, and moral support necessary to sustain a long-term research project. Her contribution to this book, however, substantially exceeded her role as faithful companion and wife. She inspired and encouraged me from the beginning to enlarge the scope of my original plan and, as my critic-in-residence, she read and commented astutely at every stage in the development of the typescript.

I also thank Elizabeth and Theo for their understanding and for the joy they bring to my life.

Abbreviations for Pater's Works

App.   *Appreciations* (London: Macmillan, 1910).

"CW"   "Coleridge's Writings," *Westminster Review* 85 (1866): 106–32.

EG   *Essays from the Guardian* (London: Macmillan, 1910).

GL   *Gaston de Latour* (London: Macmillan, 1910).

GS   *Greek Studies* (London: Macmillan, 1910).

IP   *Imaginary Portraits* (London: Macmillan, 1910).

Ltrs.   *Letters of Walter Pater*, ed. Lawrence Evans (Oxford: Clarendon, 1970).

ME 1   *Marius the Epicurean* (London: Macmillan, 1910), vol. 1.

ME 2   *Marius the Epicurean* (London: Macmillan, 1910), vol. 2.

MS   *Miscellaneous Studies* (London: Macmillan, 1910).

PP   *Plato and Platonism* (London: Macmillan, 1910).

Ren.   *The Renaissance: Studies in Art and Poetry* (London: Macmillan, 1910).

UE   *Uncollected Essays* (1903; reprint, Folcroft, Pa.: Folcroft Press, 1969).

"WM"   "Poems by William Morris," *Westminster Review* 90 (1868): 300–312.

N.B.   Wherever the source for a reference to Pater is clearly indicated in the course of the argument, only the page number is given in parentheses.

INTRODUCTION

WALTER PATER was one of the great intellectual synthesizers of the nineteenth century. With a voracious appetite for contemporary thought he read widely in the two dominant philosophic traditions of his time—British empiricism and German idealism—and he absorbed in one form or another many of the cultural and intellectual currents of the last half of the century. Consequently his texts provide an excellent cross section of his age. But in addition to being a man of his time, Pater had a taste for avant-garde thinking that made him very influential for generations to come. The Pre-Raphaelites, the aesthetes of the 1890s, and many of the early Modernist writers were profoundly affected by Pater's synthetic vision. In his *Autobiographies* Yeats said of himself and his fellow writers of the nineties, "We looked consciously to Pater for our philosophy."[1] Yeats's comment acknowledges an important role Pater played, not only for Yeats and his friends in the nineties but for Modernist writers generally; it is a role that has not yet been adequately understood or articulated.

Most of the available scholarship on Pater and the Modernists consists of traditional influence studies, including my own essays on Pater and Yeats.[2] These studies have identified a number of works by Mod-

---

1. *Autobiographies* (London: Macmillan, 1955), p. 302.
2. See the Bibliographical Appendix for a selected list of studies on Pater's influence on Modernist writers.

I

ernist writers, usually their early works, as imitative of Pater or at least influenced by him. In addition to Yeats, scholars have identified Henry James, Conrad, Joyce, Pound, T. S. Eliot, Virginia Woolf, Wallace Stevens, and others as significantly in Pater's debt, and new studies of this cultural indebtedness appear each year. Nevertheless there is still no definitive study of Pater's relationship to Modernism. Gerald Monsman comes the closest to a definitive statement when he calls Pater an "*Ur-modern*"—"a modern whose greatest contributions often lie beyond the range or compass of sources either peripheral or direct." But even Monsman hedges on the issue of Pater's centrality to Modernism: he calls him a "praeter-source" who persists in the Modernist tradition only in "unacknowledged, subliminal associations which have combined with other influences and emphases not exclusively his own."[3] What Monsman says is generally valid, but Pater was more than a mysterious, subliminal "praeter-source"; and once we step outside the limitations of a traditional influence study, we can see more precisely why Pater was often unacknowledged, how his influence merged with others, and in what manner his contribution transcended that of a peripheral or direct source.

Although Modernist writers read Pater and borrowed attitudes, ideas, and stylistic techniques from him, Pater's most important contribution to Modernist art lies not in these individual borrowings that can be identified as specifically Paterian; rather, Pater's crucial function, not only for the Modernists but for the intellectual history of post-Romantic culture generally, lies in his role as a synthesizer of some of the most important philosophic and aesthetic principles of his age, principles that were not his own exclusive property but could be found all over the cultural map of the nineteenth and early twentieth centuries. Pater's strength was his ability to synthesize the best that was thought and said into a reasonably coherent aesthetic program, a program that had a profound appeal to the Modernists.

This book is not a traditional source study, either of Pater's own sources or of Pater as a source for this or that idea, image, or technique in Modernist writing. When dealing with the features of a

---

3. "Pater and His Younger Contemporaries," *The Victorian Newsletter*, no. 48 (1975): 7.

broadly based cultural movement like Modernism, proving influence is often a tenuous affair, especially with writers like Joyce, who left us little testimony about the influences on him outside the ironic climate of his literary texts, which frequently mislead us about them.[4] Tracing individual lines of influence, then, whatever the merits of such an enterprise, is not my primary concern here.

Instead, my project is to construct from Pater's texts an intellectual paradigm that accounts for many of the distinctive features of Modernist literature. Since Modernism, like any other broad-based movement, resulted from a confluence of cultural and intellectual forces, my focus will be less on what was unique to Pater than on ideas and principles he shared with others who also could be identified as sources for the Modernists. From this perspective Pater's originality lies not in his individual ideas, temperament, or style but in the centrality and the scope of his particular synthesis. Pater's texts as a whole present a conceptual paradigm that constitutes a substantial portion of the intellectual foundations of Modernist aesthetics and that consequently elucidates many of the premises, themes, motifs, and techniques of the major Modernist texts.

The sense in which I am using the notion of paradigm resembles Thomas Kuhn's use of it in *The Structure of Scientific Revolutions*.[5] Kuhn uses the term *paradigm* in two senses, one general and abstract and the other more concrete and specific. In its broadest sense the term denotes the "strong network of commitments—conceptual, theoretical, instrumental, and methodological"—that governs the perceptions and activities of a community of practitioners. Indeed, these commitments are constitutive of those perceptions and activities, and they involve ideas, beliefs, standards, and practices within the community that shares the paradigm. Often the theoretical component is implicit in and inextricably intertwined with practice.

Kuhn's second, more specific sense of paradigm is closer to the most commonly accepted sense of the term—the recognized achievements that serve as examples that set the parameters and provide the model

---

4. See, for example, my analysis of the sources of Stephen Dedalus's aesthetics in *A Portrait of the Artist as a Young Man* in the concluding chapter below.

5. Chicago: University of Chicago Press, 1970. See especially pp. viii, 10–22, 42–51, 109–35, 174–210.

problems and solutions for a community of practitioners. These exemplary achievements often provide standards and values more effectively than theoretical articulations of the paradigm, and they can substitute very efficiently for explicit concepts, guidelines, and rules.

Although Kuhn devotes his book to the analysis of science, the historical implications of his method apply to other intellectual and cultural disciplines as well. In fact, Kuhn acknowledges that his insights derive from the historians of literature, music, the arts, political developments, and other human activities.

For Kuhn major shifts in theories, beliefs, perceptions, values, and practices in any human endeavor result not from gradual and progressive increases in our store of knowledge but from paradigm shifts that radically reorient our thinking and perceptions. Such a major paradigm shift occurred in Western thought in the late eighteenth and early nineteenth centuries, and the texts of Pater provide an exceptional opportunity to identify and articulate those theoretical and conceptual features of the paradigm that led to the Modernist revolution in the arts. My study of Pater, then, will employ primarily the more general and theoretical sense of the term *paradigm* as a shared collection of beliefs, conceptions, perspectives, and attitudes that governed the literary productions of the major Modernist writers. Although Pater's own writings could not be classified as Modernist, except marginally, in their techniques and methods, his theoretical articulation of the paradigm is one of the earliest and most comprehensive available to us.

That I focus on the more theoretical notion of paradigm in no way implies that Modernist writers were consciously implementing a theoretical program. More typically a cultural movement spreads through the influence of paradigms of the more concrete and specific sort, for example, through the influence of seminal texts like *The Waste Land* or *Ulysses*. The primary impact of concrete paradigms on actual practice, however, does not diminish the value of articulating the theoretical component.

Unlike traditional source studies, a paradigmatic approach makes no attempt to establish specific historic chains of influence, for example, by proving that Modernists took this or that idea from Pater, or that their understanding of the British and German philosophical traditions derived primarily from Pater. Paradigmatic studies focus precisely on those features of a cultural and intellectual environment that are the shared property of a generation or more.

Although this book is not a source study in the usual sense, the issue of sources is not wholly irrelevant to the project of constructing a conceptual paradigm. I am aware that my claims rest on the assumption that the major ideas of thinkers such as Hume, Kant, Schiller, and Hegel were part of the intellectual atmosphere surrounding the Modernists and that Pater was partly responsible for creating that atmosphere. I am also aware that by using the name *Pater* I point to a historic role, or rather I should say, to one of his historic roles. The role I have chosen to focus on, however, is not Pater as a source (in the ordinary sense) for the Modernists but rather Pater as one of the major formulators of the Modernist paradigm.

In contrast to the methods of traditional source studies, the paradigmatic method is at the same time a more economical and a more powerful means of studying literary history and the history of ideas. By examining the conceptual paradigm of Modernism in Pater's texts, I will be able to accomplish a number of things. First, this approach will obviate the futility of trying to prove that Pater, rather than one of many other possible sources, was responsible for the major premises that pervade Modernist writing. By using Pater to illustrate a model of a widely shared paradigm, I also can maintain both a sharply controlled focus and a broad scope of application. For example, my analysis places Pater in a somewhat different perspective than does previous scholarship, and it challenges some of the traditional views of Pater, especially those that perceive him primarily as a stylist, a priest of sensation, a formalist, or an advocate of art for art's sake. My method also demonstrates how Pater's importance to twentieth-century aesthetics lies in his role as one of the chief conduits between the philosophic origins of a new epistemology and its Modernist articulations. On a broader scale the paradigmatic method demonstrates how Modernists like Joyce are as deeply enmeshed as Pater in the major philosophical traditions of post-Romantic culture. Consequently it illuminates a particular confluence of intellectual forces common to Pater and the Modernists, a confluence that can be characterized generally as a synthesis of British empiricism and German idealism. Within this synthesis the German tradition emerges as more prominent for Pater, Joyce, and Modernism than previous scholarship has shown, especially the central role of Hegel, who remains largely neglected in Modernist studies.

Paradigmatic studies are not new to literary criticism. E. M. W. Tillyard's *The Elizabethan World Picture*, M. H. Abrams's *The Mirror and the Lamp*, and Walter Houghton's *The Victorian Frame of Mind* are only a few of the better known examples of such studies. The bewildering diversity of the international movement called Modernism, however, has discouraged attempts to identify any core of its conceptual premises. In this study of Pater I make no attempt to chart a detailed map of Modernism, but I do try to establish some useful conceptual reference points on terrain that consistently has resisted any stable scheme of orientation.

The conceptual paradigm of Modernism I construct here from Pater's texts is organized around eleven cardinal principles and constellations of corollaries clustering around each one of them. These principles, which Pater synthesized from his extensive reading in British, German, and French thought, are the subjectivity and relativity of knowledge, epistemological skepticism, the primacy of sensory experience, an observance of the Kantian limits on knowledge, aesthetic and historical idealism, a functionalist attitude toward all the products of imagination and intellect, the notion of a unified sensibility of mind, body, and feeling, an expressive orientation toward the creative process, and an ascetic devotion to aesthetic craftsmanship. Each chapter focuses on one of these cardinal principles, traces its development in Pater's texts, and suggests briefly how the principle operates in Modernist literature. In the conclusion I offer a full-scale demonstration of the operation and significance of the paradigm in Joyce's *A Portrait of the Artist as a Young Man*. I chose Joyce's *Portrait* both because it is accepted as an indisputably Modernist text and because, more than most other Modernist literary art, its irony is especially resistant to the traditional type of influence study. Almost any other major Modernist text, however, could have served my purposes.

I make no claim here for the completeness of the Modernist paradigm I construct from Pater's texts. Any piece of writing entails its exclusions; and I am well aware that, for better or worse, choosing Pater as an organizing focus excludes material necessary for a more comprehensive articulation of the paradigm. For example, other cardinal principles central to Modernist art could be associated with

Schopenhauer, Nietzsche, and Freud, writers whose texts were not assimilated into the British literary tradition through Pater. These exclusions notwithstanding, the principles I derive from Pater contribute substantially to a new understanding of both Pater and Modernism.

HELEN YOUNG pointed out long ago that in dealing with Pater's thought, one risks being swallowed up in a quagmire of contradiction and elusive reasoning.[6] Nevertheless, however imperfect Pater's attempt to unify different intellectual traditions, it was not, as T. S. Eliot claimed, "chimerical" or "blundering";[7] and if we are to understand Pater's contribution to Modernism, some reasonably firm outlines of his thought must be established. Although we may not be able to pin his protean mind, perhaps at least we can pen it within certain limits.

Pater's wide reading in the contemporary thought of his time was spurred by his need to construct a weltanschauung that, without violating the integrity of a modern mind, could adequately account for his experience of the world in general and of intellectual culture in particular. He had found untenable the well-ordered vision of reality he inherited from the eighteenth century and from the Christianity of his childhood; and he spent most of his creative energies trying to forge a satisfactory replacement. Like a Hephaestus possessed with the ideal of fusing all the metal in his shop into a single work, Pater ranged from Heraclitus to Flaubert to piece together his own philosophic/aesthetic vision.

From the tradition of Hume's empiricism Pater drew his emphasis on the primacy of sensation and the subjectivity of knowledge. Hume and his followers also encouraged in Pater an epistemological skepticism that was reinforced by his own reading of Socrates and Montaigne. Critics usually consider this empirical tradition to be the dominant strain in Pater's weltanschauung, but the influence of German idealism, though mentioned often enough, has been underestimated. By 1866, when Pater began his publishing career, he had read Goethe, Lessing, Kant, Schelling, Schiller, Fichte, Schleiermacher, and

---

6. *The Writings of Walter Pater: A Reflection of British Philosophical Opinion from 1860 to 1890* (Lancaster, Pa.: Lancaster Press, 1933), p. 7.

7. *Selected Essays* (New York: Harcourt, Brace, 1950), pp. 392–93.

Hegel, as well as Bacon, Hobbes, Locke, Berkeley, Hume, Mill, and Darwin.[8] Over the course of Pater's career Hegel influenced his thought and sensibility as much as, if not more than, Hume. Although Pater abhorred absolutes and rigid systems of all kinds and could not accept the extremes of Hegel's idealism, he accepted the phenomenological analysis of experience and the dialectical method as well as numerous other Hegelian ideas, such as the evolutionary history of intellectual culture and the notion of zeitgeist. Pater was also quite willing to abide by the strict epistemological limitations imposed by Kant's critique of reason (which reinforced his Humean notions of subjectivity and skepticism while shifting their grounds) and to assimilate a number of other notions and emphases of German idealism as they appealed to him. Pater was also assimilating German idealism from other than its primary sources—for example, through the historical critique of Scripture it spawned in the works of Renan and Baur and through Coleridge, Wordsworth, Carlyle, and Arnold.

Pater's synthesis of empiricism and idealism was part of the same emerging zeitgeist that produced the Western cultural phenomenon known as Modernism. More than a century before the radically innovative techniques commonly associated with Modernist art began to proliferate, the intellectual foundations for them were laid in the philosophies of Hume and Kant. Hume and Kant effectively shifted the focus of philosophy from issues of substance and ontology—the preoccupation with the nature of things themselves that dominated Western thought for over two thousand years—to issues of function and epistemology—the preoccupation with the nature of our perception and knowledge of things that has dominated Western thought since Kant.

This revolution in thought inaugurated by Hume and Kant constituted a paradigm shift that had a profound effect on the arts. If medieval art can be said to convey the prevailing religious conception of reality in the Middle Ages, and art from the Renaissance through the eighteenth century to convey the humanistic conception of reality that dominated those centuries, then art since the Romantic revolution

---

8. Evidence of Pater's reading is available in Billie A. Inman's *Walter Pater's Reading: A Bibliography of His Library Borrowings and Literary References, 1853–1873* (New York: Garland, 1981).

could be said to convey our modern concerns with modes of perception and conception themselves and their various forms and faculties. Rather than a spiritual vision that manifests itself in the stories, parables, figures, and icons of a religious system, or an ethical vision that manifests itself in the outward appearance, speech, and behavior of the human form, we have an epistemological vision that manifests itself in the innovative techniques of Modernist art, such as the obsession with point of view, stream of consciousness, and abstract arrangement of space, time, and mental process. The religiously inspired figures of Dante and Giotto, the full-blooded humanity of Shakespeare's and Michelangelo's characters, all give way to the psychic landscapes of Joyce and the abstract forms of Mondrian and Pollock.

As the Renaissance was the first flowering of a new vision of humanity in the arts, Modernism is the first artistic harvest of a new metaphysics with a revolutionary epistemology. In the immediate aftermath of this revolution the Romantics celebrated the new vision of humanity in their reverence for the imagination as the "human form divine"; but they did not recognize the full implications of Kant's epistemology. The Romantics mythologized the human perceptual apparatus and even endowed it at times with a transcendent existence. After midcentury, however, the transcendental elements of German philosophy were tempered by the continuing influence of the empirical tradition, and the more finite implications of Kant's epistemology, many of which Kant himself had not foreseen, were being worked out by the Oxford neo-Hegelians, such as Edward Caird, T. H. Green, Richard Nettleship, and F. H. Bradley, and later by Nietzsche, C. S. Peirce, Ernst Cassirer, and others. Rather than mythologizing the creative possibilities of our mental faculties, post-Romantic philosophers were much more interested in the various finite functions of perception and thought. More recently this interest has shifted to the preoccupation of semiotics with the structure and function of symbol systems.

Nelson Goodman offers a particularly concise overview of the "mainstream of modern philosophy" I am referring to here. According to Goodman this modern tradition

> began when Kant exchanged the structure of the world for the structure of the mind, continued when C. I. Lewis exchanged the

structure of the mind for the structure of concepts, and . . . now proceeds to exchange the structure of concepts for the structure of the several symbol systems of the sciences, philosophy, the arts, perception, and everyday discourse. The movement is from unique truth and a world fixed and found to a diversity of right and even conflicting versions or worlds in the making.[9]

Of course, this evolution can be traced from Kant through other figures as well, for example, through Hegel, Nietzsche, C. S. Peirce, Cassirer, Saussure and the Structuralists, Derrida, and Goodman himself.

Under the impetus of figures such as Pater and Nietzsche, the new epistemology infiltrated the arts and became part of the intellectual currency of the early twentieth century. Indeed, Pater's response to the intellectual environment transformed by post-Kantian thought was one of the first to cast the Romantic revolt of Western culture in terms agreeable to the Modernist sensibility. Following the lead of philosophers, particularly the British Hegelians, Pater de-Romanticized German idealism for the world of art and letters by rejecting its transcendental claims and applying its insights exclusively to the finite psychological world of individual experience. Modernist writers followed Pater in demythologizing the Romantic imagination by treating the various forms of perception and conception in a functionalist perspective.[10] By the 1920s this perspective had produced many of the

---

9. *Ways of Worldmaking* (Indianapolis: Hackett, 1978), p. x.

10. Functionalism, as I use the term in this book, refers to the post-Kantian practice of viewing all the theoretical constructions of human reason, be they philosophic, scientific, religious, mythological, historical, or aesthetic, not as representations of the substance of reality as it actually exists, but as functional hypotheses we use to comprehend our experience, hypotheses that have no authority beyond human reason and that bestow no ontological status on any of its products. A functionalist, for example, considers an idea acceptable not because it is true in any absolute sense, but because it is more useful than other ideas in organizing our understanding of the world and of experience. The functional view of metaphysics was part of the post-Kantian revolution in epistemology, and the best exposition I know of the distinction between the pre-Kantian metaphysics of substance and the post-Kantian metaphysics of function is Ernst Cassirer's *Substance and Function*, first published in German in 1910, in English in 1923, and reprinted in *Substance and Function and Einstein's Theory of Relativity* (New York: Dover, 1953). More recently Jacques Derrida has made a career of attacking metaphysics of presence, another name for philosophies of substance.

monuments of Modernist art and literature. Pater thus stands in a direct line of intellectual development between the focus of German idealism and Romanticism on the structure of the mind itself and the turn-of-the-century concern with the structure and functions of thought.

1 / Subjectivity and
the Modernist Temper

WALTER PATER'S most important contribution to the history of aesthetics was to facilitate the transition from an outward-looking metaphysics of substance to an inward-looking metaphysics of function. One major consequence of turning philosophic attention inward on the mind was a dismantling of any verifiable standard of objectivity external to the mind, either in a metaphysical realm or an empirical realm. This realization of the essential subjectivity of all knowledge, along with a concomitant skepticism and relativism, eventually resulted in the development of a number of typical Modernist literary techniques and conventions, such as the experimental obsession with point of view, unreliable narrators, stream of consciousness, ambiguity, irony, and open-ended forms. These techniques built subjectivity, relativism, and skepticism into the very structure of the Modernist literary vision.

Although subjectivity, relativism, and skepticism were not new to Western thought, Kant's epistemological revolution gave them new prominence and definition. Pater, for his part, did not advance the understanding of subjectivity in any systematic way. Like many Romantics he often failed to distinguish philosophic subjectivity, for example, of the type implied by Kant's categories of the mind, from the subjectivity of individual temperament. In early writings, such as "Winckelmann" and the "Conclusion" to *The Renaissance*, he identified the two types of subjectivity with each other and consequently merited the charge of solipsism. In his later works, however, as his understanding of German idealism deepened, he realized that a subjective philosophy need not be solipsistic, and he retreated from the total solipsism of his early work without relinquishing a prominent role for subjectivity and temperament in intellectual culture. In any case, however imperfectly or inconsistently Pater perceived the role of subjectivity in thought, he nevertheless helped propagate the new epistemology in the arts by establishing subjectivity, along with skepticism and relativity, as an authoritative and respectable aesthetic position. By endowing this cluster of philosophic assumptions with aesthetic authority, Pater prepared the way for his twentieth-century disciples to forge the innovative literary conventions to embody them.

For Pater intellectual conviction depended largely on temperament, and, like Hume, he perceived this fact to be the fundamental flaw in the pretension of all philosophy (*ME* 1:137−38).[1] Both the initial acceptance and the subsequent deployment of ideas were, according to Pater, heavily conditioned by temperament. More specifically, Pater believed, as most have come to believe in the twentieth century, that "we judge truth not by the intellect exclusively, and on reasons that can be adequately embodied in propositions; but with the whole complex man" (*PP*, 88). Consequently he held that the roots of all philosophy are "somewhere among the natural though but half-developed instincts of the human mind itself" (*PP*, 6), that the reception of ideas is really a matter of temperament and will (*ME* 1:136; *ME* 2:49, 90), and that a given philosophy, say Heraclitus's philosophy of flux, might, according to the temperament that receives it, either extinguish or kindle an interest in phenomena (*PP*, 18). In other words, faced with certain philosophical speculations, one can either accept or reject them; and if one accepts them, one can accept them with pessimism and disillusion or with optimism and hope—one can despair or one

---

1. David J. DeLaura in *Hebrew and Hellene in Victorian England: Newman, Arnold, and Pater* (Austin: University of Texas Press, 1969) shows that Newman also influenced Pater on the subjectivity of thought and belief. But, as DeLaura points out, Pater was unwilling to accept the moral and theological conclusions Newman derived from "the psychological conditions of belief" (pp. 316−21). In Montaigne, Hume, and Kant, however, Pater found rationales for subjectivity he could accept.

can resolve to make the best of it, just as the complex nature of Socrates was, as Pater notes, a source for both Cynicism and Cyrenaicism, depending on the temper of the disciple (*PP*, 87).

In his final published essay, "Pascal" (1894), Pater gives us an excellent illustration of how individual temperament works in philosophic speculation. Here he compares the responses of Montaigne and Pascal to essentially the same view of humanity. Pascal, Pater reminds us, was indebted to Montaigne's analysis of human experience (*MS*, 84–87). Montaigne's *Essays*, he says, form the "under-texture" of Pascal's *Pensées*, and Pascal accepted them as "a veritable *compte rendu* of the Satanic courses of this world since the Fall": the "paradoxical character of man and his experience"; the "relative, local, ephemeral and merely provisional character" of his standards, such as law, virtue, and happiness; the weakness of the human heart, and the "natural inconsistency of man, his strange blending of meanness with ancient greatness." In short, that "prospect of man and the *world*, undulant, capricious, inconsistent, contemptible, *lâche*, full of contradiction, with a soul of evil in things good, irreducible to law" (Pater's emphasis), is the world both Montaigne and Pascal gaze upon. Their attitudes toward it, however, the imaginative coloring each casts over the same set of circumstances, produced two radically different visions. The sanguine disposition of Montaigne takes in the whole with complacency, says Pater, and conveys a "gentle, pleasantly undulating, sunny, earthly prospect of poor lovable humanity." But under the harsh Jansenist gaze of Pascal, "under the tragic *éclairs* of divine wrath essentially implacable," with which he contemplates the depths of his own vanity and nothingness, this sunny scene becomes clouded by terror, and full of "harsh precipices, of threatening heights and depths." For Pascal it is "all or nothing"; sanctity is the only true morality; there is no middle road; and his lack of moderation leaves him, and this is perhaps Pater's severest criticism of him, "little sense of the beauty of holiness."

Wordsworth, one of the most enduring influences on Pater's sensibility and thought, figures prominently in Pater's analysis of Montaigne and Pascal. In a sense Pater has simply applied to cultural history what he learned about the emotional coloring of places and events from Wordsworth's notion of "spots of time." But Pater has elevated the central insight of the Wordsworthian "spots of time" to a philosophical level; for in his contrast between Pascal's absolutism and Montaigne's relativism Pater acknowledges two permanent dispositions in the history of thought.

This insight into the role of temperament in intellectual culture can be applied aptly to Pater's own influence on his successors. In the two generations of writers after Pater, his disciples, depending on their temperaments, tended to respond to his views in one of two ways. Either they were, like Wilde, attracted to the more negative doctrines of the flux epitomized in the "Conclusion" to *The Renaissance* and the early chapters of *Marius*, such as "Animula Vagula"; or, like Yeats, they preferred Pater's more positive yearnings to achieve through art, culture, and religion some stability amid the flux, some means of making humanity out as more than a speck in the void.[2]

Both alternatives could be found in Pater, but his own resolution leaned more toward the positive orientation of Montaigne. A philosophy of renunciation, religious or secular, could not satisfy Pater. Pascal is not his kindred spirit; rather he preferred the positive and sympathetic religious vision of Dante and the sunny skepticism of Montaigne. However much Pater may have been fascinated by the religious struggle of Pascal and his possibilities as a model for the lay religious temper he was trying to formulate for himself, he was repelled by the "perverse asceticism" of Pascal's later years. Preserving some of the "gloomy mental habits of the Middle Age," Pascal, in Pater's view, renounced the purely human disciplines and was unable to enjoy "the religion for which he had exchanged so much." Consequently he represents an inversion of the aesthetic life (*MS*, 78–81). For Pater, Wilde had also renounced too much, though in the opposite direction from Pascal;[3] and Pater considered them both to be faulty Epicurean

---

2. John Pick, in "Divergent Disciples of Walter Pater," *Thought: Fordham University Quarterly* 23 (1948): 114–28, notes both responses to Pater, as does my own "W. B. Yeats's Double Vision of Walter Pater," in *Unaging Intellect: Essays on W. B. Yeats*, ed. Kamta C. Srivastava and Ujjal Dutta (Delhi: Doaba, 1983), pp. 72–84.

3. In his review of Wilde's *Dorian Gray* Pater says, "A true Epicureanism aims at a complete though harmonious development of man's entire organism," and he criticizes Dorian and Lord Henry Wotton for lacking too much in the way of morals, hope, pleasant memories, and impressions to be true Epicureans. Wotton's cynicism particularly bothered Pater (*UE*, 127–30).

economists of life. Pater himself was, like Pascal, an advocate of ascesis; but like Montaigne he also insisted on moderation in all things.

Pater's response can be gauged even more precisely against his own assessment of the intellectual and cultural conditions he himself confronted, an assessment found in succinct form in his essay on Prosper Mérimée (1890). Here he describes the climate of disillusionment engendered by post-Kantian thought in the advanced intellects of his time. Pater opens the essay by comparing the sanguine skepticism of the eighteenth century with the disillusionment of postrevolutionary France, a disillusionment that was not confined to the political realm, for, as Pater says, "In the mental world too a great outlook had lately been cut off." "After Kant's criticism of the mind," he goes on to explain, "its pretensions to pass beyond the limits of individual experience seemed as dead as those of old French royalty. And Kant did but furnish its innermost theoretic force to a more general criticism, which had withdrawn from every department of action, underlying principles once thought eternal" (MS, 11). As a typical response to this set of intellectual circumstances Pater cites Senancour's Obermann, "the very genius of *ennui*, a Frenchman disabused even of patriotism, who has hardly strength enough to die." "The *désillusionné*," says Pater, "found in Kant's negations the last word concerning an unseen world," and discovered themselves "cut off from certain ancient natural hopes" (MS, 11–12).

As a consequence of this intellectual disillusionment, a sense of negation and theoretic insecurity were in the air, and the mind had lost "that sense of large proportion in things, that all-embracing prospect of life as a whole," that expansive perspective on life "afforded from a cathedral tower of the Middle Age." Powerful but disillusioned personalities, in Pater's view, produce a decadent quality in intellectual culture: "Deprived of that exhilarating yet pacific outlook, imprisoned now in the narrow cell of its own subjective experience, the action of a powerful nature will be intense, but exclusive and particular. It will come to art, or science, to the experience of life itself, not as to portions of human nature's daily food," but will demand of them exaggerated and artificial stimuli, extravagant and exotic passions that become ends in themselves, "almost as men turn in despair to gambling or narcotics, and in a little while the narcotic, the game of chance or skill, is valued for its own sake." Fanaticism too becomes "an end in itself, unrelated, unassociated," and science becomes a "science of crudest fact" (MS, 12–13).

For Pater Prosper Mérimée is, like Obermann, a "central type of disillusion." In him the fatal limitations of the human mind amounted to a form of bêtise, and his humanity seemed "as alien as the animals" (MS, 13, 28). Pater characterizes his work as stark and impersonal with no softening half-lights, no atmosphere of imaginative colorings. He sees the harshness of Mérimée's negative ideal as pure *mind*, lacking "what we call *soul* in literature" (MS, 37; Pater's emphasis).[4] The development of the conditions found in such figures as Obermann and Mérimée, Pater tells us, "is the mental story of the nineteenth century, especially as exemplified in France" (MS, 13). It has continued to be the mental story of the twentieth century as well; for Pater's description of Mérimée seems equally apt for, say, Beckett, a typical form of twentieth-century disillusion, or what we have come to call the post-Modern mind.

But disillusionment was not the only possible response to the post-Kantian world. Pater says others "would recover themselves [from an initial period of disillusionment], and find some way of making the best of a changed world" (MS, 12). If the disillusioned would respond by seeking the exaggerated, the artificial, and the exotic for their own sakes, a more positive response might be to seek another exhilarating, all-embracing perspective that would restore "that sense of large proportion in things" and the "prospect of life as a whole."

When Pater wrote "Prosper Mérimée," he had recovered from his own early period of disillusionment, registered most eloquently in his "Conclusion" to *The Renaissance*. Although it may not have been as extreme as what he describes in "Prosper Mérimée," the "Conclusion" clearly exhibited a sense of theoretic insecurity and negation, especially of an unseen world, a preference for the intense, the exotic, and the artificial, as well as an emphasis on passionate experience for its own sake, rather than as a portion of human nature's daily food. But in the "Conclusion" were also the seeds of recovery in a relativist

---

4. In "Style" Pater associated *mind* with intellect and structure in writing, with "logical coherency," and "architectural design"; whereas he associated *soul* with intuition and texture, with "inexplicable inspiration," "immediate sympathetic contact," with "atmosphere," "colour," or "perfume," rather than form or design (*App.*, 21–27).

temperament disposed, like Montaigne's, to make the best of a new world. As Pater says in "Style" (1888), it would be "false economy" to renounce any "means or faculty, in a world where after all we must needs make the most of things" (*App.*, 5).

By the time Pater had written "Prosper Mérimée," he had forged for himself a broad secular vision of Christian humanism that satisfied him, however tentatively, as a replacement for the exhilarating perspective from a thirteenth-century cathedral tower. Pater's own response to post-Kantian thought can be seen in the terms Marius uses to describe Aristippus's response to the philosophy of Heraclitus. For Marius, as for Pater, "the reception of metaphysical *formulae*[,] all depends . . . on the pre-existent qualities of that soil of human nature into which they fall," on the translation of abstract thought into terms of sentiment; and Aristippus's skepticism differed from that of his early Greek predecessors, says Pater's narrator, as "the mystic in his cell, or the prophet in the desert" differed from an "expert, cosmopolitan, administrator." In Aristippus, we are told, Marius found that

> an abstract doctrine, originally somewhat acrid, had fallen upon a rich and genial nature, well fitted to transform it into a theory of practice, of considerable stimulative power towards a fair life. What Marius saw in him was the spectacle of one of the happiest temperaments coming, so to speak, to an understanding with the most depressing of theories; accepting the results of a metaphysical system which seemed to concentrate into itself all the weakening trains of thought in earlier Greek speculation, and making the best of it; turning its hard bare truths, with wonderful tact, into precepts of grace, and delicate wisdom, and a delicate sense of honour. (*ME* 1: 135–37)

Aristippus thus resembles Montaigne in temperament, and, like Montaigne, serves for Pater as a model of an urbane intellectual response, as one who turned a potentially disillusioning philosophy to good advantage.

This disposition to make the best of the post-Kantian world became one of the central constituents of the Modernist temperament, opposed on the one hand to those who refused to accept the post-

Kantian limitations of human thought and on the other hand to those who accepted it but never recovered from the disillusionment it engendered. Yeats, Eliot, and Joyce all shared this more positive outlook, and despite periods of disillusionment and skepticism, they each constructed or adopted a vision to make the most of a much more limited world than humanity had previously imagined: Yeats forged his own heterodox subjective philosophy; in his later poetry Eliot effected, perhaps more legitimately than Pater, a reconciliation with orthodox Christianity in his attempt to reascend the steps of a medieval cathedral tower; and Joyce embraced a full-blown functionalist and semiotic humanism that was incipient in varying degrees in the other three.

Pater was the first major figure of English letters to respond to the post-Kantian intellectual climate in a characteristically Modernist manner. His response can be distinguished both from his Victorian predecessors' and contemporaries' by the avidness with which he embraced without hesitation or regret the new assessment of experience and its implications and from the so-called post-Modern response by his optimism and determination to make the best of it. Although it remained for Pater's successors in the twentieth century to develop the literary techniques appropriate to embody that response, the sensibility these techniques were designed to express was already present in Pater's works in remarkably well-developed form.

Pater was well aware of the modern plight; having peered into the abyss himself, he refused to accept any facile fantasies explaining it away (*ME* 2:90). In the middle of the nineteenth century he had already accepted the vision of humanity bequeathed by modern science: to Pico della Mirandola's comfortable and "childish" Ptolemaic dream he compares "our own conception of nature, with its unlimited space, its innumerable suns, and the earth but a mote in the beam; how different the strange new awe, or superstition, with which it fills our minds!" "The silence of those infinite spaces," Pater reminds us, terrified Pascal (*Ren.*, 41–42). Pater's response, however, is neither Pascal's terror nor a Beckettian silence. Instead he busily sets about constructing, if not a bulwark against the void, then a guardrail at the brink of the abyss. In the "Conclusion" he proposes art as the anodyne, and elsewhere he posits culture, especially intellectual culture in Hegel's sense of the gradual education of the human spirit.

A typical response to his confrontation with the void and its implications occurs in *Marius*, where he characterizes the "chief function of all higher education" as enhancing "one's capacity for enjoyment," the art of "so relieving the ideal or poetic traits, the elements of distinction, in our everyday life—of so exclusively living in them—that the unadorned remainder of it, the mere drift or *débris* of our days, comes to be as though it were not" (*ME* 1:53–54). This unadorned drift and debris of daily life becomes the very stuff of post-Modern writing, in the work of Donald Barthelme, for example; but Pater, while acknowledging it as part of the scheme of things, prefers to ignore it.

Though a skeptic and a relativist, Pater, like Montaigne, did not remain one of the *désillusionné*. To the extent that he acknowledges and at times contemplates the terrifying silence of infinite space, he anticipates the post-Modern temper epitomized by Beckett; but to the extent that he tries to assert against the void the highest products of an integrated human organism, the "fruit of quickened, multiplied consciousness," he anticipates the Modernist temper epitomized by Yeats, Eliot, or Joyce.

2 / ABSOLUTISM AND THE RELATIVE SPIRIT

IF ONE accepts the fundamental subjectivity of thought, especially a subjectivity founded on individual temperament, then relativism becomes a logical corollary. Truth for Pater was not one, ultimate, and absolute but multiple, local, and particular: "truth of a particular time and place, for one and not for another" (*PP*, 192). Ideas and beliefs for him had no absolute status, but were "serviceable creations" of the human mind (*PP*, 167), and, as such, they were as subject to mutability as any other product of humanity: "As the theological heresy of one age sometimes becomes the mere commonplace of the next," he says, "so, in matters of philosophic enquiry, it might appear that the all-absorbing novelty of one generation becomes nothing less than the standard of what is uninteresting, as such, to its successor" (*PP*, 154).

Pater's particular formulation of what he called the "relative spirit" of modern thought is significant because he was one of the first in English letters to recognize the lust for the absolute as the true antagonist of the relativism that was beginning to emerge again in the history of thought in a new and modern form. He also perceived this confrontation as one of the central oppositions between Romanticism and a new classicism, which later became what we know as Modernism. Pater's rhetoric in "Coleridge's Writings," for example, is as thoroughly and ardently anti-Romantic as Hulme's, Eliot's, or Babbitt's fifty years later. Like his Modernist successors, Pater liked to think that his position was classical rather than Romantic.

Although neither Pater nor the Modernists could escape the pervasive impact of Romanticism, the opposition Pater identified between absolutism and relativism has become an important distinction between different forms of neo-Romanticism. The significance of this opposition is elegantly illustrated by a contemporary relativist, Nelson Goodman, whose philosophy captures much of the essential spirit of the Modernist movement. In "The Way the World Is" (1960)[1] Goodman distinguishes between relativism and absolutism in a way that helps to characterize the Modernist quality of Pater's own philosophic response. Goodman himself opposes absolutisms of all kinds, including many concealed forms that retain some notion of absolute elements or ultimate meanings, knowable or unknowable. He finds, for example, a concealed absolutism in the distinction between analytic and synthetic propositions.

According to Goodman a typical absolutist, a Bergsonian for example, "holds that there is some way the world is," but he despairs of any adequate characterization of it: "All our descriptions are a sorry travesty," says Goodman's hypothetical absolutist; "Science, language, perception, philosophy—none of these can ever be utterly faithful to the world as it is." On the other hand, Goodman as a relativist denies that there is any way the world is, but only ways—multiple versions of the world that can be equally true—and no one version that can serve as a standard against which all other versions are judged.

Even more important for our purposes here than the distinction between absolutists and relativists is Goodman's characterization of the alternative responses typically produced by these two contrasting world views. Since the absolutist, according to Goodman,

> is concerned with the way the world is and finds that the way cannot be expressed, his ultimate response to the question of the way the world is must, as he recognizes, be silence. Since I am concerned rather with the ways the world is, my response must be to construct one or many descriptions. The answer to the question "What is the way the world is? What are the ways the world is?" is not a shush, but a chatter.

---

1. *Review of Metaphysics* 14 (1960): 48–56.

Goodman's analysis very aptly captures a distinction between the characteristically Modernist achievement of Joyce, who, through the stylistic genius of his language, constructs multiple versions of the ways the world is, and Beckett, the epitome of post-Modernism, who uses his stylistic genius repeatedly to approximate the realm of silence.

Post-Modern disillusionment frequently stems from some form of absolutism, often concealed, even if only a form of nostalgia or despair over the lack of any firm or absolute standards of value. The system-building optimism of Modernism, on the other hand, tends to be less disillusioned and more relativistic, pluralistic, and constructive. If silence is the logical conclusion of absolutism, the noise and clatter of construction, the chattering ventures of Modernism busily erecting multifarious universes of discourse constitute the logical fate of relativism.

Although Pater contained within himself the potential for both constructive relativism and disillusionment, and even fostered both responses in succeeding generations,[2] his own solution fell decidedly into the relativist camp. Despite many adjustments of his position and many careful restatements of it, Pater maintained his relativist stance throughout his career, and it was accompanied by an unrelenting opposition to absolutism. His position on relativism and absolutism appears in remarkably well-developed form in the first publication of his professional career, "Coleridge's Writings" (1866). It evolved with some significant alteration in "Winckelmann" the next year and again in its most influential formulations in the "Preface" and "Conclusion" to *The Renaissance* (1873). Pater's relativism and his bias against absolutes, however, were equally strong at the end of his career, as evidenced in *Plato and Platonism* (1893). For the formulation and development of Pater's version of the "relative spirit" we must turn to these works.

"Coleridge's Writings" can be considered one of the opening salvos

---

2. For views of Pater as a forerunner of both Modernism and post-Modernism see Harold Bloom, Introduction to *Selected Writings of Walter Pater* (New York: New American Library, 1974), p. xxxi; J. Hillis Miller, "Walter Pater: A Partial Portrait," *Daedalus* 105, no. 1 (1976): 97–98; and Gerald Monsman, *Walter Pater's Art of Autobiography* (New Haven: Yale University Press, 1980), p. 5.

of the Modernist movement in literature and the arts.[3] Less a review of Coleridge's prose than a manifesto of his own, this essay was one of the first attacks of the Modernist vanguard against the shibboleths of a passing age. Although Pater was in many ways part of that passing age himself, he was also one of the first to begin undermining some of its most cherished conventions. In "Coleridge's Writings" alone, Pater takes aim, from a vantage point occupied by forces of the age to come, at targets vital to Romanticism, Victorianism, and pre-Kantian metaphysics of substance. The essay focuses not so much on Coleridge, who is used as a pretext and a whipping post to flay absolutism of all kinds, as on what Pater calls the "relative spirit" of modern thought.

Although Pater never quite conceals that he himself was wrestling with some of the same problems as Coleridge, he castigates Coleridge's penchant for abstraction and absolutes and prefers for himself what he considers to be the more instinctive practice of Wordsworth or Goethe's immersion in individual, sensuous experience. Pater believed, as he later emphasized in the "Conclusion," that art could accommodate the relative spirit better than philosophic abstraction could; and in "Coleridge's Writings" he allies art with science and opposes them to religion and speculative philosophy because the former two deal with experience in the concrete while the latter deal with abstractions. Pater himself had a strong inclination toward abstraction; nevertheless his polemics against the absolute and the abstract persisted throughout his career. He considered the "metaphysical prejudice for the 'Absolute'" to be, as he put it in 1886, the equivalent of "the false intellectual conscience" (*EG*, 32); and in his first published essay Pater chose to single out Coleridge as a prime example of this false intellectual conscience.

His attack on Coleridge's absolutism was two-pronged: first he assaulted his metaphysics and then through them his aesthetics. Because Coleridge tried to assert something "the human spirit has done with"—a "religious philosophy" (112)—he suffered, according to

---

3. "Coleridge's Writings" first appeared in the *Westminster Review* 85 (1866): 106–32. Pater published a substantially altered form of this essay in *Appreciations*; but because the revisions, excising many of his early views of Christianity and German philosophy, partially obscure the importance of the essay in Pater's own development and in the development of the Modernist sensibility, I have used the 1866 version.

Pater's diagnosis, from "a distemper of the eye of the mind" (117), and his entire intellectual effort was a futile attempt to counter the march of an "irresistible modern culture" (115). Although Pater later changed his mind about religion, in this essay he asserts that a religious faith never could "appeal with any success to any genuinely human principle," and that the Catholic Church and humanity are two fundamentally opposing powers "that divide the intellect and spirit of man" (114–15).

Because he hungered for eternity, Coleridge, like Luther and Newman, ignored the lessons of history, "tended to depreciate historical testimony," and refused to employ a true historical method (129–30). By the historical method Pater meant the methods that were being applied to the textual criticism of the Bible. In the essay he specifically mentions Ferdinand Christian Baur, the Protestant theologian and Hegelian who founded the historical school of biblical criticism that transformed nineteenth-century intellectual life. Baur's essays on the history of dogma were published posthumously in the years surrounding publication of Pater's Coleridge essay.

Coleridge erred, in Pater's view, by applying a Schellingean transcendental philosophy "to the questions of theology and art criticism" (117). This effort Pater judges to be outdated and doomed from the start, for Coleridge sought "for something fixed where all is moving" (132). According to Pater, Coleridge was fortunate that he failed in his "disinterested struggle against the application of the relative spirit to moral and religious questions," because his struggle was "against the increasing life of the mind itself" (108).

Pater felt that Coleridge's metaphysical flaws also marred his aesthetics, which he considered even more rigid than his philosophy. Coleridge's aesthetics were "an attempt to reclaim the world of art as a world of fixed laws" (118) and a "fanciful and bizarre attempt to rationalize art, to range it under the dominion of law" (120). In other words, like his metaphysics, Coleridge's aesthetics were infected with absolutism.

Particularly offensive was Coleridge's organicism, which Pater considered to be an exaggeration of unity, an affirmation in the sphere of art of the absolute, which congeals thought and obscures the true interest of art because it conceives artistic creation as a mechanical process. In addition to its absolutist overtones, organicism implied for Pater a creative process much too controlled to be able to capture the fugitive nature of modern experience. The idea of a work of art germinating from a seed offended Pater: he could consider the artistic process "no blind ferment of lifeless elements to realize a type" (122). Later, however, Pater silently changed his mind about organicism, and he began to cite it as a positive attribute of artistic works.

More than three decades after the Coleridge essay, Pater launched another major attack on absolutism in *Plato and Platonism*. His antagonists this time were the Eleatic philosophers Xenophanes, Parmenides, and Zeno, but the tone and tenor of his argument had changed little from his earlier encounter with Coleridge. Pater condemns Eleatic rationalism as the beginning of Scholasticism in Western thought and as an illness from which the philosophical mind has never quite recovered. As a result of growing up in this destructive tradition that dissipates sense, we have experienced, according to Pater, some regrettable loss (31). Parmenides' "impossibly abstract doctrine" set the European mind on a vain and diseased quest "after a kind of knowledge perhaps not properly attainable," Pater says, and this "strange passion for nonentity," this "infectious mania" for annihilation, self-negation, and "moral suicide" left the mind never quite sane again (38–40).

Pater's attack on absolutism in the Coleridge essay, in *Plato and Platonism*, and elsewhere was a polemic that shored up his relativism. Like Nelson Goodman, he perceived absolutism as the logical antagonist to his relativism, and he had to exorcise its ghosts in order to assert the new, modern, relative spirit. That Pater performed his exorcism more than once suggests that the ghosts of absolutism in his scheme of things were not easily banished. Pater nevertheless maintained his relativist position to the end. As late as *Plato and Platonism* he rejected Plato's objectification and deification of ideas as "creators of our reason" in favor of Socrates' pragmatic attitude toward abstract universals as creations of human reason "in service to, and valid only in and by, the experience they recorded, with no *locus standi* beyond" (167).

Pater never rejected ideas and abstractions outright but considered them contingent, like the experience out of which they grew, and not to be taken seriously as absolute or eternal verities in any sense. For Pater the mark of a "complete culture in the handling of abstract questions" is a "certain shade of levity and unconcern," a humanism that "does not weep over the failure of a theory of the quantification of the predicate" ("CW," 111). Through his loophole of levity he is able to admit certain abstract thinkers, such as Plato and eighteenth-century skeptical philosophers like Hume, into the compass of European culture because they did not, in Pater's view, take their abstractions too seriously. But Coleridge is excluded, along with Luther and Newman, because he does take his theories too seriously and becomes melancholy under the burden of their weight.

Pater's own conception of relativism in "Coleridge's Writings" was not systematically developed, for it was based on an unstable fusion of positivism, empiricism, and German idealism. Although he notes that "the positive method makes very little account of marks of intelligence in nature," whereas German idealism, like Greek philosophy, finds "indications of mind everywhere" (118–19), Pater was apparently unaware that some of the positivist elements of his own thinking were incompatible with elements he absorbed from the German idealists and with his Humean emphasis on the primacy of sensation.

The positivistic orientation of Pater's relative spirit is evident in the way he links evolution, history, and science. Darwin, whose *Origin of Species* had appeared six years prior to the Coleridge essay, is invoked in the opening paragraph, in which Pater presents the inevitable flux of intellectual and cultural history as a Darwinian rise and fall of "ideas, moralities, modes of inward life," which nature evolves and represses in turn. Pater saw evolutionary theory as one of the observational sciences under whose influence "the idea of 'the relative' has been fecundated in modern times" (106–7). Although Pater's relativism is contrary to Comte's quest for certainties, that did not stop Pater from employing Comte's strategy of attempting to apply the methods of the natural sciences to the social sciences and moral behavior. Having applied Darwin to cultural history, Pater then uses the Comtean argument that since "the moral world is ever in contact with the physical[,] the relative spirit has invaded moral philosophy from the ground of the inductive sciences. There it has started a new analysis of the relations of body and mind, good and evil, freedom and necessity." Pater then uses evolutionary theory to chart the ever-increasing complexity of the human organism along with its intellectual heredity and environment (107–8). Ironically, the more obviously deterministic elements of Darwin do not seem to bother Pater as much as those he finds in Coleridge's organicism.

In "Coleridge's Writings" the positivistic methods of observation and analysis are the preeminent critical tools the relative spirit receives from modern science. Refined by "a continual analysis of facts of rough and general observation into groups of facts more precise and minute," scientific truth is for Pater fugitive, relative, full of fine gradations (107–8). Pater naively believes at this point that science gives unambiguous answers to questions about the limits of knowledge. If current perspectives on scientific thought make Pater seem unduly optimistic, we must remember that Pater shared the optimism of his age in the accomplishments of science, an optimism that did not wane until well after the turn of the century.

At the same time that Pater was urging a scientific and positivistic view of cultural history under the aegis of Darwin and Comte, he was also drawing from another major source of evolutionary theory in the nineteenth century, a source whose premises, assumptions, and methods differed radically from the tradition of scientific positivism. That source was Hegel; and in the Coleridge essay Pater's views of cultural history were informed as much by Hegel and his followers as they were by Comte and Darwin. Although he specifically criticizes Kant and Schelling, by this time Pater had already absorbed substantial portions of German philosophy into his own thinking; and in the same essay where he invokes a positivist vision of history he also invokes the Hegelian historians in his critique of Coleridge's historical sense of Christianity. He cites as the only valid treatment of Christian dogma the historical methods of Baur and Renan. Coleridge, according to Pater, had many elements of the historical method—"learning, inwardness, a subtle psychology, a dramatic power of sympathy with modes of thought other than his own"—but he had a "strange dulness of the historical sense": he accepted the "true historical origin of the dogma" as justification of its present existence, and he could not "regard the books of Scripture simply as fruits of the human spirit." Thus he did not envisage his historical material within a true historical method as the German biblical critics did by subjecting the origins of Christian doctrine to rigorous critical scrutiny. This true historical method Pater considered the most fruitful of all applications of the relative spirit (129–31).

Sitting side by side with the positivist and the idealist elements are elements drawn from the empirical tradition of Berkeley and Hume, with its focus on the flux of individual sensory experience. This empirical orientation is evident throughout the essay in Pater's emphasis on the fugitive nature of experience and, in contrast to Coleridge's Romantic penchant for the abstract and the absolute, his own more classical preference for the "here and now" (132). While Pater complains that Coleridge "withdraws us too far from what we can see, hear, and feel" (124), he admires Wordsworth because of his more instinctual temperament and Goethe because he neglected "no touch of the world of form, colour, and passion" (108).

Despite its contradictory elements, the general thrust of Pater's relativism in the Coleridge essay is clear, and it provided him with a permanent philosophical position that guided all his subsequent thought and writing. By 1866 Pater had accepted the assessment of the new "modern spirit" that "nothing is or can be rightly known except relatively under conditions" and that the proper domain of this spirit is not the infinite and eternal but the concrete relations of experience and "the world of form, colour, and passion." Opposed to any form of transcendentalism or absolutism that seeks to "arrest every object in an eternal outline," or "that makes what is abstract more excellent than what is concrete," Pater's relative spirit, "by dwelling constantly on the more fugitive conditions or circumstances of things, breaking through a thousand rough and brutal classifications, and giving elasticity to inflexible principles, begets an intellectual finesse, of which the ethical result is a delicate and tender justness in the criticism of human life." It is a disinterested "power of distinguishing and fixing delicate and fugitive details," no mere impressionism, but a cognitive function, a genuine "faculty for truth." Rather than forcefully fixing all the elements of our disparate experience under a single system, the gentler relative spirit settles for partial truths and "cries out against every formula less living and flexible than life itself." Only in this way can we achieve "a more exact estimate of the subtlety and complexity of our life"; and "hard and abstract moralities" must yield to this new spirit. In contrast to the deadening effect of rigid absolutes, the relative spirit is a form of intellectual pluralism Pater identifies with the life of the mind itself (107–8, 131–32).

The relative spirit also had some important implications for style.

Pater believed that while the relative spirit may sacrifice some precision of form, it compensates with its greater intricacy of expression (108). Consequently, under the impulse of the relative spirit, modern prose style would become a much more appropriate vehicle to convey the subtlety, complexity, flexibility, and fugitive nature of experience.

Many weaknesses mar Pater's essay on Coleridge, including inconsistent and confusing thinking, unwarranted generalizations, an irritating and condescending pity, an eagerness to shock conventional orthodoxy with the latest avant-garde thought, and an insufficient assimilation of his wide reading. In the end Pater was no more disinterested than Coleridge—he too had an axe to grind. Nevertheless "Coleridge's Writings" is still a remarkable accomplishment, precocious for the generation that came of age in mid-Victorian England. Despite its flaws, in it Pater recognized the lust for the absolute as the true antagonist of the relative spirit and saw this confrontation as one of the central oppositions between Romanticism and a new classicism. So notwithstanding his unfair treatment of Coleridge, Pater's choice of him as the first conquest in his crusade for the relative spirit was altogether appropriate; and as a manifesto and an opening salvo of a new cause in English letters, Pater's essay announces prophetically and emphatically the beginning of a new movement.

Although the initial formulation of Pater's relativism in the Coleridge essay was an important manifesto both for himself and for the history of Modernist thought and aesthetics, it was neither his final nor his most influential formulation; it underwent significant alteration and development in "Winckelmann," the "Conclusion," and the "Preface." Beginning with "Winckelmann," an important shift takes place in Pater's philosophical allegiance: positivism drops out almost completely from his philosophical orientation, and his relativism becomes a much more stable compound of empiricism and German idealism. With this shift of philosophic allegiance, Pater became one of the first Modernists. By tracing his transition we can gain a good deal of insight not only into Pater's own thought and development but also into the genesis of Modernism.

In "Winckelmann," published a year after "Coleridge's Writings," Pater began to eliminate some of the inconsistencies of the earlier essay. The relative spirit survives intact, but its foundation in the positivistic methods of history and the observational sciences evaporates. Pater's sense of history is no longer informed by Darwin's evolutionary science but almost exclusively by Hegel's neo-Kantian mode of evolutionary history and philosophical "science." As a result of dropping his positivistic orientation, many of the contradictions in "Coleridge's Writings" stemming from the conflict among the positivistic, empirical, and neo-Kantian elements disappeared. Instinct, intuition, and sense could now be asserted more confidently over observation and analysis as the primary faculties of artist and critic alike; and there was a corresponding de-emphasis of the intellect in art. The model of Goethe, not surprisingly, becomes even more prominent than in the Coleridge essay.

Although Pater's revised formulation of the relative spirit was evident in "Winckelmann," its most influential and definitive articulation came the following year (1868) in the paragraphs at the end of his essay on William Morris that became the "Conclusion" to *The Renaissance*. In the original context of the Morris essay, Pater introduces these paragraphs as his response to a hypothetical challenge to "see what modern philosophy . . . really does say" about experience and truth and their relation to "the desire of beauty" ("WM," 309). Philosophy, it turns out, has little more to say about truth than art.

The opening of the "Conclusion" appears to pick up on relativism where Pater left it in the Coleridge essay: he opens with a broad affirmation of the relative spirit—"To regard all things and principles of things as inconstant modes or fashions has more and more become the tendency of modern thought" (*Ren.*, 233)—and then he moves to the flux of the physical world, the world of molecules and atoms that yields to the scrutiny of the positive method. But almost as directly he leaves this world behind in favor of an effervescent phenomenal world, the flux of images formed in the mind's eye:

> At first sight experience seems to bury us under a flood of external objects, pressing upon us with a sharp and importunate reality, calling us out of ourselves in a thousand forms of action. But when reflexion begins to play upon those objects they are dissipated under its influence; the cohesive force seems suspended like some trick of magic; each object is loosed into a group of impressions—colour, odour, texture—in the mind of the observer. (*Ren.*, 234–35)

31

These images, the "inward world of thought and feeling," became the focus of the "Conclusion" and of all Pater's work thereafter.

Denying even a positivism as narrowly circumscribed as Wittgenstein later outlined in his *Tractatus*, Pater then carries this inner vision into complete solipsism:

> And if we continue to dwell in thought on this world, not of objects in the solidity with which language invests them, but of impressions, unstable, flickering, inconsistent, which burn and are extinguished with our consciousness of them, it contracts still further: the whole scope of observation is dwarfed into the narrow chamber of the individual mind. Experience, already reduced to a group of impressions, is ringed round for each one of us by that thick wall of personality through which no real voice has ever pierced on its way to us, or from us to that which we can only conjecture to be without. Every one of those impressions is the impression of the individual in his isolation, each mind keeping as a solitary prisoner its own dream of a world. (*Ren.*, 235)

Although Pater never consistently maintained this degree of solipsism in his later writings, these passages indicate quite clearly that he has abandoned any positivistic foothold in a physical world.

Pater then contends that rational analysis can tell us little, and he rejects any philosophical orthodoxy, either positivistic or idealistic—Comte and Hegel are specifically mentioned (*Ren.*, 237). Pater's rejection of philosophical orthodoxy, however, does not constitute a rejection of philosophy itself, only of its claims to any form of ultimate truth. Pater still allowed a prominent role for philosophy, not for a philosophy that sought substantive truths, either physical or metaphysical, but for a relativistic, pragmatic philosophy whose primary function was to aid the observation of experience. Philosophy, or any system of ideas, always remained subservient to experience for Pater: "Not the fruit of experience, but experience itself, is the end," and the "theory or idea or system which requires of us the sacrifice of any part of this experience, in consideration of some interest into which we cannot enter, or some abstract theory we have not identified with ourselves, or of what is only conventional, has no real claim upon us" (*Ren.*, 236–38).

So by the time he wrote the "Conclusion" in 1868, Pater had abandoned positivism and science as allies in his campaign against the abstract and the absolute, and he had consolidated a position that asserted the relative and functional nature of philosophy and theory, but he strictly subordinated them to the primacy of sensory experience itself.

Between the time that Pater had written the "Conclusion" originally for the William Morris essay in 1868 and the time he wrote the "Preface" several years later, he had written most of the essays that comprise *The Renaissance*; and as he progressed through these essays, he developed, qualified, and modified a number of his major positions. He softened his religious skepticism and his extreme solipsism, for example. He also became preoccupied with other issues besides subjectivism and relativism. When Pater wrote the "Preface," he must have realized how far he had traveled intellectually since writing the "Conclusion" several years earlier, for the "Preface" seems to look back chronologically to the Coleridge essay as well as the "Conclusion" by taking up issues—the attack on abstraction, the relative spirit, and the role of analysis—that had not been dealt with explicitly to any extent in the other essays written for *The Renaissance*. In other words, Pater seems to have written his "Preface" with his eye on the "Conclusion" in an effort to tie everything together, at least philosophically, and to include some issues he considered important but had not managed to explore sufficiently in other essays. The apparent similarities between the positions in the "Preface" and "Conclusion," however, mask the progression and development of Pater's thinking over a four- or five-year period; for in the "Preface" there are subtle but nonetheless significant shifts in Pater's relativism and subjectivism.

On the surface the "Preface" appears simply to apply Pater's philosophical relativism and solipsism to criticism and aesthetics. "Beauty," says Pater, "like all other qualities presented to human experience, is relative; and the definition of it becomes unmeaning and useless in proportion to its abstractness. To define beauty, not in the most abstract but in the most concrete terms possible, to find not its universal formula, but the formula which expresses most adequately this or that special manifestation of it, is the aim of the true student of aesthetics" (*Ren.*, vii–viii).

To this aesthetic relativism Pater adds a description of the art critic's function that appears to be consonant with the solipsism of the "Conclusion." The true aim of criticism, he claims, is "'to see the object as in itself it really is'"; but the way to achieve this goal is to "know one's own impression as it really is, to discriminate it, to realise it distinctly." The critic must ask, "What is this song or picture, this engaging personality presented in life or in a book, to *me*? What effect does it really produce on me? . . . How is my nature modified by its presence, and under its influence? The answers to these questions are the original facts with which the aesthetic critic has to do; and, as in the study of light, of morals, of number, one must realise such primary data for one's self, or not at all" (*Ren.*, viii; Pater's emphasis).

Readers of the "Preface" from its publication in 1873 to T. S. Eliot perceived in these passages an irresponsible, solipsistic, aesthetic impressionism, especially irresponsible, from Eliot's point of view, because Pater applied his impressionistic criticism to all sorts of non-aesthetic concerns in life, such as the judgments of character and morals, and based these judgments solely on the subjective impressions of the observer. After all, Pater does say that the most important trait a critic should have is not an intellectual knowledge of beauty in the abstract, but "a certain kind of temperament, the power of being deeply moved by the presence of beautiful objects" (*Ren.*, x). This criterion could countenance a very wide range of reactions, not all of them admirable, nor even proper to aesthetic experience.

Our own perspective from the late twentieth century, however, makes it easier to see how the earlier critics of Pater's aesthetic impressionism misread him. They should have been tipped off by Pater's inclusion of science and mathematics ("light" and "number"), as well as character and morals, as proper subjects of aesthetic criticism that he was not speaking of aesthetics and criticism alone, but of perception in general, perception in a somewhat phenomenological vein. The fundamental position underlying the "Preface" is not subjective impressionism but Hegelian phenomenology.[4]

---

4. Wendell V. Harris in "Arnold, Pater, Wilde, and the Object as in Themselves They See It," *Studies in English Literature, 1500–1900* 11 (1971): 733–47, shows in somewhat different terms from my own how Pater's "Conclusion" and "Preface" moved away from Arnold's confidence in objective perception, in seeing an "object as in itself it really is," into a realm of the mind that was relative, subjective, and to some

When we look beneath the apparent solipsism and impressionism that glitters on the surface of the "Preface," we find an essentially phenomenological base; and in his emphasis on the effects of works of art on the observer, we can consider Pater as one of the earliest advocates of modern reader-response theory. "The function of the aesthetic critic," Pater says, "is to distinguish, to analyse, and separate from its adjuncts, the virtue by which a picture, a landscape, a fair personality in life or in a book, produces this special impression of beauty or pleasure, to indicate what the source of that impression is, and under what conditions it is experienced" (*Ren.*, ix). Here Pater has characterized what is essentially the phenomenological encounter between the perceiving subject and the aesthetic object.

Whereas Pater allowed solipsism free reign in the "Conclusion," his deepening understanding of Kantian epistemology in general and Hegel in particular led him in the "Preface" to impose certain restraints on the subjectivity of his aesthetic critic. For one thing, he tried to circumscribe the subjectivity of an observer's response through education. The ideal critic's temperament is schooled to be a highly refined receptor of aesthetic impressions by exposure to the master works of our civilization: "Nor is there singing school but studying / Monuments of its own magnificence," as Yeats put it in "Sailing to Byzantium." "Our education becomes complete," Pater says, "in proportion as our susceptibility to these impressions increases in depth and variety" (*Ren.*, ix). The type of aesthetic education Pater alludes to here he adopted from Schiller and Hegel.

Another check to a purely subjective response Pater offers in the "Preface" is a certain kind of objectivity akin to Kant's requirement for universality in aesthetic experience. He implies this objectivity in his own method when he says that a critic's goal is reached when he has disengaged this or that special virtue of an artist "and noted it, as a chemist notes some natural element, for himself *and others*" (*Ren.*, ix–x; my emphasis). The chemist analogy implies a system of relations or a system of knowledge that is not purely individual but is shared by

---

extent transcendent. But Harris seems to be thinking of transcendence in Plato's sense rather than Kant's. Billie Inman, in a paper delivered at the Pater session of the 1981 Modern Language Association convention, explicitly identified the theory of Pater's "Preface" as essentially Hegelian.

others. Art criticism then, as assimilated through repeated exposure to the masterpieces of our culture, would constitute such a shared system of relations and values that would enable one to make discriminations and judgments that would be understood and recognized as having validity, even though they may not be wholly accepted by others. In other words, relative to a historically evolved system of knowledge, aesthetic facts of the kind Pater describes—affective facts of the reader/observer—can be shared and intelligibly communicated from one observer to another.

A source for this kind of objectivity, an objectivity bestowed by a system of relations into which a fact or object enters, can be found in Kant's *Critique of Judgment*.[5] Here Kant insists that aesthetic judgments, though subjective in that they are addressed to the capacity for feeling pleasure or pain in the observer, are also universal. By universal Kant means that a judgment of beauty imputes but does not postulate the assent of others. In other words an aesthetic judgment assumes that a similar judgment can be reached by others possessing the faculties of aesthetic judgment, even though a particular judgment may not be accepted by another.

So Pater's aesthetic critic, when he makes a critical judgment, makes it not for himself alone, a prisoner of his own dream of a world, but he assumes, because he shares with others certain faculties and educational experiences that together construct a system of relations and values, that his judgment can be communicated and will make sense to someone else. The observer need not agree with the judgment. To make sense, in this case, means to fit with the data, not only of the work itself, but of the entire phenomenological experience, both objective and subjective, including the temperament and presuppositions of the critic. To put this another way, the goal of the critic is not necessarily to secure the reader's agreement but to secure his under-

---

5. Cassirer also in *Substance and Function*, especially pp. 271–308, demonstrates in terms of Hegelian phenomenology how subjective sense perceptions become objectified by virtue of their insertion into a system of relations. Although Cassirer is concerned primarily with mathematics and the natural sciences in *Substance and Function*, his analysis applies to all experience. "All consciousness demands some sort of connection," he says, "and every form of connection presupposes a relation of the individual to an inclusive whole, presupposes the insertion of the individual content into some systematic totality" (296–97).

standing. To do this he must make use of various conventions that have traditionally linked one solitary prisoner with another, and these conventions, such as language, shared educational experience, philosophical tradition, method, and the functional logic of the entire human organism—sense, emotion, and intellect—enable something (how much or how little is an open question) to penetrate that thick wall of personality that surrounds each one of us.

So when Pater's aesthetic critic proposes to extract that particular virtue, formula, or active principle that "expresses most adequately this or that special manifestation" of beauty in an artist's work, and then to trace the active principle in the works (*Ren.*, vii–viii, xi), he is not proposing a solipsistic reverie or learned soliloquy, but a genuine act of criticism that takes place in a cultural community. The act is relative and subjective, but relative to a system, or indeed systems, of relations that transcend individual experience, and subjective in the sense that the judgment takes place in the mind of the observer.

In the "Preface," then, *mind* is not the hermetically sealed chamber it was in the "Conclusion"; instead, it shares certain faculties, systems of knowledge, and educative experiences with others. Pater may not have articulated this view explicitly in the "Preface," but it is implicit in his rhetoric and allusions, particularly the unacknowledged allusions to Kant, Schiller, and Hegel.

Eliot's criticism of Pater for applying aesthetics to matters of morals, though justified in one sense, fails to see that the larger issue of a new theory of perception and knowledge governs the polemics of the "Preface." If we see the "Preface" not as merely advocating impressionistic criticism but as espousing a new epistemology, then morals, as well as science and mathematics, have a legitimate place there alongside aesthetics.

Between the "Conclusion" and the "Preface," then, Pater tempered his solipsism and provided his relativism and subjectivism with a base in a Hegelian phenomenology modified by his native empiricism. In doing this he created some chinks in the prison walls, chiseled out by his emerging realization and understanding of a new epistemology and a new vision of human nature.

3 / EPISTEMOLOGICAL SKEPTICISM

SKEPTICISM IS as old as philosophy itself; but in the history of modern thought since the Renaissance, skepticism in various forms has been a natural accompaniment to the simultaneous rise of science and decline of religious belief. Montaigne provided perhaps the most influential formulation of early modern skepticism; but toward the end of the eighteenth century when the possibility of knowledge itself was subjected to severe critiques by such philosophers as Hume and Kant, skepticism took a new turn in which judgment was suspended not only over the truth of any particular assertion or belief but also over the very ability of our cognitive faculties to arrive at any kind of truth.

Although skepticism in many forms has been with us for centuries, it was not until the early twentieth century that literary techniques were forged specifically to embody the severely circumscribed powers of our mental and perceptual faculties in a post-Kantian world, techniques that suggest the problematic nature of truth, knowledge, and perception and that convey a world view that is subjective, relative, and ultimately indeterminate. Examples of epistemological skepticism abound in the literature of the twentieth century from Yeats and Conrad to Beckett and Barthelme. Beckett explored this issue perhaps as much as anyone. *Waiting for Godot* and *Endgame*, for instance, provide lucid metaphors for the sharply circumscribed epistemological potential of modern man. *Endgame* in particular constitutes a dramatic metaphor for the hermetically sealed mind Beckett describes in *Murphy* (107–13), and as such it echoes Pater's description of the self in the "Conclusion," a self imprisoned by the "thick wall of personality through which no real voice has ever pierced" from without and whose "whole scope of observation is dwarfed into the narrow chamber of the individual mind" (*Ren.*, 235). Indeed, the entire corpus of Pater's writings offered his successors a broad examination of the skeptical mind and temper in a modern formulation that has maintained its appeal over several generations.

Pater's religious doubts, although part of his skeptical outlook, are not germane to my argument here, which will focus only on his philosophical skepticism.[1] While religious skepticism was an important issue to Pater personally and to his Victorianism, it was not crucial to the development of Modernist aesthetics. Epistemological skepticism, on the other hand, was perhaps the most critical philosophic issue in the evolution of Modernism.

Pater characterizes his own skepticism as the "wholesome" modern variety found in Hume and Mill that appeals to the authority of sense over reason, as opposed to the skepticism of Greek rationalism that appealed to the authority of reason over sense (*PP*, 31). But Pater actually explores many more varieties of skepticism than is suggested by this misleading and oversimplified contrast between Greek rationalism and modern empiricism. In *Marius* alone he delves into the various forms of skepticism found in the thought of Heraclitus, Aristippus, the Stoics, and Lucian. In the "Conclusion" he deals with skeptical empiricism, and in two chapters of the unfinished *Gaston de Latour* he examines in detail the thought of Montaigne. His section on Plato's dialectical method in *Plato and Platonism* explores Socratic skepticism and the appropriateness of the prose essay as the preeminent literary vehicle to carry the modern skeptical vision.

The broadest formulation of Pater's skepticism can be found in a passage from the "Animula Vagula" chapter of *Marius the Epicurean* (1885), in which Pater's protagonist resolves to "entertain no theory of conduct which did not allow its due weight to this primary element of incertitude or negation, in the conditions of man's life" (*ME* 1:133). This skeptical principle remained part of the philosophy of Marius

---

1. Pater's religious skepticism is examined judiciously and comprehensively by David J. DeLaura in *Hebrew and Hellene* and by U. C. Knoepflmacher in *Religious Humanism and the Victorian Novel* (Princeton: Princeton University Press, 1965).

even on the threshold of Christianity, as it did for Pater in his own reconciliation with Christianity. Although this "primary element of incertitude or negation" constitutes the essential core of Pater's skepticism, he gleaned the particulars from a variety of sources, including Hume, Montaigne, Socrates, and the negative sides of Kant and Hegel. Montaigne especially had a firm hold over Pater's imagination in the last two decades of his life.[2]

Whatever forms of skepticism Pater engaged, two common elements characterize the forms he eventually adopted for himself and for the fictional heroes of his novels. First, the skepticism is precipitated by an awareness of death and the inability to reconcile it to the scheme of things inherited from childhood. Second, the skepticism is both a prelude to a more positive and all-embracing vision and a persistent negative element in that vision. The early skepticism is never renounced, but, as in Hegel's dialectic, brought into and reconciled with the larger vision.

The intellectual developments of both Marius and Gaston de Latour reveal a good deal about Pater's own skeptical thought. By the time Pater was twenty-three, he had experienced the deaths of five close relations, including the death of his father when Pater was two and the death of his mother when he was fourteen.[3] Likewise, the early experience of death figures prominently in the intellectual life of both Marius and Gaston. For Marius the death of his mother first "made him a questioner," and he began to have intimations that the religion of his childhood might be merely "one form of poetic beauty, or of the ideal, in things," that it might be merely "one voice, in a world where there were many voices it would be a moral weakness not to listen to" (ME 1:43–44). Later Marius's outrage over the death of his friend Flavian made his childhood religion and any doctrine of the immortality of the soul seem untenable. And since his natural inclination toward the sensuous in life would brook no melodramatic mysticism, he was propelled into an austere intellectual materialism in the doctrines of Heraclitus (ME 1:123–25). Gaston de Latour is vaulted out of the

2. Montaigne figures prominently in Pater's essays on Charles Lamb (1878) and Pascal (1894) and in Gaston de Latour.

3. Michael Levey, The Case of Walter Pater (London: Thames and Hudson, 1978) pp. 29–31, 45, 49–51, 91.

secure beliefs of his childhood into a more indifferent adult world by the death of his grandmother. This death marks his transition from a sheltered medieval world in the shadow of Notre-Dame de Chartres to the idealized but somewhat jaded secular world of Ronsard's poetry, which asserted "the latent poetic rights of the transitory, the fugitive, the contingent" (*GL*, 57).

Subsequent to the disillusionment triggered by the death of someone close to their affections both Marius and Gaston, like Pater, passed through a phase of skeptical thought en route to a more encompassing vision. According to Pater, this skeptical phase is the "first step" of speculative thought and one that "can never be retraced": the child's natural sense of self-evident principles can never be recaptured.[4] Marius's major encounter with skepticism is with the philosophy of Aristippus of Cyrene and Gaston's is with Montaigne, as for Pater Hume had fulfilled the role of early skeptical mentor. Gaston's ultimate philosophical destination is unclear, but Marius progresses beyond the Cyrenaicism of Aristippus through a more fully developed form of Epicureanism, which he then merges with Stoicism to bring him to the vision afforded by early Christianity.

After his initial contact with Christianity Marius again encounters skeptical relativism when he listens to a conversation of Lucian, but his response is ambiguous. Although he makes no attempt to renounce such skeptical thought, it does nothing to assuage the "terror of isolation" he experiences among the decaying graveyards outside Rome. Instead of responding rationally, Marius merges Lucian's conversation with a blood-red sunset reflecting off the gravestones and an image he recalled from "a certain Christian legend he had heard": "an image, almost ghastly in the traces of its great sorrows—bearing along for ever, on bleeding feet, the instrument of its punishment" (*ME* 2:170–71). At this point it seems that Marius's skepticism, although triggered by the fact of death, offers no consolation for it. So without retracting his allowance for the "primary element of incertitude or negation" in the human condition, Marius looks beyond skepticism to Christianity to propitiate the fear and longing prompted by the awareness of death. The skepticism remains, but it is tran-

---

4. Houghton Library MS 3 "[The history of philosophy]."

scended and harmonized into a larger vision. And as the skepticism of Aristippus and Lucian evolves into a broader sympathetic vision for Marius, so for Pater the skepticism of Hume was incorporated into a larger vision synthesized from a number of sources, but particularly from an idiosyncratic selection of elements from Hegel and Christianity.

Although the role of death and the persistence of skepticism within a larger, more positive vision remained constant in most of Pater's skeptical thought, other elements did not; and the evolution of his position can be traced through four major formulations: the "Conclusion," Marius's encounter with the philosophy of Aristippus, Gaston's encounter with Montaigne, and the section on dialectical method in *Plato and Platonism.*

The "Conclusion" enunciates the earliest and the most extreme form of Pater's skepticism; in his own development it corresponds to Marius's encounter with Aristippus, who serves as a thinly disguised Hume. As noted in the previous chapter, Pater observes in the "Conclusion" that philosophy has little more to say about the truth of experience than art has. He is willing to grant that the purely physical world of atoms and molecules yields to the scrutiny of the positive method; but he also recognizes, as did Wittgenstein much more rigorously half a century later, that positivistic knowledge of the physical world says very little about the phenomenal world of human experience we all inhabit, the world of images in the mind's eye. On this level all is undulate and fleeting; the illusion of objectivity dissolves in Humean fashion into a group of discrete impressions in the mind of the observer. The impressions of the mind, mere "relics" of moments already receding into the past, are the sole basis of our comprehension of experience. Rational analysis only confirms that this is indeed the situation, and beyond that it can tell us nothing. Pater's solution, or at least his way of coping with this state of affairs, was to burn with a "gemlike flame," that is, to tune the sensory apparatus to a fever pitch in a "desperate effort to see and touch," to "grasp at any exquisite passion," to get "as many pulsations as possible into the given time." In this endeavor only art ensures that our passion will be genuine and that it will involve quality as well as quantity (*Ren.*, 233–39).

This formulation of skepticism is the one most often associated with Pater; however, while it had a substantial impact on writers of the nineties, such as Wilde, it did not satisfy Pater's Modernist successors. Yeats said the gemlike flame was an "insufficient motive,"[5] and Eliot engraved the desolation of this solipsistic vision on the modern consciousness in *The Waste Land*:

> *Dayadhvam*: I have heard the key
> Turn in the door once and turn once only
> We think of the key, each in his prison
> Thinking of the key, each confirms a prison
> Only at nightfall, aethereal rumours
> Revive for a moment a broken Coriolanus.

Eliot manages to camouflage Pater's presence here, as he often does elsewhere, with more obvious allusions to Dante and Shakespeare and a well-placed footnote on F. H. Bradley; but none of these sources links solipsistic isolation and the prison image as Pater does.[6]

Pater, however, also became dissatisfied with this extreme form of skepticism; he sought some firmer ground, which, if still relative, at least provided a functional foothold that did not give way under his feet. He found an emotional foothold in Christian ritual and an intellectual one in various formulations, most of them vague, of universals in human experience.

In *Marius the Epicurean* Pater's skepticism is more tempered. It still retains its foundation in sensory experience, but now only as a stage in a philosophical quest for consolations that the strict Humean sensationalism of the "Conclusion" could not offer. Art, the anodyne of the "Conclusion," is more broadly defined as *culture* in *Marius*, and it encompasses ethical and intellectual ideals, along with pleasure and passion, as legitimate goals of a circumscribed epistemological outlook. Hegel also becomes more prominent in *Marius*. In addition to providing a model for assimilating an early skepticism into a more

---

5. *The Oxford Book of Modern Verse: 1892–1935*, comp. W. B. Yeats (New York: Oxford University Press, 1936), p. ix.

6. If Eliot's passage alone is not explicit enough about the relationship of solipsism to the prison image, the quote from Bradley in Eliot's own footnote to the passage makes it perfectly clear. David DeLaura also has noted Pater's relation to these lines in *The Waste Land* in "Echoes of Butler, Browning, Conrad, and Pater in the Poetry of T. S. Eliot," *English Language Notes* 8.3 (1966): 220–21.

positive system, Hegel also provides a historical grounding for individual speculation that breaks down the total solipsism of the "Conclusion."

The stages of Marius's skepticism proceed in two steps, marked by his encounters with the philosophies of Heraclitus and Aristippus. What Marius assimilates from Heraclitus, however, does not strictly follow from the doctrines of this pre-Socratic philosopher who distrusted the senses in favor of an absolute Logos. Although Pater was well aware of this, he preferred, like Plato and many others, to associate Heraclitus mainly with his doctrine of the flux. Consequently he has Marius "learn" from Heraclitus two things that are actually inconsistent with the principles of his first skeptical mentor: first, that "the individual is to himself the measure of all things," and second, that he must "rely on the exclusive certainty to himself of his own impressions" (ME 1:133). Eliot's epigraphs to "Burnt Norton" quote Heraclitus's own observation on precisely this misinterpretation of the Logos: "Although the Logos is common to all," says Heraclitus, "most live as though they have an understanding of their own." Pater, however, clearly wished to associate Heraclitus and the flux with the empiricism that governed his own early skepticism.

At this stage Marius perceives the skeptical doctrine of the flux as a necessary "preliminary step towards a large positive system of almost religious philosophy" (ME 1:130), a perception not evident in Pater's own "Conclusion" but maintained in all his subsequent skeptical thinking. So after his encounter with the philosophy of Heraclitus, Marius moves on to Aristippus of Cyrene.

In contrast to Heraclitus, Aristippus was a skeptic of the "wholesome," modern variety. He rejected metaphysical enquiry and "left off in suspense of judgment as to what might really lie behind . . . the flaming ramparts of the world"; and he exhibited a much more "subtly practical worldly-wisdom" (ME 1:134–35). Aristippus also recognized the subjectivity of all knowledge; but in him an acrid and depressing theory that reduced all things to fleeting shadows was transformed into a practical pursuit of pleasure and experience. Pater attributes to Aristippus, who actually focused primarily on physical pleasure, the later ethical and intellectual applications of Cyrenaicism developed by Epicurus.

Pater's intellectual portrait of Aristippus is drawn in a way that suggests a parallel between the doctrines of Aristippus/Epicurus and those of Hume and John Stuart Mill. "Every age of European thought," says Pater's narrator, "has had its Cyrenaics or Epicureans, under many disguises" (ME 1:144). Pater introduces Aristippus, a contemporary of Plato, as being, like Hume, a practical-minded cosmopolitan who relies on sensation as the only form of certain knowledge. Pater also seems to imply an analogy between the relationship of Aristippus to his absolutist forbears, especially Heraclitus, and of Hume to his predecessor Bishop Berkeley, who gave his empiricism a divine foundation as Heraclitus had founded his flux upon the Logos. Despite radical differences in tone and complexion between Pater's Epicureanism and Mill's Utilitarianism, Mill's application of Hume's empiricism to ethical and intellectual matters appears to be the implicit parallel to the more fully developed Epicureanism of Pater's Aristippus. In Pater's scheme, then, Heraclitus, Aristippus, and Epicurus would be earlier incarnations of Berkeley, Hume, and Mill.

Like Pater's Aristippus, Marius himself did not stop at the obvious goal of physical pleasure; but, like Epicurus and Mill, he cultivated primarily ethical and intellectual ideals of pleasure, and he resolved to pursue not hedonism but "a general completeness of life" as his "practical ideal" (ME 1:142), a completeness that, far from excluding everything but hedonistic pleasure, would be "comprehensive enough to cover pleasures so different in quality, in their causes and effects, as the pleasures of wine and love, of art and science, of religious enthusiasm and political enterprise, and of that taste or curiosity which satisfied itself with long days of serious study" (ME 1:151). Marius sums up his ideal as "the precept of 'culture'": "—Be perfect in regard to what is here and now" (ME 1:145; Pater's emphasis).

Marius's precept of culture had its negative, skeptical component aimed at "ascertaining the true limits of man's capacities"; but it was, we are told, "for the most part positive, and directed especially to the expansion and refinement of the power of reception; of those powers, above all, which are immediately relative to fleeting phenomena, the powers of emotion and sense" (ME 1:147).

Marius's ideal of culture seems to restate the substance of the "Conclusion," and it does; except that art is now redefined more broadly as culture. But even more significantly, the skeptical element of Pater's philosophy, so much more prominent in the "Conclusion," is now cast in a more subordinate role as the negative prelude to a positive philosophy of experience: as Hume's skeptical emphasis on sensation gave way to broader cultural and ethical visions in Mill's Utilitarianism, so Aristippus gave way to New Cyrenaicism.

Despite Pater's reassertion of solipsism in *Marius*, there is another element that carries the Epicureanism of Marius beyond that of the "Conclusion" and grounds it in something outside the individual mind. Neither Marius's philosophy nor Pater's was forged from private experience alone. Pater clearly specifies that Marius retraces "in his individual mental pilgrimage the historic order of human thought." He says that each of his predecessors "served in turn to give effective outline to the contemplations of Marius" (*ME* 1:134). But the same can be said of Pater himself, as evidenced by the parallels he continuously works in his writings between the philosophies of one age and another, especially between ancient and modern thought. Pater's model in such an enterprise was, of course, Hegel, whose belief that all philosophy contributed to the gradual evolution of thought and the human mind Pater accepted for himself.[7] The latest development in this evolution, represented for Pater by Hegel, would embrace all previous thought.

So by the time Pater wrote *Marius*, he had added three significant modifications to the skepticism of the "Conclusion": a more broadly defined culture replaced art as a means of enhancing experience; the role of negative skepticism was more precisely defined and relegated to a subordinate and preliminary status; and the individual intellectual pilgrimage was grounded in a common quest evolving through history. This last element particularly contradicts the Cyrenaic emphasis on the here and now exclusively.

In *Gaston de Latour* Montaigne's skepticism functions as the negative prelude to a more positive system. Pater found in Montaigne a mature, modern, skeptical temper akin to his own, a temper that would require less fictional distortion than would the tempers of Heraclitus or Aristippus to serve as a thinly disguised way station in his own devel-

---

7. In "Pater on Plato: 'Subjective' or 'Sound'?" *Prose Studies* 5 (1982): 222, William F. Shuter links Pater's practice of working parallels between different ages not only to Hegel but to "a number of Pater's sources" and to "many nineteenth-century historians who followed in the footsteps of Niebuhr."

opment. In his intellectual portrait of Montaigne Pater does not regress to the extreme solipsism of the "Conclusion" but continues to provide safeguards against total subjectivity. In *Gaston* he offers two checks against solipsism. One is Montaigne's postulate of the self as the model for humanity. Since he perceived "every man carrying in him the entire form of [the] human condition" (93), like Pater, he could claim both that the individual mind is "the unique organ, and the only matter, of knowledge" (105) and that it also represented "the pattern of the true intellectual life of everyone" (106). The other check against solipsism in *Gaston* is Pater's application of Hegel's notion of zeitgeist to Montaigne's thought. Pater says that the "spirit" of Montaigne's essays "doubtless had been felt already in many a mind" and that they provided an ex post facto theoretic justification for the new intellectual currents of his time (83).

The subjective, skeptical relativism of Montaigne seems very much like the philosophic situation described in the "Conclusion"; but Pater's attitude toward these philosophic circumstances and the tone of the discussion are more positive. This shift reflects both Pater's emotional and intellectual acceptance of these circumstances and his movement toward finding some philosophic and religious ground beneath the flux that, without denying or contradicting the new epistemology, would provide some ballast and some means of orientation and navigation in a world where all was motion. By the time Pater had written the early essays that formed *The Renaissance*, the relativistic world of modern thought no longer depressed him. He had accepted its assessment of both the external world and the internal world of thought and feeling, and he was learning how to deal with it. How much Pater's attitude toward a universe of flux had changed from his original formulation in the Morris essay can be gauged by his characterization of Montaigne's vision of a similar flux. In *Gaston de Latour* Pater tells us that Montaigne, being of sanguine temperament, was not depressed by his vision of "the littleness of man" (95). What appealed to Gaston, and presumably Pater, was the optimism of Montaigne, his capacity, amid the intellectual insecurities of a relativistic universe, to be charmed by the unpredictability of human nature (89).

The skeptical mind and temper continued to fascinate Pater, and his own position on skepticism continued to develop until it became a matter of style, a style for discourse and for the intellectual life itself.

This is particularly true of Pater's most complete and mature discussion of skepticism—his analysis of Plato's dialectical method in *Plato and Platonism*.

In Pater's analysis the main thrust of Plato's philosophy is a fusion of Eleatic absolutism with the practical morality of Socrates. This fusion in turn spawned two distinct philosophic traditions. Plato's doctrine of ideas with its insistence on absolute certainty in the pursuit of truth and knowledge lured like-minded system builders and mystics: it inspired Aristotle and scholastics in all ages, as well as Spinoza and Neoplatonists in all ages. Descartes, Hegel, and Schelling are also part of this company. The other tradition traceable to Plato orients itself around his "actual method of learning and teaching," the dialectic of his dialogues, with its tentative inconclusiveness of the mind reasoning with itself. This side of Plato appealed to skeptics in all ages, such as Lucian, Cicero, Abelard, and Montaigne (192–94). Pater is part of this company. "If Platonism from age to age," says Pater, "has meant, for some, ontology, a doctrine of 'being,' . . . for others Platonism has been in fact only another name for scepticism, in a recognisable philosophic tradition" (194).

On the surface this oversimplified partitioning of Plato's influence seems both arbitrary and coarse; nevertheless its defects make an important point about the attitude of Pater, and of the modern mind in general, toward Plato's thought. Pater was not alone in rejecting Plato's metaphysical absolutism while assimilating much else in Plato's works that appealed to him. Marxism is only the most obvious example of antimetaphysical thought deeply indebted to Plato via Hegel, as was Pater himself. In some ways Pater tried to do for Platonism what he tried to do for Christianity in *Marius*—to make it possible for the modern mind. Pater says that when most of us talk about Socrates we are really talking about the Platonic Socrates (98); but in Pater's case, it would be more accurate to say that his primary interest was in the Socratic Plato. In *Plato and Platonism* Pater's discussions of Socrates, like his attack on Eleatic absolutism, attempt to vindicate his own views and beliefs and formulate a Platonism he can be comfortable with.[8]

---

8. In "Plato and Pater: Fin-de-Siècle Aesthetics," *British Journal of Aesthetics* 12 (1972): 369–83, I. C. Small points out that while Pater added some original touches

Pater's Socrates adjusted the focus of philosophy from the material cosmos to the study of human nature. His Promethean act was to bring philosophy down from heaven to earth and to give this new orientation "a religious or mystic character" (81). His greatest wisdom was his "consciousness of ignorance," his profound skeptical awareness of the limitations of human nature in the pursuit of knowledge (82). Socrates was also aware that "we judge truth not by the intellect exclusively, and on reasons that can be adequately embodied in propositions; but with the whole complex man" (88), and that cosmic order could be discovered "by any one who, in good faith with himself, and with devout attention, looks within" (81).

Pater's Socrates may be more of a subjective, skeptical relativist than the evidence permits; but since our primary interest is Pater, not Socrates, Pater's version of Socrates is more to the point. For Pater Socrates served as a practical, earthy counterbalance to Plato's opulent mysticism, the counterbalance Pater needed to reconcile Plato to the tradition of modern skepticism. This tradition for Pater was inaugurated by Montaigne; and Pater's Socrates is Socrates seen through lenses colored by Montaigne. Montaigne's *Que scais-je?* does more than simply carry on the tradition of Socrates for Pater; it re-creates it for the modern temper.

The modern mind for Pater could never be "sanguine about any form of absolute knowledge, of eternal, or indefectible, or immutable truth." Although the modern age may thirst for intellectual security, in the end it "cannot make up its mind." Plato may promote ideals in the modern world, but not "eternal and immutable ideas." The skeptical modern mind has had "to check wholesomely the pretensions" of any certainties of either metaphysics or empirical science. And what better means is afforded to us than the dialectical spirit, that other inheritance from Plato, which retains to the end "its diffidence and

---

of his own, his treatment of Plato followed in part a tradition, spawned by his Oxford colleague Benjamin Jowett, that viewed Plato's dialogues as literature rather than as a system of philosophy and that viewed Socrates as a literary character. William Shuter in "Pater on Plato" goes much further than Small and traces many of Pater's supposedly idiosyncratic views in *Plato and Platonism* to the "informed" scholarship of his time. Neither Small nor Shuter, however, indicate the extent to which Pater's discussion of Plato, Socrates, and the dialectical method of the dialogues is adapted from Hegel's *Lectures on the History of Philosophy*.

reserve, its scruples and second thoughts." The "condition of suspended judgment" implicit in dialectical thinking corresponds for Pater to "the expectation, the receptivity, of the faithful scholar, determined not to foreclose what is still a question." In Pater's view, for the true "philosophic temper" the "survival of query will still be the salt of truth" (*PP*, 194–96).

As much as the skeptical nature of the dialectical spirit appealed to Pater, he was fascinated more with the appropriate literary vehicle for that spirit. He opens his discussion of Platonic dialectic by identifying three traditional modes of philosophic discourse, each determined by its matter and its mode of viewing truth. The earliest form, metrical composition, conveyed a philosophy that was intuitive, oracular, and enigmatic. Pythagoras, Parmenides, Empedocles, and Lucretius all used this form. According to Pater's analysis, the philosophic poem was succeeded by its opposite, the formal treatise, well suited for the detailed exposition of dogmatic systems, "the dry bones of which rattle in one's ears," says Pater, "the natural out-put of scholastic all-sufficiency." Its practitioners include Aristotle, Aquinas, Spinoza, and Hegel. Situated midway between these two was the third form, evolved to convey the "perfected philosophic temper." This form is the essay, which Pater calls the "characteristic literary type of our own time" and the "invention of the relative, or 'modern' spirit," as developed and honed by Montaigne. The prose essay is the "strictly appropriate form of our modern philosophic literature," and it is "precisely the literary form necessary to a mind for which truth itself is but a possibility, realisable not as general conclusion, but rather as the elusive effect of a particular personal experience." Although the philosophical essay is "seemingly modest" in its aim, according to Pater, it has "really large and adventurous possibilities" (174–75).

The literary ancestor of the essay is the Platonic dialogue. The dialogue form, which remained in use along with the essay, for example, with Bruno, Berkeley, Hume, and Landor, had many of the same virtues of the essay. Structurally it lent itself to a "many-sided but hesitant consciousness of the truth" (176);[9] it was an organic embodi-

---

9. Pater notes that Berkeley misused the form as a means, not of exploring truth, but of popularizing "certain very dogmatic opinions" (*PP*, 176).

ment and idealization of Socrates' method of teaching and learning; and its validity lay ultimately in its capturing in literary form the endless dialogue of the mind with itself.

For Pater the dialectic of Platonic dialogue takes both writer and reader on a never-concluding, circuitous journey, where the only truths arrived at are those arrived at for oneself, and the journey itself reproduces the actual movement of thought. It is the "very converse of mathematical or demonstrative reasoning, and incapable therefore of conventional or scholastic form, of 'exactness,' in fact." The dialogue proceeds toward truth "not by the analysis and application of an axiom, but by a gradual suppression of error, of error in the form of partial or exaggerated truths" (179). With this dialectical method we must "go where the argument carries us," says Pater quoting Socrates, "as a vessel runs before the wind." This method, Pater claims, is "a part of the continuous company we keep with ourselves through life," and it participates in the accidental, informal, and unmethodical nature of that life (185). The pursuit of truth is to be preferred to its possession. The proper function of dialectic is not to finally arrive at truth, but to clear the ground, to "put one into a duly receptive attitude towards such possible truth, discovery, or revelation, as may one day occupy the ground" (188). Yeats said much the same about the operations of reason—that it clears away the rubble at the mouth of Sybil's cave, but it is not the Sybil. This is precisely where Pater leaves his hero at the end of *Marius the Epicurean*—at the mouth of the cave, not in possession of Christian truth but at the end of a life dedicated to refining the organs of perception and to rejecting any impediments to the total openness of his entire receptive capacity. Philosophy, for Pater, does not provide propositions or systems "but forms a temper" (188).

Pater was aware, of course, that his analysis confutes Plato's emphasis on the absolute and eternal forms of knowledge. But Pater insists that Plato, despite his demand for certainty, recognizes, or at least leads his reader to recognize, that truth is ultimately subjective; that since it "depends a good deal on the receiver," it "must be, in that degree, elusive, provisional, contingent, a matter of various approximations" (187). Besides, Pater argues, Plato presents a paradox to his readers: his desire for "infallible certainty," for absolute truth is embodied in a method of the "utmost possible inexactness, or contingency." "The Philosopher of Being, or, of the verb 'To be,' " Pater concludes, "is after all afraid of saying, 'It is' " (188–89).

The justice of Pater's reverie over Plato is not at issue here, but the reasons for its bias are. Because Pater believed that all truth and knowledge are subjective, relative, contingent, and uncertain and that the mind is "not an exact mechanism," he had to conclude that Plato's absolutes were, after all, matters "of immediate intuition, of immediate vision" and as such they were therefore "incapable of analysis" and "incommunicable by words" (189–90). The dialectical method, on the other hand, as a limited method of reasoning, takes into account the inconclusiveness of truth and the limitations of the human mind. In Pater's analysis a Platonic dialogue corresponds finally to "that whole, life-long, endless dialogue which dialectic, in its largest scope, does but formulate, and in which truly the last, the infallible word, after all, never gets spoken" (192).

Pater's impassioned pleas for a mode of discourse that could accommodate the epistemological skepticism of modern thought did not go unheeded. By the time *Plato and Platonism* appeared in the mid-1890s, the prose essay, one of the prime literary achievements of Victorian literature of which Pater's work is a culmination, was going out of fashion. But if the prose essay itself did not become the norm for twentieth-century writers, prose fiction and the dialectical structure of thought did become preeminent in the literary productions of Pater's successors, and the new techniques of modern prose fiction generally embodied Pater's ideals for the prose essay.

Joyce in all his works, but particularly in *A Portrait of the Artist*, embodies the subjective, skeptical relativism of Pater's vision, where all is fleeting, contingent, and inconclusive, where truth, subjective, elusive, provisional, and approximate, is realized only as personal experience. In *Portrait* certainties are checked at every turn as each of Stephen's victories is subverted in turn. As with Pater, not truth but only the gradual suppression of error prevails through a dialectic oscillation that does not so much form a system as temper a soul.

Joyce's rigorous adherence to the viewpoint of a single character provides a structural metaphor for philosophic subjectivity. The narrator of *Portrait* is effaced to the point that no alternatives to Stephen's versions of things are even suggested as possible. We have only the subjective consciousness of Stephen himself; and the many conflicting interpretations of the novel attest that Joyce did his utmost to remove all standards of reference and value other than Stephen's own. This type of "objective" narration acknowledges a vision of humanity that is relative, epistemologically skeptical, and (paradoxically) subjective.

Ulysses and fiction after Joyce are replete with even more techniques and devices that reflect the epistemological skepticism of the age, or to use a more fashionable term, the ultimate indeterminateness of experience. All of these various devices of twentieth-century fiction—unreliable and multiple narrators, objective points of view, juxtapositions of various forms of discourse without authorial comment, streams of consciousness, and the fictional fables of Beckett—fulfill the spirit of Pater's requirements for a modern prose that captures the lifelong dialogue of the mind with itself, that does not foreclose what is still a question, and in which the last, infallible word never gets spoken.

4 / The Primacy of Sensation

In his influential essay on Pater in *The Last Romantics*, Graham Hough, like many of Pater's critics before and after him, emphasizes the primacy of sensation as the bedrock of Pater's thought.[1] This claim cannot be made, however, without qualification; for the primacy of sensation and experience for its own sake was not as pure a concept for Pater as it was, say, for T. E. Hulme. On the contrary, there was a considerable amount of alloy in its composition. The undue emphasis placed on the empiricism of Pater's thought results from the disproportionate influence his "Conclusion" to *The Renaissance* has had from the furor it first created at Oxford in 1873 down to the present.[2] The "Conclusion" was the purest formulation of Pater's empiricism, but it was modified considerably in later writings, where intellect and abstraction played increasingly larger roles. In *Marius* and *Plato and Platonism* particularly, Pater tried to fuse sense and intellect into a unified aesthetic sensibility. Although he never managed to articulate a consistent and unified view on the relations between sense and intellect, he did modify and contradict his early views repeatedly. The

---

1. Graham Hough, *The Last Romantics* (New York: Barnes and Noble, 1961), pp. 134–74.

2. Helen Young pointed this out long ago in her *Writings of Walter Pater* (1933). "The *Conclusion* to the Renaissance studies, which Pater wrote in 1868," she says, "was a short-lived philosophy for Pater, but a lasting one in its influence" (19–20).

"Conclusion" nevertheless has continued to represent the essence of Pater's empiricism.

As Pater's most widely anthologized piece, the "Conclusion" and its empirical orientation had a substantial impact on the art and aesthetics of several succeeding generations. In its insistence on the primacy of sensation, for example, the "Conclusion" fostered the emphasis in Modernist writing on the fragmentary nature of experience, and it helped to undermine the notion of the unitary personality, which had become subject to the same forces of fragmentation as sensory experience. Along with philosophies like Bergson's, the "Conclusion" also helped to promote a cult of the concrete that attracted writers like T. E. Hulme, Pound, the Imagists, William Carlos Williams, and many of the New Critics.[3]

Drawn primarily from the British empirical philosophers Berkeley, Hume, and Mill, the primacy of sensation formed the ground of Pater's attacks on secular and religious absolutism; it was the main weapon in his own arsenal of Romanticism to counter the rationalism of previous centuries. Pater's career, from one point of view, can be seen as a lifelong attempt to provide through an emphasis on the senses a corrective to the excessive rationalism that dominated Western culture from medieval Christianity through the eighteenth century. For Pater the Renaissance marked the beginning of this reawakening of the senses, which had lain dormant since classical times. Accordingly in his first two published essays, "Coleridge's Writings" and "Winckelmann," Pater attacked Christianity and the abstract as enemies of sense. Al-

---

3. Herbert Schneidau in *Ezra Pound: The Image and the Real* (Baton Rouge: Louisiana State University Press, 1969) argues that Pound should not be lumped with Hulme and imagists like Amy Lowell who fostered the cult of the concrete. Rather, he sees Pound as having assimilated more of Ernest Fenollosa's emphasis on relations over things than Hulme's emphasis on the concrete image, and he would place Pound among those who, like Eliot and Joyce, sought universals through concrete particulars (77). Schneidau acknowledges, nevertheless, that Pound's polemics emphasized particulars much more often than universals (93), an emphasis that, in my own view, prevented the *Cantos* from achieving the level of universality of *The Waste Land* or *Ulysses*. Also, Schneidau concludes his argument with a very Hulmean assertion about Pound that contradicts Fenollosa's idealism, the assertion that Pound's goal was a knowledge that was "direct" rather than "conceptual" (188) and achieved "by making words 'strike the senses as nearly as possible' as experience itself would" (201).

though shortly after these essays he began with varying degrees of success to readjust his estimate of the relations between sense on the one hand and abstraction and Christianity on the other, he never renounced the primary emphasis on sensory experience he had assimilated from the British empiricists.

In opening his career with an assault on abstraction, Pater was beginning where Berkeley had begun his *Treatise Concerning the Principles of Human Knowledge*. Berkeley opened his famous work by attacking notions of abstraction held by Descartes and Locke. The notion of abstraction totally apart from any of the particulars that gave rise to it was inconceivable to Berkeley. Insisting that all things exist only in being perceived, he denied the distinction between primary and secondary qualities in things and the existence of an unknown and unseen material substratum in which the primary qualities, such as extension, figure, and motion (as opposed to the secondary qualities, such as color, sound, and taste), supposedly inhered. For Berkeley things or objects were nothing but images or impressions of the senses, and these sensations were our most elementary ideas. Other ideas could be formed from sensation, but sensory impressions were primary and more vivid than any ideas derived from them.

Hume advanced Berkeley's analysis, minus the elaborate deus ex machina Berkeley required to explain the ultimate source of all our sensations and ideas, by continuing to give priority to sensory impression. Simple ideas for Hume were exact copies of impressions. Lacking Bishop Berkeley's religious vision, the atheistic Hume found experience to be only a series of discrete impressions. Where Berkeley found order imposed on our impressions by a Divine Mind, Hume found only illusions. For Hume our impressions were internal and fleeting; they moved in perpetual flux with inconceivable rapidity. At the level of ideas this flux was even more extreme; and in the end Hume remained skeptical about knowledge derived from either sensation or reason.

Adhering rigorously to his fundamental assumption that discrete sensations provide the elementary building blocks for whatever knowledge we have, Hume demonstrated that deductive reasoning, that is, the pure relations of reason, did not apply to experience and that any attempt to apply them to experience was untenable. Identity and cause and effect in particular became targets for Hume's skepticism.

His undermining of these two fundamental relations of thought had far-reaching consequences in the history of Western thought, consequences that passed through Pater into the aesthetics of Modernism.

Hume did not deny the relations of identity and cause and effect, but he insisted that they had no ontological or rational foundation, that instead they were grounded in subjective habits of mind. In other words, Hume explained cause and effect in terms of the psychology of perception rather than in terms of actual connections between objects or in terms of rational proofs.

Hume focused on causation because he saw it as the most important relation we use both in everyday life and in scientific thinking. According to Hume, "All reasonings concerning matters of fact seem to be founded on the relation of *Cause and Effect*. By means of that relation alone we can go beyond the evidence of our memory and senses" (*Enquiry*, 26; Hume's emphasis).[4] When he examined this relation closely according to his strict adherence to sensation and perception as the foundation of all knowledge, Hume concluded that we could neither observe a necessary connection between two objects nor could we prove its existence by reason. "Upon the whole," says Hume, "necessity is something, that exists in the mind, not in objects"; and when he carefully examines specific instances of cause and effect, he finds only three relations—contiguity, succession, and constant conjunction—with no element of necessity. "We have no other notion of cause and effect," he argues, "but that of certain objects, which have been *always conjoin'd* together, and which in all past instances have been found inseparable" (Hume's emphasis). "We only observe the thing itself," Hume insists; and we cannot infer on the basis of this observation that what has been conjoined in the past may also conjoin in future instances of the separate objects or events. Consequently, within the dictates of reason no future event can be predicted on the basis of past experience. When we do predict occurrences on the basis of previous experience, we do so with faculties other than reason. "We suppose," says Hume, "but are never able to prove, that there

---

4. All references to Hume's *Enquiry Concerning Human Understanding* are to L. A. Selby-Bigge's 3d edition, revised by P. H. Nidditch, of *Enquiries Concerning Human Understanding and Concerning the Principles of Morals* (Oxford: Clarendon Press, 1975).

must be a resemblance betwixt those objects, of which we have had experience, and those which lie beyond the reach of our discovery" (*Treatise*, 91–94, 165).[5]

Hume, of course, is aware that we make predictions based on causal evidence all the time, and quite properly so. When we make such predictions, however, they are not based on anything we can observe in the physical world or demonstrate by deductive reasoning. In place of the traditional ontological and rational foundations for cause and effect, Hume offers the principle of "Custom or Habit," by which he means the feeling produced in the mind by the repeated observance of one event following another. "Custom, then," says Hume,

> is the great guide of human life. It is that principle alone which renders our experience useful to us, and makes us expect, for the future, a similar train of events with those which have appeared in the past. Without the influence of custom, we should be entirely ignorant of every matter of fact beyond what is immediately present to the memory and senses. (*Enquiry*, 43–45)

For Hume "experience only teaches us, how one event constantly follows another; without instructing us in the secret connexion, which binds them together, and renders them inseparable" (*Enquiry*, 66).

Hume wished to define cause and effect in such a way that everyone could agree with it and so end all philosophical dispute over it and over the doctrine of necessity it entailed. Hume also wanted to demonstrate that his analysis of causation held for both the physical world and the mental world, that is, for both the relations between physical objects and between the will and its effects. Ultimately Hume wanted to capitalize on the success of the experimental method in the natural sciences for moral and psychological enquiry; but before he could do that, he had to put science on the same footing as the philosophy of mind and morals.

Hume knew, however, that his arguments sharply circumscribed the limits of human knowledge and exposed the "narrow extent of science when applied to material causes" (*Enquiry*, 93). He was also

---

5. All references to Hume's *A Treatise of Human Nature* are to L. A. Selby-Bigge's 2d edition, revised by P. H. Nidditch (Oxford: Clarendon Press, 1978).

well aware that by making cause and effect a feeling produced in the mind by custom and habit, he was placing it on very skeptical grounds. If reason could not be trusted, sensory experience was not infallible either.

Hume's analysis of the relation of identity was no less skeptical or devastating to the traditional foundations of knowledge than his analysis of cause and effect. Hume's views on identity effectively challenged the long-standing myth of the unitary personality by reducing the identity of the individual to a mere bundle of discrete sensations. If all knowledge is based on the perception of discrete sensations, Hume's argument runs, then there are no certain means of determining whether the sense data of one perception is identical with the data of another perception. In other words, nothing can assure us of the uninterrupted, continuing existence of anything in the external world, whether it is an object or a person. Since *the mind never perceives any real connexion among distinct existences*" (*Treatise*, 636; Hume's emphasis), we know only what we perceive when we perceive it, and the rest is all a fictitious construction of memory and imagination, "the fiction of a continu'd existence," as Hume calls it (*Treatise*, 205). When Hume looks into the mind he finds "nothing but a bundle or collection of different perceptions, which succeed each other with an inconceivable rapidity, and are in a perpetual flux and movement" (*Treatise*, 252); he sees no justification other than habit or custom for positing a single and unified self that is continuous and unvarying over time and to which any succession of perceptions could be assigned. "When I turn my reflexion on *myself*," says Hume, "I never can perceive this *self* without some one or more perceptions; nor can I ever perceive any thing but the perceptions. 'Tis the composition of these, therefore, which forms the self" (*Treatise*, 634; Hume's emphases). According to Hume, the imagination has simply acquired a habit based on experience that transforms a continuous flux of impressions and ideas into a notion of personal identity (*Treatise*, 253–55). "Identity," says Hume, "is nothing really belonging to these different perceptions [of the mind], and uniting them together; but is merely a quality, which we attribute to them" (*Treatise*, 260).

Hume's philosophy had a number of different effects on subsequent thinkers. Hume himself said (understating the case for his eighteenth-century contemporaries), "We may, perhaps, find that it is with difficulty we are induced to fix such narrow limits to human understanding" (*Enquiry*, 93–94); and extreme skepticism of the type we find in Pater's "Conclusion" was a rather late development of British empiricism. In his own lifetime Hume's philosophy was received sympathetically only in France. Initially philosophers either denied Hume's premises and arguments, as did Thomas Reid, the Scottish philosopher of common sense, or like Kant, they tried to find a new ground for identity and causation in the structures of the mind itself. Later empirical thinkers like the Mills and Bentham tried to extend and apply the insights of Hume's epistemology to a number of areas of intellectual inquiry in their synthesis of the doctrines of Locke, Berkeley, Hume, and others under the aegis of Utilitarianism.

On occasion Pater acknowledged his debt to the empirical tradition. In *Plato and Platonism*, for example, he refers to the "wholesome" modern skepticism of Hume and Mill; and in *Marius the Epicurean* Pater has his protagonist agree with Berkeley that it is easier to conceive of matter as thought than to conceive of mind as matter. Marius's rationale, however—that "because mind was really nearer to himself: it was an explanation of what was less known by what was known better"—avoids Berkeley's recourse to Divinity (*ME* 2:69–70). Perhaps Pater's most emphatic endorsement of empiricism generally, and of Hume in particular, is his reference in "Sir Thomas Browne" (1886) to the "great stride" of philosophy that "ends with Hume" (*App.*, 159).

More emphatic than his explicit endorsement of these philosophers, however, is the extent to which he drew from them in his own thinking and works. The subjectivity of knowledge, the primacy of sensation over abstraction, the relation of idea to sensation, the perpetual flux of our impressions and ideas, the disintegration of personality, skepticism about any form of certain knowledge, pleasure and the pursuit of completeness and perfection of life as an end in itself—all this derives, with modifications from other sources and Pater's own temperament, from these three major empiricists. Of these Hume appears to exert the largest influence, especially in Pater's early works. Mill assumes more prominence in the Epicureanism of Marius, particularly in the chapter called "New Cyrenaicism." Despite Pater's skepticism and his general lack of interest in Utilitarianism, much of the philosophic rationale, if not the tone and temper, of his "true" Epicureanism could be found in the doctrines of John Stuart Mill. In Marius's Epicureanism, for example, we find Mill's notions that pleasure and freedom from pain are the only things desirable as ends and that pleasure must be judged in terms of quality as well as quantity. We also find pleasure defined not merely in sensory terms but also in terms of Mill's emphases on intellectual pleasure and on the social welfare of the community.

Pater's empiricism, like Abelard's described in "Two Early French Stories," sought "to find a ground of reality below the abstractions of philosophy, as one bent on trying all things by their congruity with human experience" (*Ren.*, 8). He wanted for himself, as for Marius, a theory with "no basis of unverified hypothesis," a philosophy of the here and now which makes no recourse to a metaphysical "future after all somewhat problematic" (*ME* 1:149). Pater found his verifiable ground in human sensation. Reality for Pater, as for Hume, was at bottom nothing more than a "series of fleeting impressions" (*ME* 1:146). Knowledge in this scheme of things was limited to "what we feel," to "direct sensation"; and since Pater, like his Marius (but unlike Hume), believed that the phenomena of the senses never deceive us and that we can never deceive ourselves about them (*ME* 1:138–39), he resolved to "live in the concrete" (*ME* 1:164), to "hold by what his eyes really saw," and to reject any facile fantasies about this world or another (*ME* 2:90). As a writer he would record an "exact and literal transcript" of what passed before him, and his "philosophic scheme" would be "but the reflection of the *data* of sense, and chiefly of sight" (*ME* 1:164–65; Pater's emphasis).

In the "Conclusion" Pater gives us the fullest exposition of his early empirical position. As we saw in previous chapters, after a brief flirtation with positivism in "Coleridge's Writing," Pater was content to leave the physical world of molecules and atoms behind in favor of the phenomenal world of sensory images, where "each object is loosed into a group of impressions—colour, odour, texture—in the mind of the observer." The "Conclusion" opens with this transition from an outer world to an inner world, thus paralleling a similar shift in the focus of philosophy that had been taking place over the previous century. "That clear, perpetual outline of face and limb," says Pater, "is but an image of ours, under which we group" our impressions of elements without; it is a momentary "design in a web, the actual threads of which pass out beyond it." It is this image or gestalt that has Pater's passionate allegiance.

Pater's "inward world of thought and feeling," of "sensations and ideas," closely follows Hume's analysis of experience. There are no fixed certainties in this world. The flux, the "race of the mid-stream," the "drift of momentary acts of sight and passion and thought," is even swifter than in the world without. This is a world not of solid objects but of unstable impressions, "which burn and are extinguished with our consciousness of them." Experience itself is reduced to a "swarm of impressions"[6] in the mind (*Ren.*, 234–35). Like Hume, Pater denies that rational analysis can carry us very far; it can only confirm that experience indeed is nothing but a continuous succession of fleeting moments.

Pater also accepts the implications of Hume's sensationism for the notion of the unitary personality. Although at one point Pater would contain the "swarm of impressions" that constitutes individual experience within a solipsistic "wall of personality," he also acknowledges that the self shapes itself and dissolves itself as continuously and as rapidly as the impressions that constitute it. "The passage and dissolution of impressions," in other words, correspond to "that continual vanishing away, that strange, perpetual weaving and unweaving of ourselves" (*Ren.*, 236). In his first version of the "Conclusion" Pater was even more explicit and emphatic about the dissolution of the self. There he says that the vision of experience as a flux of sensation elicits the "image of one washed out beyond the bar in a sea at ebb, losing even his personality, as the elements of which he is composed pass into new combinations. Struggling, as he must, to save himself, it is himself that he loses at every moment" ("WM," 311).

If we pursue this empirical analysis of experience and personality into twentieth-century literature and aesthetics, we find that Hume's understanding of fundamental relations like identity and cause and effect not only has had far-reaching consequences on subsequent phi-

---

6. The phrase "swarm of impressions" appears in the original version of the "Conclusion" and in the 1873, 1888, and 1900 editions. The 1893 and 1910 editions substitute the phrase "group of impressions" (*The Renaissance: Studies in Art and Poetry: The 1893 Text*, ed. Donald L. Hill [Berkeley: University of California Press, 1980], pp. 187, 273, hereinafter referred to as the Hill edition).

losophy down to the present day but also has had a profound impact, transmitted through influential formulations such as Pater's "Conclusion," on Modernist literary techniques. Hume's analysis spawned an authoritative philosophic tradition that prepared the way for the breach with Aristotelian aesthetics, whose conceptions of character and plot depend heavily on the concepts of unitary personality and cause and effect. Hume's skepticism, along with his emphasis on perception as a discontinuous succession of sensory impressions, provided a rationale for the widespread Modernist techniques of discontinuous juxtaposition and various forms of narration based on psychological perception rather than plot and character. It also led to the gradual dissolution of the individual personality in modern fictional characters. One of the hallmarks of Modernist art is the fragmentary nature of its vision of experience. This fragmentation is usually attributed to the nature of life in the pluralistic, urbanized, industrialized society of the twentieth century; but almost two hundred years earlier Hume's phenomenalism provided the philosophical foundation for the fragmented world view rendered in techniques such as stream of consciousness and the multiple perspectives of Modern art.

Virginia Woolf was one of the first to call explicitly for techniques like these to replace the Aristotelian conventions. In her essay "Modern Fiction," written in 1919, she insists that the traditional conventions and forms, such as plot, comedy, tragedy, and detailed physical descriptions, are no longer capable of capturing life where Hume relocated it—"close to the quick of the mind." She exhorts her fellow writers to develop techniques like those Joyce used in *Portrait* and *Ulysses*, techniques that will express life as a flux of sensation and ideas: "Let us record the atoms as they fall upon the mind in the order in which they fall, let us trace the pattern, however disconnected and incoherent in appearance, which each sight or incident scores upon the consciousness."[7] Woolf's call for new techniques of psychic portraiture may have been based on Joyce's success with Stephen Dedalus and Leopold and Molly Bloom, but behind those successes lay Hume's analysis of experience.

The typical Modernist technique of discontinuous juxtaposition,

---

7. *Collected Essays* (London: Hogarth Press, 1966), 2:106–7.

employed in poems like Pound's *Cantos*, Eliot's *The Waste Land*, and Crane's *The Bridge*, is just one more way writers have responded to a world in which the bonds of cause and effect have been loosed and life itself is perceived as a rapid succession of discrete impressions. In place of cause and effect Modernist writers use principles such as psychological or verbal association and symbolic or mythic structures as substitutes for the older aesthetic principles of cohesion. Joyce's use of association, his use of the Daedalus myth in *Portrait*, and his use of the *Odyssey* in *Ulysses* are prime examples of these new techniques, as is Eliot's use of fertility myths and the grail legend in *The Waste Land*.

As experience in Modernist literature was fragmented and discontinuous, so was the individual personality, even to the point of dissolution. Yeats, who like many others saw the new, fragmented vision of experience emerging suddenly around the turn of the century, said, "Nature, steel-bound or stone-built in the nineteenth century, became a flux where man drowned or swam; the moment had come for some poet to cry 'the flux is in my own mind.'" Yeats's image of the drowning man here echoes Pater's own image for the dissolving personality; and a few paragraphs later Yeats explicitly invokes Pater: "Did Pater foreshadow," he asks, "a poetry, a philosophy, where the individual is nothing, the flux of *The Cantos* of Ezra Pound?"[8] Although Yeats failed to see Hume behind Pater, he at least acknowledged the role of the empirical vision of the flux in dissolving our comfortable notion of the unitary personality.

Pirandello particularly made significant use of the notion of a fragmented, discontinuous personality. In his masterpieces *Henry IV* and *Six Characters in Search of an Author*, the protagonists present no single, identifiable self but only different masks or roles at different times, in different circumstances, and to different people. Under the impetus of Browning, Wilde, Pound, and others, Modernist writers generally became increasingly concerned with masks and personae in contrast to the more traditional concern with character and personality.

---

8. *The Oxford Book of Modern Verse*, pp. xxviii, xxx.

> "It was the mask engaged your mind,
> And after set your heart to beat,
> Not what's behind,"

replies Yeats's persona in "The Mask" to his more conventional lover, who wants him to "put off" the mask and reveal the "true" self beneath. " 'What matter,' " the persona concludes, " 'so there is but fire / In you, in me?' " [9]

In addition to masks and personae, the fragmented personality or the divided self has become commonplace in Modernist literature. Conrad's Lord Jim, who cannot reconcile his ideal of himself with his actual behavior, is one of the earliest examples of the disintegration of the self. In *The Waste Land* Eliot carries this disintegration further in the figure of Tiresias, who approximates Hume's description of the self as a mere succession of discrete perceptions. Post-Modern literature completes the destruction of the unitary personality by expunging and, in effect, denying the existence of any identifiable self, fragmented or otherwise, as in Beckett's *Unnamable* or any of the many disembodied voices that narrate contemporary fiction.

Another Modernist tradition fostered by the empiricist notion of knowledge being built up out of simple sensations is the cult of the concrete and the pursuit of experience for its own sake. Through influential formulations, such as Pater's "Conclusion," Hume provided philosophic sanction for the claim of the more empirically oriented Modernists, such as Bergson, Hulme, Pound, the Imagists, and John Crowe Ransom, that sensation is primary and ideas secondary.

T. E. Hulme's essay "Bergson's Theory of Art" is perhaps the most extreme manifesto of this cult. Hulme accepted Bergson's position that ordinary perception, which could see only through the veil of conventional categories, perceived only certain stock or fixed types: "Our faculties of perception are, as it were, crystallised out into certain moulds. Most of us, then, never see things as they are, but see only the stock types which are embodied in language." The artist, on the other hand, "is able to emancipate himself from the moulds which language

---

9. *The Poems of W. B. Yeats*, ed. Richard J. Finneran (New York: Macmillan, 1983), p. 95.

and ordinary perception force on him," and as a result he is "able to see things freshly as they really are" and "to convey over the actual things he sees or the emotions he feels." He captures the freshness and individuality of a thing, rather than its universal qualities or significance. He tries to hand over sensation "bodily"—direct and unmediated as the intuitions of original experience. By avoiding the stereotyped forms of language and perception the artist can communicate his "actual contact with reality." This direct communication of reality, this "life-communicating quality," as Hulme calls it, is the essence of the aesthetic experience.[10]

A later development of Hulme's position can be found in John Crowe Ransom's well-known essay "Poetry: A Note on Ontology." Here Ransom insists on a "physical poetry," a poetry of things rather than ideas. Drawing on a basic empiricist tenet, he asserts the image as the raw material of the idea. In its primitive state the image has a "primordial freshness" as it is "discovered" in its "natural or wild state." The proper function of the aesthetic imagination is to "contemplate things as they are in their rich and contingent materiality." The idea, on the other hand, is an "image with its character beaten out of it." The "Platonic world of ideas," according to Ransom, "fails to coincide with the original world of perception, which is the world populated by the stubborn and contingent objects." Platonic poetry, the poetry of ideas, subordinates things or images to ideas so that they become mere illustrations or ornaments of ideas. Ransom calls this type of poetry "predatory" because it reduces everything to the scientific or the universal and through abstraction destroys the individuality, the uniqueness, the freshness, the very thingness of things.[11] Ransom's appeal to the oversimplified opposition between poetry and science goes back as far as Coleridge, and its corollary opposition between the concrete and the abstract led Ransom into his paradoxical description of a poem as "a *logical structure* having a *local texture*" (Ransom's emphases). He goes on to say that texture is the essentially

---

10. Quotations from "Bergson's Theory of Art" are taken from *Speculations: Essays on Humanism and the Philosophy of Art*, ed. Herbert Read (New York: Harcourt, Brace, 1924), pp. 141–69.

11. Quotations from "Poetry: A Note on Ontology" are taken from *The World's Body* (Baton Rouge: Louisiana State University Press, 1968), pp. 111–42.

poetic element and that, like wallpaper in a house, it is "logically un-related to structure."[12]

The cult of concrete experience at the expense of intellectual ab-straction helped to revivify the practice of poetry in the twentieth cen-tury, but it also led to a number of theoretical dead ends in Modernist aesthetics and to an obfuscation of the very nature of abstraction and its role in perception and art. Murray Krieger has extensively ex-plored many of the theoretical paradoxes of New Criticism in *The New Apologists for Poetry*; but aside from its inherent paradoxes, the cult of the concrete ignored the abstracting nature of the entire human perceptual and conceptual apparatus. So-called immediate sensation is already highly selected and abstracted from the bewildering chaos of data that bombards the senses every second. While sensation may differ from ideas or conceptual abstractions in the nature of the ab-straction involved, what we abstract from the raw data presented to the senses is even more radically transformed perhaps than the trans-formation of sensation into conception. In other words, sensations may be closer to ideas than to an object world, as Pater seems to have understood when he agreed with Berkeley that it is easier to conceive of matter as mind than of mind as matter. Pater also understood that any apprehension that emphasizes one of our faculties at the expense of others is likely to be only half alive. Even William Carlos Williams's "red wheel barrow / glazed with rain water / beside the white chick-ens" is nothing without its introductory abstraction, "so much de-pends upon"; and if the reader knows something about Imagism, New Criticism, and the polemical context, the poem is many times more alive and fresh and original than if the reader responds simply with pure unsullied sensation.

Other notions bequeathed by Bergson and Hulme have been equally troublesome. By making special claims for the artist's mode of percep-tion Bergson, in his attempt to defend art in a scientific age, actually hindered the progress of aesthetics by obscuring some real affinities art has with other modes of knowing. Bergson, for example, insists that the unique intuitive genius of the artist puts us into direct contact with reality in its most concrete form, whereas conventions and ab-

---

12. "Criticism as Pure Speculation," in *Critical Theory Since Plato*, ed. Hazard Adams (New York: Harcourt, Brace, Jovanovich, 1971), pp. 886–87.

67

stractions deaden reality and distance it from us. Bergson's view, however, obscures a number of obvious considerations. First, creativity is not peculiar to artists. It is a term we use to define the capacity to be strikingly original and to show us how to perceive experience in fresh and unique ways, whether it be through the images, scenes, characters, and plots of literary artists, or through the fresh and original abstract insights of philosophers or scientists. No serious claim can be made that Joyce gave us more fresh and original insight into reality than Freud, Einstein, or Wittgenstein. Second, conventions and abstractions are not in themselves deadening and opaque. They are as vital to knowledge and experience as concrete images, and a cliché can be just as stale whether it be an image or an abstraction. It is now generally recognized that all communication depends on conventions, which can be used in fresh, ingenious, and novel ways, as well as in stale, deadening ways. The prejudice against conventions fails to recognize that language is one of our most creative systems of conventions and that without it there would be much less contact with reality, direct or otherwise. Pater, in contrast to Hulme, did not confuse conventions and abstractions with clichés as the great deadeners of perception (*GL*, 158).

In a number of passages Pater did adumbrate views of the artist later held by Bergson. In "Winckelmann," for example, he says, "The basis of all artistic genius lies in the power of conceiving humanity in a new and striking way, of putting a happy world of its own creation in place of the meaner world of our common days, generating around itself an atmosphere with a novel power of refraction, selecting, transforming, recombining the images it transmits, according to the choice of the imaginative intellect" (*Ren.*, 213–14). But even here Pater does not totally subscribe to the naïve empiricism of Bergson or Hulme. Pater had no illusions about direct contact with reality. Rather he realized that the artist's powers operate in accordance with the "imaginative intellect," a notion he defined in Hegelian terms, and that in order to achieve his novel conception of experience, the artist has "to employ the most cunning detail, to complicate and refine upon thought and passion a thousandfold" (*Ren.*, 214).

However much the "Conclusion" may have contributed to various Modernist techniques and the cult of the concrete, in *Marius the Epicurean* Pater himself moved away from the strict Humean empiricism of that essay. Initially Marius arrives at a position very similar to that of the "Conclusion"; since a life based on sensation could not lead beyond itself with any certainty, Marius resolves to fill every present moment of his life "with vivid sensations, and such intellectual apprehensions, as, in strength and directness and their immediately realised values at the bar of an actual experience, are most like sensations" (*ME* 1:144). In other words, he will confine himself to Hume's very limited reality of sense impressions and ideas that are more or less direct copies of these impressions.

But, as Pater says, "*Let us eat and drink, for to-morrow we die!*—is a proposal, the real import of which differs immensely according to the natural taste, and the acquired judgment, of the guests who sit at the table" (*ME* 1:145; Pater's emphasis). Although Pater and Marius began with the maxim "*Life as the end of life,*" it was "not pleasure, but a general completeness of life" that was "the practical ideal to which this anti-metaphysical metaphysic really pointed" (Pater's emphasis). His goal would be "insight through culture, into all that the present moment holds in trust for us, as we stand so briefly in its presence" (*ME* 1:142–45). From this point Marius moves well beyond the limits of Hume's empiricism to a broader Stoic concern with general humanity, to Christian pity and sympathy, and to a resolve to add nothing to the store of human unhappiness in the world.

The inspiration and authority for Pater's scheme for Marius's intellectual development came from a number of different sources. Berkeley and Hume provided the foundation of his development in sensation; but Hume's skepticism, along with Kant's critique of knowledge, also provided the negative phase of Marius's aesthetic education that carefully circumscribed the limits of human knowledge. The more positive elements, on the other hand, were provided primarily by Mill, Schiller, and Hegel, who enabled Pater to move, however inconsistently, beyond the skepticism of Hume and the world of immediate sensation to a "world of intellectual discipline" and "impassioned contemplation," where pleasure was not merely sensuous, but intellectual, ethical, and moral as well. Although Mill's Utilitarianism differs radically in its tone and emphasis from Marius's Cyrenaicism, Mill at least provided Pater with a precedent for applying the insights of empirical philosophy to social, ethical, and intellectual matters. The actual tone and orientation of this application, however, derived more from Schiller and Hegel, who built upon Kant's rather than Hume's foundation. From Schiller came the notion of a primarily aesthetic education, with *aesthetic* defined very broadly in epistemological terms; and Pater's whole scheme of development from negative to positive, as well as his comfortable accommodation of a life of the spirit to the life of sense, had its precedent in the doctrines and dialectics of Hegel.

The Hegelian world of the rational spirit seems very distant from the empirical world of Berkeley and Hume with its reality reduced to impressions and ideas that are copies of impressions. Hume did deal with the relations of thought, but he was very skeptical of them, and he reduced the most important of them, causation and identity, to clusters of discrete sensations. Pater, on the other hand, unconcerned with philosophical rigor, was much more comfortable in the company of the intellectual spirit. Although throughout his career he continued to emphasize the primacy of sensation and to maintain that intuition and the concrete are more natural than intellect and the abstract (*PP*, 155–56), he had a temperamental predisposition for things contemplative and intellectual that was at least equal to his avowed obsession with sense, and perhaps even more compelling in him, if we judge not by what he says, but by the nature of his most powerful passages. We do not remember Pater for his exquisite rendering of concrete, sensuous detail; others, Keats for example, far outstrip him in this capacity. His most memorable passages are not physical descriptions of Florian Deleal's childhood home, of Aurelian Rome, or of Botticelli's paintings; rather they are passionate renderings of a whole complex organism responding to artifacts of intellectual culture. This characterizes his greatest passages, such as the "Conclusion," the famous description of the Mona Lisa, and passages from his essays on Winckelmann, Wordsworth, Plato, and style.

Pater's position on the relations between sense and intellect can be ascertained more clearly in the light of two opposite reactions to Kant, one represented by Hegel and the other by Bergson and T. E. Hulme. Kant's model of the mind had severed the understanding at one extreme from the realm of pure reason and at the other extreme from the ding an sich, the thing-in-itself, the object in the external world that impinges on the senses. Hegel's critique of Kant tried to salvage pure reason on the new epistemological grounds Kant established, while the critique implicit in the Bergson-Hulme position tried to salvage our contact with the actual physical objects of the world. Pater had little desire either to salvage direct contact with actual physical objects or to follow Hegel into the realm of absolute spirit. Like Nietzsche, he occupied a position equally disposed to the Dionysian impulses toward sense and the Apollonian impulses toward abstract intellect; but in the end he was content with the realm of pure phenomena without any absolute assurances from either reason or a material world beyond our sense impressions. Reason and the abstract played an important functional role for Pater, but neither were they deified, as in German idealism, nor were they rejected outright in favor of an impossible ideal of direct contact with reality, as with Bergson and Hulme. Pater recognized that the senses, as well as the intellect, altered, shaped, conditioned, and abstracted from the actual data that impinged upon them. But he did not thereby despair of any fresh understandings of experience, nor did he engage in, as Keats put it in his famous discussion of *negative capability*, "any irritable reaching after fact and reason." Whatever Pater rejected in Kant, he appears to have accepted Kant's limitations on knowledge at both extremes; and he knew that freshness was gained not by direct contact with reality, but by a new orientation in the mind and sensibility of the perceiving subject.

Pater's attempt to resolve the tension between sense and intellect in his thought resulted in his efforts to develop the concept of a unified sensibility, a concept central to Modernist art. Pater's contribution to this concept is the subject of a later chapter. Here it will suffice to note that a unified sensibility is one that fully integrates and harmonizes the operations of sense, emotion, and intellect. In *Marius*, for example, Pater foresees "true aesthetic culture" as a "new form of the contemplative life" operating in a "world of perfected sensation, intelligence, emotion" (*ME* 1:148). If Pater's early views anticipated the antipathy toward abstraction shared by Bergson, Hulme, Pound, the Imagists, and the New Critics, all of whom drew very heavily from the empirical tradition, his later views anticipated other Modernists, such as Yeats, Joyce, Eliot, Virginia Woolf, and Wallace Stevens, who achieved a more balanced fusion of idealism and empiricism.

Despite Pater's movement toward a unified balance between concrete sensation and abstract thought, his own formulations of the relations between sense and intellect were problematic. This was partly due to his persistent polemical emphasis on the primacy of sensation, an emphasis he maintained in the midst of his equally persistent and contradictory fascination with the rational spirit. Nevertheless, Pater's polemics on the primacy of sensory experience, particularly in its most influential formulation in the "Conclusion," firmly established him in the minds of many as the apostle of sensation; it is this side of Pater, the Pater of the "Conclusion," that contributed significantly to the cult of the concrete and to the fragmented worlds and personalities of Modernist art.

5 / THE LIMITS OF IDEALISM: KANT AND SCHELLING

UP TO this point I have dealt primarily with one side of Pater—the Pater who abhors absolutism and who embraces sensation, relativity, subjectivity, and skepticism in all things. This is, by and large, the Pater of the "Conclusion," the Pater worshiped by Wilde and other aesthetes in the nineties, and the Pater whose reputation survived into the first half of the twentieth century. There is that other side to Pater, however, that is equally important to his Modernist successors, a much more intellectualized Pater who investigated in both his criticism and fiction many forms of idealism from Parmenides to Hegel: he deals with the Eleatics and Platonic idealism in *Plato and Platonism*; with the idealism of early Christianity in *Marius*; with late medieval Christianity and the Platonism of Giordano Bruno in *Gaston de Latour*; with the Platonism of Pico della Mirandola and Michelangelo in *The Renaissance*; and with a pathological Spinozan idealism in "Sebastian van Storck." From his first published essay on Coleridge's religious and philosophical absolutism to his last published essay on Pascal's religious asceticism, Pater was obsessed with the idealistic temperament, even while he was often setting himself in opposition to it. A list of Pater's explicit treatments of idealism, however, does not suggest the extent to which it pervaded his own temperament; for whether Pater was espousing idealism or sensation at any given point, all of his works embody a dialectical tension between the poles of sense and intellect, a tension which in him, as in Yeats, was never wholly reconciled or harmonized. The terms of this opposition sometimes varied—expressed at different times as an opposition between Christian and Hellenic, Apollonian and Dionysian, or empirical and idealist—but the essential dialectical tension always remained at the core of Pater's temperament and thought.

In contrast to the skeptical empiricism that led to his emphasis on sensation, the other side of the Paterian temperament was decidedly rationalist, a Pater who in his last published essay could appreciate the imaginative force, if not the literal truth, of Pascal's assertion, *"Toute notre dignité consiste donc en la pensée"* (MS, 83). If Pater was restrained by his empiricism from wholeheartedly embracing the constructs of reason, he nevertheless had a constitutional affinity for them. At times his emphasis on sensation and his views on abstract thinking flatly contradict each other, as in *Plato and Platonism* where he both affirms and denies the efficacy of intellectual abstraction; but in his own writing, whether critical or fictional, he is much more eloquent about ideas than about sensuous beauty.

Richard Wollheim, one of the few critics to capture accurately both the balance and the ambivalence of Pater's intellectual temper, identifies "two separate elements" in his philosophic attitude in a way that suggests the place of intellectual culture in Pater's scheme of things: "There is, first," says Wollheim, "his sense of the folly, of the futility of metaphysical speculation. . . . And, secondly, there is Pater's awareness of the fascination that such systems have always had, perhaps always would have, for the human mind." According to Wollheim, Pater reconciled these two elements not theoretically but with "the suggestion . . . that we should always look at metaphysical speculation as an exaggeration, or as a projection, of certain recognized ways we have of feeling, or thinking, of talking about the world around us."[1] Wollheim here is referring to Pater's own practice of translating abstract thought into terms of individual temperament, a translation that moderates

---

1. *On Art and the Mind* (Cambridge: Harvard University Press, 1974), pp. 158–59. In *Plato and Platonism* Pater says, "Platonism is not a formal theory or body of theories, but a tendency, a group of tendencies—a tendency to think or feel, and to speak, about certain things in a particular way" (150).

the harshness of abstraction and fleshes out its dry bones: for example, the way the severity of Heraclitus's thought is moderated by the "subtly practical worldly-wisdom" of Aristippus. "It has been sometimes seen, in the history of the human mind," says the narrator of *Marius*, "that when thus translated into terms of sentiment—of sentiment, as lying already half-way towards practice—the abstract ideas of metaphysics for the first time reveal their true significance. The metaphysical principle, in itself, as it were, without hands or feet, becomes impressive, fascinating, of effect, when translated into a precept as to how it were best to feel and act; in other words, under its sentimental or ethical equivalent" (*ME* 1:135).

It would appear that Pater's interest focuses chiefly on the practical consequences of metaphysical thought; but this assessment is not quite accurate and needs more refinement. Given Pater's insistence on the subjectivity of knowledge, that is, "that the reception of this or that speculative conclusion is really a matter of will" (*ME* 1:136), his translation of thought into sentiment places metaphysics between a prior subjective disposition toward accepting them and a subsequent and equally subjective conversion of them into terms of individual sentiment, and this sentiment is itself a halfway house toward action. Pater's contemplative nature seldom proceeds beyond this halfway house, but his formulation of the role of metaphysics nevertheless indicates an interest less in the abstractions themselves than in their practical consequences. "The truth is," says Wollheim, "that for Pater all metaphysics is essentially Janus-like. It faces two ways. It faces backwards to its origins in feeling and thought or language. But it also faces forward toward its consequences in practice. . . . To discern the practical equivalent of a metaphysical theory is not just to be in a better position to predict its consequences: it is integral to assessing, indeed to understanding, it." [2]

Wollheim's assessment is accurate as long as we limit the practical consequences of metaphysical thought to the understanding of experience. Pater was much more temperamentally disposed toward contemplation than action, and despite his own comments about practical equivalents of abstractions, the effects of metaphysical thought

---

2. *On Art and the Mind*, pp. 164–65.

that preoccupy his writing are not practical, ethical actions but rather "how it were best to feel"—in other words, how metaphysics, converted into sentiment, conditions and tempers the individual human spirit. Pater regarded philosophic speculation, then, pragmatically—in terms of its utility or function in helping us to understand and appreciate experience and in terms of the consequences of that understanding on the shaping of an individual temper. Even in the "Conclusion," one of Pater's most antimetaphysical essays, philosophy is valued insofar as it can enhance our experience of life, rouse the human spirit, "startle it to a life of constant and eager observation," and "help us to gather up what might otherwise pass unregarded by us" (*Ren.*, 236–37).

If we overlook Pater's heavy emphasis on the individual and his lack of philosophical rigor, we can find in his attitude toward philosophic speculation an anticipation of later, more successful attempts to fuse empiricism and idealism by philosophers such as Nietzsche, Cassirer, and the American pragmatists, particularly Dewey, all of whom contributed substantially to the philosophic and aesthetic foundations of Modernism. In *Substance and Function* Cassirer distinguishes between popular notions of pragmatism, which, like Benthamism, identify the concept of truth with the concept of utility, and a more rigorous philosophical pragmatism, which characterizes his own thought and that of "Dewey and his school." The latter, a "finer and more subtle interpretation" of pragmatism, according to Cassirer, perceives the practical consequences of philosophic speculation not in purposes external to thought but in its contribution to the development of philosophic thought and the "progressive unification of the manifold": "We call a proposition 'true,'" says Cassirer,

> not because it agrees with a fixed reality beyond all thought and all possibility of thought, but because it is verified in the process of thought and leads to new and fruitful consequences. Its real justification is the effect, which it produces in the tendency toward progressive unification. Each hypothesis of knowledge has its justification merely with reference to this fundamental task; it is valid to the degree that it succeeds in intellectually organizing and harmoniously shaping the originally isolated sensuous data.[3]

---

3. *Substance and Function*, pp. 317–18.

Although Pater did not share Cassirer's optimism for the progressive unification of thought, Cassirer's attitude toward the function of speculative thought as providing the organizing principles for the sensuous manifold is very close to Pater's, and it indicates how far he had proceeded beyond the utilitarianism empirical philosophy had fostered in other nineteenth-century thinkers.

Like Cassirer, Pater views the formative powers of various intellectual disciplines—philosophy, art, morality, science, myth, and religion—in a functionalist perspective. He even admired Raphael for the functional prowess of his intellect: "We have here," Pater proclaims, "the sort of intelligence to be found in Lessing, in Herder, in Hegel, in those who, by the instrumentality of an organized philosophic system, have comprehended in one view or vision what poetry has been, or what Greek philosophy, as great complex dynamic facts of the world" (*MS*, 56).

Pater's remark about Raphael points to the source of his functionalism—the German idealists. Nothing in Hume and the empirical tradition accounts for either Pater's confidence in the employment of intellectual schemes or his obsession with abstraction in all his works. Pater's notion of ideas is much closer to Hegel than to Hume. For Hume ideas were built up out of sensation, and a simple idea was an image of a sensation. For Pater, on the other hand, ideas were abstract schemes that organized sensations and gave them meaning. Although Pater could never accept any of Hegel's metaphysical absolutes and infinites, he was open to his analyses of phenomenal experience, culture, art, history, and philosophy. Pater was always wary of metaphysical abstractions—he considered them "bad masters"—but taken in the right spirit they were "very useful ministers towards the understanding, towards an analytical survey, of all that the intellect has produced"; and in such thinking he found the German mind especially rich (*EG*, 30).[4]

Inspired by German thought, Pater endowed the rational intellect with formidable power. As with Coleridge, his polemics of pleasure and sensation obscured a deeply rational soul. In *Plato and Platonism* he assigns philosophy the "continuous purpose" of discovering beneath the "apparent chaos" of experience a "unity in variety," a "*cos-*

---

4. In *Marius* Pater notes how the indifference of the Cyrenaics made them masters rather than servants of intellectual systems (*ME* 2:23).

mos—an order that shall satisfy one's reasonable soul" (52; Pater's emphasis). Pater meant *philosophy* in a post-Kantian sense, however. As we saw earlier, in the essay on Prosper Mérimée, Pater accepted the more limited perspectives of the post-Kantian world, where philosophies of substance were supplanted by philosophies of function. "What is really new in a new organism is the new cohering force," Pater says. "As, in physical organisms, the actual particles of matter have existed long before in other combinations" (*GS*, 215), so too with cultural and intellectual entities all the elements have been used before, and "nothing but the life-giving principle of cohesion is new; the new perspective, the resultant complexion, the expressiveness which familiar thoughts attain by novel juxtaposition. In other words, the *form* is new" (*PP*, 8; Pater's emphasis).

If the *matter* of philosophy remains constant, what provides the shape? What is the source of the new perspective? Pater's answer is human reason (guided, of course, by individual temperament). If the outer world consists of mere matter that can be molded into various forms, and if the realm of metaphysical absolutes is dismissed as unknowable, then what determines the configuration of the matter must come from within the mind. "To enforce a reasonable unity and order," says Pater, "to impress some larger likeness of reason, as one knows it in one's self, upon the chaotic infinitude of the impressions that reach us from every side, is what all philosophy as such proposes." Although it would fain discover a preexistent reality, philosophy actually projects the "light of intelligence upon the at first sight somewhat unmeaning world we find actually around us" (*PP*, 35–36).

Although Pater talks nostalgically about the old philosophies of substance, he claims their formative power, whether projected or discovered, is similar to the power of the fine arts to mold material things and the power of moral discipline to mold lives. This power consists in a "delightful adaptation of means to ends, of the parts to the whole," that endows "the entire scene about one, bewildering, unsympathetic, unreasonable, on a superficial view," with a "welcome expression of fitness" (*PP*, 36). Modern science too embraces this formative spirit, though it may exist only "in fancy," "in the expansion of a large body of observed facts into some all-comprehensive hypothesis, such as 'evolution'" (*PP*, 37).

While Pater's exposure to German thought reinforced and partly formed his own habits of intellection and gave him a confidence in the powers of reason and in the utility of abstract schemes and conceptions, on the other hand, Kant's model of the mind based on a priori categories, Schelling's transcendental philosophy, and Hegel's logical absolutism were all tempered considerably by Pater's native empiricism, which relegated ideas to a subordinate role that was not absolute or transcendental in any sense, but purely functional.

A clearer perspective on Pater's pragmatic idealism can be established by looking more closely at his relationship to German thought. Billie Inman's study of Pater's reading has demonstrated conclusively the extensiveness of Pater's immersion in the works of German philosophers and critics, and in works inspired by them.[5] Most of them he read as an undergraduate and a fellow at Oxford, where in Pater's time Hegel's *Philosophy of History* was becoming popular. By the 1870s Oxford had spawned its own school of neo-Kantians and neo-Hegelians: William Wallace was there; Benjamin Jowett had tutored Pater; and Pater's friends included T. H. Green, Richard Lewis Nettleship, and Edward Caird.[6] By the mid-1880s, when *Marius the Epicurean* was published, "British thought," Helen Young says, "had been shaken by science; roused out of positivism, relativism, and agnosticism; inoculated with German metaphysics."[7] So Pater was exposed to German thought in a number of ways, and his immersion in it was as thorough as his immersion in the British empirical tradition from Bacon to Mill.

In general Pater's attitude toward German idealism and his attempt to reconcile it with his native empiricism were very much in step with the British philosophers of his time who were sympathetic toward the Germans. Caird and Green, for example, emphasized a "healthy Hegelian habit of doing full justice to the finite," and British Hegelians in general preferred a more logical and concrete universal to Hegel's Romanticized realm of the absolute spirit.[8]

---

5. Inman's book of brief but useful summaries of key works Pater is known to have read now constitutes the logical starting point for a study of his debt to the German idealists.

6. Young, pp. 13–15, 36, 41, 90 n. 79.

7. Young, p. 15.

8. Young, p. 92 n. 93; p. 108.

No definitive relationship between Pater and any of the German idealists can be established on the basis of his library borrowings, his allusions to them in his own writing, or his own brief, inadequate, occasional discussions of them in his essays. A full-scale exploration of Pater's ties with German thought warrants at least a book-length treatment of its own and remains a major gap in Pater scholarship.[9] Sorely needed is a major study of Pater and Hegel alone by someone who knows them both equally well. My purpose here is only to indicate Pater's attitude toward the German philosophers, the general outlines of how he adapted their thought, how his own thought and sensibility were shaped by their influence, and the importance of Pater's assimilation of German thought for Modernism. This can be accomplished by looking at a sampling of Pater's relationship to German thought, a sampling that brings out two sides to that relationship—one negative, directed primarily at Kant and Schelling, that establishes the limits of Pater's commitment to idealism, and the other positive, directed primarily toward Schiller and Hegel, that establishes a number of the Paterian principles and attitudes that helped shape Modernist literature and thought.

KANT

PATER'S RELATIONSHIP to Kant is somewhat problematical. Although he is reputed to have said that one must "read Kant *whole*" (Pater's

---

9. A number of scholars deal with Pater and German thought, but none of the studies are definitive in any way. In addition to the studies by Inman and Wollheim cited already, they include: Robert Currie, "Pater's Rational Cosmos," *Philological Quarterly* 59 (1980): 95–104; Peter Allan Dale, *The Victorian Critic and the Idea of History: Carlyle, Arnold, Pater* (Cambridge: Harvard University Press, 1977), pp. 169–245; Bernard Fehr, "Walter Pater und Hegel," *Englische Studien* 50 (1916): 300–308; Wendell V. Harris, *The Omnipresent Debate: Empiricism and Transcendentalism in Nineteenth-Century English Prose* (DeKalb: Northern Illinois University Press, 1981), pp. 338–59; John Smith Harrison, "Pater, Heine, and the Old Gods of Greece," *PMLA* 39 (1924): 655–86; Hans Proesler, *Walter Pater und sein Verhältnis zur deutschen Literatur*, diss. Albert Ludwigs Universität, 1917 (Freiburg: Werkstätten für Platkate u. Kalender, 1917); William Shuter, "History as Palengenesis in Pater and Hegel," *PMLA* 86 (1971): 411–21; Anthony Ward, *Walter Pater: The Idea in Nature* (London: MacGibbon and Kee, 1966).

emphasis),[10] Pater himself, if he read all of Kant, does not seem to have assimilated him whole. He views Kant mainly as a skeptic for his demolition work on the traditional foundations of metaphysics. In his own writing Pater accepts and abides by the strict limitations of Kant's epistemology, but his reading reflects more interest in the implications of those limitations for religion and morals. Although he undoubtedly read Kant on one of his visits to Germany and was clearly familiar with the main tenets of the *Critique of Pure Reason*, his British library borrowings indicate more interest in works like the *Foundation of the Metaphysic of Morals* and the *Critique of Practical Reason* than in the other two famous critiques. He also read Schleiermacher and Fichte, who both explored the religious and moral implications of Kant's epistemology. Fichte was also much more interested in the individual ego than was Kant himself.[11] Nevertheless, despite his interest in Kantian moral philosophy, Pater dismissed the crucial concept of the categorical imperative as arbitrary and groundless.[12]

Pater grappled with Kant's thought at the outset of his publishing career in "Coleridge's Writings" (1866). In this essay, as we saw in chapter 2, Pater parades an inconsistent and immature (or perhaps *premature* is a better word) synthesis of idealism with his positivism and empiricism, all of which were major philosophical crosscurrents at Oxford in his time. Pater had not yet carefully assimilated his wide reading, and he was not as aware of the contradictions in his own thinking as of those in the writers he attacked. Although Pater never fully resolved the conflicting influences of the philosophic traditions he absorbed, after the Coleridge essay his philosophic positions rapidly matured, perhaps as a result of laying bare some of the more blatant contradictions in that essay. Although Pater never became a systematic Kantian, by the time he wrote the first version of the "Conclusion" as part of his essay on William Morris two years after the Coleridge essay, he was abiding more consistently by the epistemological limits Kant imposed on both metaphysics and matter. Nevertheless, despite the immaturity and confusion of his views in "Coleridge's Writ-

---

10. A. C. Benson, *Walter Pater* (London: Macmillan, 1906), p. 194.
11. Inman, *Pater's Reading*, pp. 14–19, 21–25, 58–60, 68–71.
12. Houghton Library MS 17 "[Moral philosophy]."

ings," the essay represents the opening of one of the largest conduits of German thought into the English literary tradition since Coleridge and Carlyle.

In "Coleridge's Writings" Pater's polemics against Coleridge's absolutism focus mainly on Kant and Schelling. Notwithstanding his absorption of some of Kant's epistemological premises, he sharply rebukes the elements of Kant he finds in Coleridge's works. Even though the relative spirit he opposes to Coleridge's absolutism is compounded of, among other things, a Kantian epistemological emphasis on functions and relations over substance, he nevertheless rejects Kant and transcendental philosophy in general. In his first essay Pater seems unaware of how much Kant and the idealists have already informed his own thought. Although he is unwilling to relinquish the world of fact and sense to abstract Kantian categories, he seems perfectly willing to employ Kantian premises to undermine metaphysical speculation of all kinds. He also tries to lump Kant as an enemy of the concrete with all kinds of transcendentalism, including Hindu mysticism, even though Kant himself, an archrationalist, was ardently antimystical.

To look more closely at Pater's argument, after he ponders the intricate and paradoxical complexity of man's modern condition in his opening speculation on the relative spirit, Pater asserts that what experience gives us is "not the truth of eternal outlines effected once for all" but the truth of relations, "a world of fine gradations and subtly linked conditions shifting intricately as we ourselves change." " 'Ontology,' " he confidently declares, "is the misconception of a backward school of logicians." Despite this bold, Kantian denial of metaphysics of substance, he goes on to oppose any abstract transcendentalism. This kind of thinking (he refuses to grant it the status of philosophy) is characteristic of "the Hindoo, lost to sense, understanding, individuality." In contrast he proposes Goethe, "to whom every moment of life brought its share of experimental, individual knowledge," as the "true illustration of the speculative temper" (108).

So by the rough type of categorical violence Pater claims to abhor, he divides philosophy into two camps, one exemplified by the Hindu and the other by Goethe. In this way he is able to combine the a priori categories of Kant with Eastern mysticism and save "the world of form, colour, and passion" from the ravenous jaws of abstraction (108). Later in the essay Pater does say that it was Coleridge's own confusion about the division of reason and understanding that cast a mystical glow over Kant's idealism. Consequently Coleridge "got no farther than the old vague desire to escape from the limitations of thought by some extraordinary mystical faculty." Nevertheless Pater still had little use for what he called Kant's "harsh division" between reason and understanding, and he found it the "most sterile" part of his philosophy (128–29).

In his effort to preserve the world of sense and matter, Pater also refused to accept "Kant's fine-spun theory of the transformation of sense into perception." Even though he understands the difference between Kant's phenomenalism and Hartley's materialistic theory of association, he nevertheless finds Coleridge's Kantian notion of imagination, as distinct from the more mechanical and Hartlean fancy, as nothing more than a "vigorous act of association." In other words, Coleridge's essential distinctions between imagination and fancy totally elude Pater, who prefers to believe that Kant's theory of perception "has not been able to bear a loyal induction." "Even if it were true," Pater adds, "how little it would tell us; how it attenuates fact!" (120–21). Pater objects to Kant's analysis primarily because his theory abstracts too far from sense perception.

Pater obviously approved of Kant's restraint of speculative reason, especially his destruction of "the rational groundwork of theism"; but then Kant introduced some formidable abstractions of his own, such as the understanding and the practical reason. Pater approvingly cites Heine's critique of Kant: "Kant distinguishes between the theoretical and the practical reason, and, with the practical reason for a magic wand, he brings to life the dead body of deism, which the theoretical reason had slain" (128). So even though Pater could sympathize with one side of Kant's philosophy, in the end Kant was one who, like the Hindu, found what is more abstract more excellent than what is concrete.

In addition to the Coleridge essay Pater also discusses Kant in an unpublished and undated manuscript that has been given the misleading title "The history of philosophy." [13] The manuscript actually deals

---

13. Houghton Library MS 3. On the basis of a reference to *Cardinal* Newman, Billie Inman suggests an approximate composition date of 1879 (*Pater's Reading*, p. xl). The immaturity of Pater's philosophic views in the essay, however, suggests that

with the epistemological revolution effected by Berkeley, Hume, and Kant that shifted the focus of philosophic speculation from issues of ontology to issues of epistemology and to a critique of the mind itself and its various faculties. In contrast to the Coleridge essay where Kant is allied with absolutism, in "The history of philosophy" Kant becomes a skeptical empiricist and a follower of Berkeley. The conclusion of the essay highlights the role of Berkeley in the tradition of modern skepticism that includes Descartes, Hume, Berkeley, Kant, Fichte, and Hegel; but the main thrust and body of the essay employs the arguments of Kant.

Pater opens the essay with a dismissal of all previous speculative thought expressed with a confidence that echoes Kant's dismissals in the *Critique of Pure Reason* and the synoptic *Prolegomena to Any Future Metaphysics*. Then after discussing the character of modern skepticism generally, Pater devotes almost half of the essay to brief histories of the "three fixed subjects of the older moral or metaphysical science"—God, the universe or cosmos, and the soul. Pater's very interest in these subjects of "older" philosophies of substance derives from and is framed by Kant's demolition of them in the *Critique of Pure Reason* as proper objects of knowledge and his relegation of them, as Pater notes, to "ideas of reason." Pater, like many other post-Kantians, does not see the relegation of such subjects to "ideas of reason" in the positive light that Kant himself did—as a means of preserving moral and metaphysical speculation from the inroads of scientific empiricism. Rather he perceives Kant's critique as primarily destructive: Pater says that the development of the ideas of God, the universe, and the soul represents "the history of philosophy as constructively written. But the history of philosophy may be and has been brilliantly written in a destructive spirit."

After appealing to Kant's critique of these ideas, however, Pater shifts his ground and deserts Kant in favor of Berkeley's empiricism.

---

the original composition date might have been earlier, perhaps around the date he wrote "Coleridge's Writings" (1865), which evidences a similar philosophic immaturity and alludes to some of the same philosophic issues, including Kant's "'three categories of totality,' God, the soul, and the universe" ("CW," 128), which provide the structure for the argument of the manuscript essay. If this is the case, the reference to Cardinal Newman would have been added later.

The three fixed subjects of constructive philosophy, Pater argues, have been opposed by the spirit of modern skepticism, which is based on an appeal from understanding "to the testimony of sensible experience." For Pater in the end it is not Kant's a priori categories that explode the pretensions of previous metaphysics but the testimony of the senses. Kant's analysis, in other words, leads Pater quite illegitimately to the empirical idealism of Berkeley, where "the solidly realized conception of the understanding is dissipated into a certain number of concrete sensible experiences." But, as with Kant, Pater is much more interested in Berkeley's contribution to the "negation" of previous thought than in the theological foundations of his metaphysics, which Pater characterizes as dictated by the "necessities of [Berkeley's] ecclesiastical position" and "a matter much less easy to enter into." So Kant's a priori categories and Berkeley's God as the ultimate perceiver suffer similar fates in Pater's much more skeptical scheme of things, a skepticism much closer to that of Hume than any other modern philosopher.

Pater continues to develop his argument by asserting that Berkeley's "main point has never really been answered" and that no "real philosophical antidote" has since been proposed. Although Pater does not explicitly identify what he perceives as Berkeley's "main point," the context suggests the very broad distinction between modern idealism generally and all forms of realism; that is, Berkeley's "main point" is the idealist premise that things exist only as perceived and have no foundations beyond perception. Pater, however, construes this point so broadly as to encompass the very different epistemological premises of both Kant and Berkeley. He claims that Berkeley's skepticism about the material world led to the "stronger wave of skepticism" led by Kant against the substantial reality of the mind. This claim is true in one sense, for it was the skepticism of Hume, which followed Berkeley's, that shook Kant out of his "dogmatic slumber." But Pater makes it clear that he has confused Kant's premises with Berkeley's when he says that after Kant's critique of the mind, "what remained of our actual experience was but a stream of impressions over the supposed but wholly unknown mental substratum which no act of intuition or reflexion could ever really detect." He also claims that the effect of such a skeptical idealism might be to send us back to outward phenomena with renewed vigor and "with a great sense of relief after the long strain of a too curious self-inquiry." These arguments are based mostly on Hume and totally ignore both Berkeley's theological metaphysics and Kant's claims to have established a science of the mind.

For Pater, then, one of the primary functions of idealism, whether Berkeley's empirical idealism or Kant's critical idealism, is to support a Humean skepticism. It is apparently this function that he refers to when he says that Berkeley's idealism has become "one of the recognized first steps in every intellectual theory since," for at the beginning of "The history of philosophy" Pater says that the "first step" of speculative thought is always "an act of skepticism." So for Pater, Heraclitus, Descartes, Berkeley, Hume, Kant, Fichte, and Hegel are all alike in that they all begin with the first skeptical step.

In conflict with his skeptical emphasis, Pater concludes this essay with the unlikely suggestion that the empirical inductive method developed since Bacon "might yet achieve the ideal of cosmos Greek thinkers thought they had achieved" through the aegis of reason alone. Clearly the contradictions, inaccuracies, and general shabbiness of this essay result from Pater's attempt to link Kant forcibly with British empiricism. The attempt was seriously flawed, as Pater must have realized, and he wisely never published the essay.

Pater's misunderstanding of Kant was not peculiar to himself, however. Until the last quarter of the nineteenth century British thinkers in general had a very imperfect grasp of Kant's thought. Like Pater, they perceived Kant's philosophy mostly as a negative, skeptical force checking the pretensions of reason, metaphysics, and theology, while they ignored Kant's more positive claims to have established a science of mind that preserved philosophic speculation, religion, moral philosophy, and aesthetics from the destructive forces of positivism and empiricism (which is how Kant perceived his own achievement in the face of Hume's skepticism). Pater was also typical of British Kantians in rejecting Kant's transcendental, a priori categories, while accepting the epistemological limits they circumscribed.[14]

---

14. For discussions of nineteenth-century views of Kant see Young, pp. 10–15; Proesler, p. 75; Harris, pp. 31–37; and René Wellek, *Immanuel Kant in England, 1793–1838* (Princeton: Princeton University Press, 1931).

Hans Proesler claims that Pater absorbed Kant primarily through Goethe, who shared Pater's preference for concrete experience over abstract philosophy and who also accepted Kant's limitations on human knowledge without embracing their metaphysical foundations. Pater, according to Proesler, understood neither Goethe nor the aims of critical philosophy very well, but nevertheless assimilated part of Goethe's version of Kant.[15] Pater lends some credence to Proesler's view in his essay on Winckelmann, where he draws extensively from Goethe. Of Goethe's debt to Kant Pater says, "Kant's influence over the culture of Goethe, which he tells us could not have been resisted by him without loss, consisted in a severe limitation to the concrete" (*Ren.*, 181–82), which is precisely how Pater interprets Kant in "The history of philosophy." Although there is no doubt some truth to Proesler's claim that Goethe was the source of Pater's version of Kant, the issue is clearly more complex than Proesler implies; for Pater had read Kant himself and his view of him also coincides with the distorted image of Kant that prevailed in Britain until the late nineteenth century.

Pater's version of Kant undoubtedly came from all of these sources, and since Goethe's Kant and the British Kant fit rather conveniently into his own scheme of things, he probably felt that his views on Kant were accurate and authoritative; and they did not change much over the course of his career, even though his understanding of German idealism matured considerably through the continuing influence of Hegel. The statements he makes about Kant in "Prosper Mérimée," cited in chapter 1, indicate that as late as 1890 his view of Kant's influence as primarily negative and skeptical had not altered. And in *Plato and Platonism* he maintains this position: in contrast to the absolutist paradoxes of the Eleatics, Pater claims that Kant identified the "'antinomies,' or contradictions, or inconsistencies of our thoughts . . . as actually inherent in the mind itself—a certain constitutional weakness or limitation there, in dealing by way of cold-blooded reflexion with the direct presentations of its experience" (*PP*, 28).

Pater apparently had plans for Kant in a third novel that would complete a trilogy along with *Marius the Epicurean* and *Gaston de*

---

15. Proesler, pp. 78–82.

Latour. According to manuscript notes, the protagonist of this novel was to be a young man coming of age at the beginning of the nineteenth century. The youth, who would anticipate the spirit of the century, would be influenced by his early reading of Kant and the adventurous possibilities it opened up for the reconstruction of modern thought.[16] It appears that Kant was to play a role similar to the roles played by Heraclitus for Marius and by Montaigne for Gaston, that is, the role of early, skeptical mentor who clears the mind of preconceptions inherited from either childhood or intellectual history. This skepticism would serve as a prelude to the construction of a new, positive vision linking the mind of the protagonist with the latest intellectual revolution.

Throughout Pater's career, then, Kant consistently represented for him that "first step" of speculative thought, the "act of skepticism" that was a prelude to building a more positive philosophic vision. While Pater accepted the limitations Kant imposed at both boundaries of human knowledge, the limits of sensation and the limits of reason, he rejected their philosophical foundations in Kant's transcendental categories. Pater's unwillingness to enter into the realm of Kant's transcendental categories was a consequence of his native empiricism and his own passion for sensory experience. In the end Kant's critique of metaphysics and the mind was acceptable to Pater because it coincided with what he felt instinctively, a skepticism that had been reinforced if not formed by Hume.

At the same time that Pater guided his intellectual journey by the star of Hume's skepticism, however, his immersion in Kant introduced idealist elements into his own thinking that were alien to Hume. For example, despite his rejection of a priori categories, Pater did assimilate, as early as "Coleridge's Writings," a neo-Kantian preference for relations over substance in thought that apparently contravenes Hume's undermining of such key relations as identity and cause and effect. And in *Plato and Platonism,* instead of Pythagoras's postulation of numerical law as independent of human thought, Pater prefers Kant's view of number as an element of perception, if not an a priori category (52).

---

16. Houghton Library MS 31 "[Thistle]."

SCHELLING

IN CONTRAST to his ambivalence toward Kant, Pater's attitude toward Schelling was more consistent, even though his arguments were no less confused. Pater's attitude toward Schelling also typifies the fate of the Romantic transcendentalism that German idealism had inspired in England during the first three decades of the nineteenth century.[17] While Pater could sympathize with the poetic quality of Schelling's visionary ideal,[18] he could not accept a philosophy that transcended the bounds of both the sensible world and the limits of reason established by Kant. In other words, Pater could accept the general conclusions, if not the premises, of a critical idealism that defined the limits of knowledge, a critique provided by Kant and Hegel, but he could not accept a transcendental idealism that operated beyond these limits, even though both Kant and Hegel sanctioned such operations of pure reason. Again Pater's native empiricism restrained him from pursuing German thought into any realms of the transcendental or the absolute. In short, whatever in German thought could not be applied to concrete experience and our understanding of that experience had little appeal to Pater.

In the Coleridge essay Pater's critique of what he calls Schellingism in Coleridge's thought is even more severe than his treatment of Kant. His attack focuses primarily on what he calls Schelling's philosophy of nature, which Pater defines as that "mode of conceiving nature as a mirror or reflex of the intelligence of man," or vice versa, the essential point being "a 'rapport' in every detail, between the human mind and the world without it" (118, 121). This definition is so broad, however, that it encompasses most philosophy before Kant, including that arising from Newtonian physics. While he also defines Schellingism in the usual, more limited, and Romantic sense as the poetic "*vivification* [Pater's emphasis] of nature . . . the conception of nature as living, thinking, almost speaking to the mind of man," he goes well beyond this conception of nature to include all forms of intuitive and pantheistic philosophies since Greek mythology, as well as deism and Hegel's work, under the aegis of Schelling's philosophy of nature. For

---

17. Wellek, pp. 245–62; Harris, 313–59.
18. Proesler, p. 87.

Pater deism and pantheism are "two ways of envisaging those aspects of nature which appear to bear the impress of reason or intelligence. There is the deist's way, which regards them merely as marks of design, which separates the informing mind from nature as the mechanist from the machine; and there is the pantheistic way, which identifies the two, which regards nature itself as the living energy of an intelligence of the same kind as, but vaster than, the human." As another example of this philosophy, he includes the Hegelian formula "Whatever is, is according to reason; whatever is according to reason, that is" (118–19). This attempt to lump the Romantic conception of nature, historical pantheism, deism, and Hegel under the concept of Schellingism results only in confusion and renders the concept impotent.

Pater himself seems to be confusing reason and intuition in his critique of the idealists. He voices two major objections to his very broadly defined "Schellingism." First, he cannot accept its claim that "the ideas of the mind must be true, must correspond to reality." This notion may be a great aid to faith, Pater admits, but only "if one is not too nice in distinguishing between ideas and mere convictions, or prejudices, or habitual views, or safe opinions" (127–28). Here Pater fails to perceive the essence of critical idealism, as he confuses the premises of philosophies of function with philosophies of substance. Both Kant and Hegel distinguish between logical necessity and empirical necessity, a distinction Pater consistently fails to make. With both Kant and Hegel the ideas of the mind, that is, the categories or relations of thought itself, such as number or cause and effect, "must correspond to reality" because they are the forms of understanding through which we perceive reality. This form of logical necessity makes no claims about the nature of things themselves but only about our perception of the relations of things, which must conform to our perceptual apparatus.

Pater's second objection is to the intuitiveness of Schelling's philosophy of nature. Pater soon changed his mind about intuition as he moved away from positivism and as Goethe and Wordsworth became his touchstones for the truly integrated perspective of the "supreme artistic view of life"; but in "Coleridge's Writings" Pater was still in the grip of positivism. Instead of a philosophy of nature like Schelling's, Pater preferred a "true science" based on observation and analysis.

His conception of science, however, was also muddled:[19] "The positive method," he says, "makes very little account of marks of intelligence in nature"; rather, he adds vaguely, "it absorbs them in the simpler conception of law" (119). At the same time, however, in contrast to the older philosophies that accepted mind and nature as mirror images of each other, Pater posits a Kantian view that emphasizes "the artifice and invention of the understanding" (121) and regards the old view of universal forms as "the modification of things by the mind of the observer" (118). There are two serious problems with this version of modern thought. First, the "positive method" from the seventeenth century to the present has not been averse until recently to the notion that the mathematical formulas of science are *there* in the operations of nature, that one is the mirror image of the other.[20] Second, Pater's invocation of the Kantian model is inconsistent both with his own rejection of a priori categories and with his preference for the "positive method" of scientific observation and analysis. As in his discussion of Kant, in his critique of Schellingism there is a good deal of confusion between positivism and German idealism.

Pater's second major engagement with Schelling's form of transcendentalism occurs at a critical point in *Marius the Epicurean*. Despite his fundamental opposition to Schelling, Pater flirted, as I pointed out at the beginning of this chapter, with many forms of Neoplatonic idealism, a tradition in which Pater places Schelling (*PP*, 169, 193). In the chapter entitled "The Will as Vision" Marius recognizes the allure of a philosophy like Schelling's, but upon subsequent reflection he is compelled to dismiss it as too facile despite the world of possibilities it might open up. Marius's experience in "The Will as Vision" is something like an epiphany, except it is not based on the empirical and phenomenological premises of the "Conclusion," which inform most critics' views of the Paterian privileged moment, but rather on a Schellingistic philosophy of nature. The epiphany occurs toward the end of Marius's intellectual journey, after he has explored the various philosophies of Heraclitus, Aristippus, Epicureanism, and Stoicism,

---

19. Young notes that Pater took over the "conception of scientific method . . . in its vague, general outline from his contemporaries" (p. 84).

20. This is the central argument of Edwin Arthur Burtt's *The Metaphysical Foundation of Modern Science* (1932; Garden City, N.J.: Doubleday, 1954).

but before he approaches the threshold of Christianity. The function of the epiphany is to make Marius more receptive to the transcendental possibilities offered by Christianity; but Marius's second thoughts about the epiphany also foreshadow his unwillingness in the end to actually cross the threshold into the Catholic Church.

Pater characterizes Marius's epiphany as one of "those divinations of a living and companionable spirit at work in all things." That Pater had Schelling in mind is suggested by Marius's progress from the "instinctive divinations, to the thoughts which give them logical consistency" (*ME* 2:68). In *Plato and Platonism* Pater credits Schelling with formulating, "as a philosophic, a Platonic, theory," the Romantic pantheism that inspired Goethe, Wordsworth, and Shelley (169).

As in the "Conclusion," the epiphany begins in the material world: "In this peculiar and privileged hour, [Marius's] bodily frame . . . was yet determined by a far-reaching system of material forces external to it, a thousand combining currents from earth and sky." Assuming a receptive posture akin to Shelley's sensitive plant, the "seemingly active powers of apprehension" in Marius's physical being became "but susceptibilities to influence. The perfection of its capacity might be said to depend on its passive surrender, as of a leaf on the wind, to the motions of the great stream of physical energy without it" (*ME* 2:68).

Although this epiphany begins in the material world like the reverie of the "Conclusion," whereas the "Conclusion" moves quickly from the physical world to a phenomenal world, from an object world to a world of perceptions, Marius's experience leaps just as quickly by means of analogy into a world of transcendental, pantheistic thought: "And might not the intellectual frame also . . . be a moment only, an impulse or series of impulses, a single process, in an intellectual or spiritual system external to it, diffused through all time and place— that great stream of spiritual energy, of which his own imperfect thoughts, yesterday or to-day, would be but the remote, and therefore imperfect pulsations?" Marius speculates whether the entire material world might not be a reflection or a creation of "that one indefectible mind, wherein he too became conscious, for an hour, a day, for so many years." At the height of this almost mystical experience, the "purely material world, that close, impassable, prison-wall, seemed [to Marius] just then the unreal thing, to be actually dissolving away all around him: and he felt a quiet hope, a quiet joy dawning faintly, in the dawning of this doctrine upon him as a really credible opinion" (*ME* 2:68–70).

Just how strictly Pater abided by Kant's limits of knowledge even in this moment of vision can be determined by noting how carefully Pater's language circumscribes the experience. The impassable wall between perception and things themselves (the "purely material world") only *seems* to become unreal and dissolve. And the Schellingistic doctrine dawns upon Marius not as truth or knowledge, but merely as "credible opinion." In the end, although Marius was made richer by this experience and even though it remained one of his most valued moments, it is never admitted into the realm of experience known in the Kantian sense; rather it is relegated to Kant's realm of "pure reason," whose products do not qualify as truth or knowledge but function as useful guides to the understanding in the form of heuristic hypotheses or ideals. Thus Pater will only grant that the epiphany provided Marius with "a definitely ascertained measure of his moral or intellectual need, of the demand his soul must make upon the powers, whatsoever they might be, which had brought him, as he was, into the world at all" (*ME* 2:71–72). The extent to which this experience provides Marius with a practical guide for his experience in the world, a guide without any more foundation than the categorical imperative Pater rejects, is suggested by the question posed at the end of the episode: "Must not all that remained of life," Pater's narrator asks, "be but a search for the equivalent of that Ideal, among so-called actual things—a gathering together of every trace or token of it, which his actual experience might present?" (*ME* 2:72).

If Marius's epiphany is so carefully circumscribed as it occurs, it is all but negated upon further reflection. In the next chapter Marius ruminates at length on his experience related in "The Will as Vision," whose very title suggests the same realm where Kant's categorical imperative operates. Although the narrator acknowledges that the experience altered Marius's mental perspective permanently and gave the external world a weaker hold over him (*ME* 2:75) and that Marius, like many others, yearned "for the trace of some celestial wing across" an "unpeopled sky," he had to object, nevertheless, to doctrines others assumed "with too much facility, too much of self-complacency." For Marius, the narrator insists, "it was clear, he must hold by what his eyes really saw." His epiphany served in the end only to restrain him from foreclosing on "a variety of human disposition and a consequent variety of mental view, which might—who could tell?—be correspondent to, be defined by and define, varieties of facts, of truths, just 'behind the veil,' . . . a world wider, perhaps, in its possibilities than all possible fancies concerning it" (*ME* 2:90–91). Christianity was one such "variety of human disposition" that opened up a world of possibilities for Marius and for Pater, and Schellingism was another. But despite their ennobling ideas and the possibilities of a noumenal world they offered, by the strict dictates of Pater's Kantian epistemology, both Christianity and Schelling's philosophy of nature remain "fancies" of the human mind that belong to a realm of pure reason operating beyond the world of experience.

Pater's antipathy toward Schelling's pantheism, like most of his attitudes toward German idealism, was part of the intellectual climate of his time.[21] But his rejection of Schelling's form of transcendentalism does not constitute a rejection of German idealism as a whole nor, as Wendell Harris claims, of philosophical speculation in general. In *The Omnipresent Debate: Empiricism and Transcendentalism in Nineteenth-Century English Prose* Harris says that Pater's rejection of transcendentalism and his emphasis on sensation and experience "sanctioned the retreat from the philosophical trenches" that characterized the fin de siècle. He also claims that before the end of the century the British idealists, such as Stirling, Caird, Green, and Bradley, "did not in the main much affect English thought beyond the regions in which professional philosophers dwell."[22] Whatever other merits Harris's book may have, this view of Pater and the turn of the century can do nothing but impede our understanding of Modernism and its roots. By this point in my argument it should be clear that whatever Pater may have rejected philosophically, he at no time retreated or sanctioned a retreat from the philosophical trenches. On the contrary, he injected a sorely needed dose of philosophic thought into the veins of a desiccated British literary tradition. Richard Wollheim is much closer to the truth than Harris when he says, "By the standards of

---

21. Young, p. 11.
22. Harris, pp. 37, 338, 346–47.

his time, though barely of ours, Pater lived the life of a professional philosopher."[23]

Unless we understand the nature and source of Pater's philosophic injection, we cannot properly understand the place of Pater, Wilde, Yeats, Joyce, or Eliot in a continuous literary tradition. All these writers, even Wilde, struggled with the same philosophical crosscurrents of empiricism and idealism. In an 1891 essay Yeats admired the "jewelled paragraphs" of "The Will as Vision,"[24] and T. S. Eliot's debt to F. H. Bradley is well known. Even granting that Eliot did not read Bradley until after 1900,[25] the British idealists still had a substantial impact on literary as well as philosophic thought, with Pater himself as the chief conduit of that thought. Harris arrives at his conclusion because he, like so many of Pater's critics, only acknowledges the Pater of the "Conclusion" and because he limits his study to the Romantic transcendentalism of German thought and neglects the critical idealism of Kant and Hegel. Harris ignores critical idealism by design, but it is nevertheless a strategy that obscures for him how Pater and the British idealists at Oxford demythologized the form of transcendentalism that appealed so much to the Romantics. Pater's role in this intellectual movement is illustrated by his relationship to Kant on one hand and to Schelling on the other. By accepting the limits established by Kant's critique of knowledge and, at the same time, rejecting its transcendental grounds and the transcendental flights of reason and imagination in philosophies like Schelling's, Pater brought German thought closer to his native empiricism. Even though he employs fallacious arguments in "Coleridge's Writings" to formulate his responses to Kant and Schelling, those responses nevertheless circumscribe the limits of his own idealism, limits that he maintains consistently thereafter and that govern his more positive use of Schiller and Hegel.

---

23. *On Art and the Mind*, p. 158.

24. *Letters to the New Island*, ed. Horace Reynolds (1934; reprint, Oxford: Oxford University Press, 1970), pp. 137–38.

25. Lyndall Gordon, *Eliot's Early Years* (Oxford: Oxford University Press, 1977), p. 49.

6 / Aesthetic Idealism: Schiller

SCHILLER'S IMPACT on Pater was more decisive than either Kant's or Schelling's. Perhaps Schiller appealed more to Pater because he also combined an aesthetic with a philosophic temperament, although he was both a better artist and a better philosopher than Pater. Schiller knew Kant well—much better than Pater did—and like Schelling he pushed Kant's philosophy in the direction of Hegel and a Romantic transcendentalism with an emphasis on absolute beauty and the indeterminate freedom of the aesthetic condition. Pater himself, as we have seen, had a very limited understanding of Kant. Schelling's development of Kant's aesthetic seems to have had little impact on Pater, and Hegel, although he influenced Pater more extensively than Schiller, subordinated art to religion and philosophy in the realm of absolute spirit. Schiller's language and transcendentalism, however, were more moderate than Schelling's, thus requiring less modification by Pater to adapt them to his own sensibility, and Schiller's privileging of the aesthetic, precisely because it fused sense and intellect, is much closer to Pater's position than is Hegel's preference for the more purely intellectual disciplines that most escape the limitations of sensuous experience. Of all the Germans Pater read, except perhaps Winckelmann and Goethe, Schiller's style, subject matter, and combination of philosophic and aesthetic temperament had the closest affinities to Pater's own inclinations, and Schiller offered a Kantian philosophic sanction to the relations between sense and intellect that Pater explored throughout his career.

Despite the remarkable similarities between their views of aesthetic experience, surprisingly little has been said about Pater's debt to Schiller.[1] One reason for this lacuna in Pater scholarship is suggested by Billie Inman's observations that "Schiller's ideas are inextricable from Hegel's, Kant's and Fichte's at some points" and that Pater was well versed in all three "before he read Schiller."[2] Whether Pater read Hegel, Kant, and Fichte before Schiller is open to debate, for Pater may have read Schiller on one of his many visits to Germany, where his sisters lived from his undergraduate years until 1869, when they took a house with Pater in Oxford.[3] In any case, by Inman's account, Pater read Schiller's critical and philosophical works by late 1865,[4] before his first essay was published; and whether or not he took certain ideas from Schiller, Kant, Fichte, or Hegel, or, we might add, from Goethe or Schelling, Schiller nevertheless provided Pater with a cogent and appealing formulation of the aesthetics of German idealism, particularly in his letters *On the Aesthetic Education of Man*, one of the most important aesthetic manifestos of the movement. Furthermore, Pater's

---

1. Currie says Pater acquired a "romantic schema of epistemological history" from Schiller among others (100–101), and Inman says that letters twenty through twenty-seven of *On the Aesthetic Education of Man* "illuminate" a number of Paterian notions, such as the disinterested aesthetic observer, music as the ideal art form, the idea of art for art's sake in the "Conclusion," the idea of *being* in "Wordsworth," and more generally, "Pater's whole conception of the aesthetic outlook" (*Pater's Reading*, 101). Inman also notes that in "Winckelmann" Pater cites Schiller as a model for "spiritual adventurers" (116) and derives from him the notion that "the wholeness of the aesthetic personality came from balancing diverse or opposite forces" (137–38). Finally, she speculates that Schiller may have had an important influence on the ideal aesthetic temperament of Pater's "Diaphaneitè" (75). Note: The incorrect accent mark on *diaphanéité* is Pater's, and I have retained it throughout.

In the introduction to their edition and translation of Schiller's *On the Aesthetic Education of Man: In a Series of Letters* (English and German facing) (Oxford: Clarendon Press, 1967), Elizabeth Wilkinson and L. A. Willoughby number Pater among those influenced by Schiller; but since they apparently were familiar only with *The Renaissance*, they ignore some of Pater's profounder affinities with Schiller and perceive Pater's views as superficial distortions of Schiller (clvi–clxxxi).

2. Inman, *Pater's Reading*, pp. 100–101.

3. Levey, pp. 77–78, 87–88; Monsman, *Walter Pater*, Twayne's English Authors Series (Boston: Twayne, 1977), pp. 15, 39–40; Benson, p. 9; Thomas Wright, *The Life of Walter Pater* (1907; New York: Haskell House, 1969), 1:162, 178, 240.

4. Inman, *Pater's Reading*, p. 100.

views on aesthetic experience at a number of points are closer to
Schiller's than to other German thinkers, and so many of Pater's positions echo Schiller's *Aesthetic Education* that whether his original
source for various ideas was Schiller or someone else, his reading of
the *Aesthetic Education* must have solidified, if not generated, many
of his own views and attitudes.

The list of issues and viewpoints from Schiller's *Aesthetic Education* that show up in Pater's writing is impressively long: it includes the
pressing need for a unified sensibility in modern thought; Goethe as
the model poet; the ideal, cultivated sensibility as contemplative, receptive, and indifferent, almost passive; music as the ideal art form;
truth as internal rather than external; an emphasis on images of perception, on appearances in Kant's sense, over external objects, and on
ideas over sensory images; the artist as an alien figure cleansing his
age;[5] and, most importantly, the nature, character, and privileging
of aesthetic experience itself with its various emphases on dialectic
thought, on the reconciliation of oppositions (particularly the oppositions of sense and intellect and of matter and form), on play and the
autonomy of the aesthetic, and on the relation of aesthetic experience
to moral life. There were elements of Schiller's *Aesthetic Education*
that Pater could not accept, such as any notion of absolute beauty or
transcendental freedom; but even here Pater did accept some of the
more finite implications of these concepts, such as the privileging of
the aesthetic over other forms of experience. If many of these ideas
from the *Aesthetic Education* could be found elsewhere in German
thought, nowhere could they be found in such a concise and appealing form.

A number of Pater's individual debts to Schiller are considered in
other chapters of this book. The most important issue, however, the
nature, character, and privileging of aesthetic experience, is worth
pursuing here because it is a key issue in Modernist thought that Pater
transformed in significant ways.

The ultimate source of the aesthetic as a privileged mode of knowing and experiencing is Kant, whose analysis of the aesthetic faculties
is crucial to his philosophic position. One of the first to develop some

---

5. Pater's imaginary portraits "Denys L'Auxerrois" and "Apollo in Picardy" particularly illustrate this motif.

of the implications of Kant's transcendental analysis, Schiller adapted Kant's arguments for his own purposes and arrived at a view of the aesthetic as the highest function of human nature. This view contributed substantially to the privileging of aesthetic experience in late nineteenth- and early twentieth-century thought, including the development of the *art for art's sake* movement, which was in part a popularized misunderstanding of the aesthetics of German idealism.[6]

The degree of Schiller's fidelity to Kant and the logical consistency of the *Aesthetic Education* itself have been debated by philosophers and literary critics alike; and opinions have varied over a wide range. Schiller has been considered the faithful disciple of Kant who inspired Hegel's dialectical elaboration of Kant's epistemology, but he has also been viewed as a dilettante who made a travesty of his mentor's philosophical rigor. Likewise, the *Aesthetic Education* has been regarded as a muddle of Kantian and pre-Kantian ideas as well as a perfectly unified work of artistic and philosophic genius.[7] My own view, guided by my interest in Schiller's relationship to Pater, does not coincide exactly with any previous view, but it does incline toward that tradition of Schiller scholarship that finds some inconsistencies both in his use of Kant and in the logical structure of the *Aesthetic Education*. In particular, I find three different notions of the aesthetic that are not completely harmonious and consistent with each other: the notion of play, the notion of the aesthetic as an enabling condition for all other forms of experience, and the notion of an aesthetic education leading from sensuous to moral experience. All three of these notions also show up

---

6. For the role of Schiller and other German idealists in the development of the aesthetic movement in the late nineteenth century see Rose Frances Egan, *The Genesis of The Theory of 'Art for Art's Sake' in Germany and England, Smith College Studies in Modern Languages*, vol. 2, no. 4 (1921), 1–61, and vol. 5, no. 3 (1924), 1–33.

7. In the Introduction to their edition of the *Aesthetic Education* Wilkinson and Willoughby ardently defend Schiller as both philosopher and artist, but they also give a good overview of Schiller's reputation from his contemporaries to the mid-twentieth century. For more recent evaluations of Schiller, see Dieter Henrich's "Beauty and Freedom: Schiller's Struggle with Kant's Aesthetics," *Essays in Kant's Aesthetics*, ed. Ted Cohen and Paul Guyer (Chicago: University of Chicago Press, 1982), pp. 237–57; and Eva Schaper's "Schiller's Kant: a Chapter in the History of Creative Misundertanding," *Studies in Kant's Aesthetics* (Edinburgh: Edinburgh University Press, 1979), pp. 99–117.

in Pater's writing. Since neither my qualifications nor my present purposes prompt me to enter the ongoing debate about Schiller's philosophic merit, I will confine myself to the more modest task of indicating the relationship between Schiller's privileging of aesthetic experience and the invocation of that privilege by Pater and his Modernist successors.

Schiller is best known in the history of aesthetics for uniting the sensuous drive (*Stofftrieb*) and the formal drive (*Formtrieb*) in the play drive (*Spieltrieb*). The sensuous drive proceeds from our physical and sensuous nature and links us with the world of time and matter, a mutable and finite world that "binds the ever-soaring spirit" (81).[8] The sensuous drive furnishes us with particular instances by which we passively apprehend the world around us. Excluding spontaneity and freedom, the sensuous drive binds us to the external necessity of nature's laws and determines our condition in time. The object of the sensuous drive is "life, in the widest sense of this term" (101). The formal drive, on the other hand, proceeds from our rational nature and absolute existence, and it links us with a realm of logic and reason, an immutable and infinite realm in which the spirit is free. The formal drive furnishes us with laws by which we actively comprehend our world. It annuls time and change, brings harmony and unity to diversity, and elevates the actual to the universal and the necessary. Through the formal drive we rise "to a unity of ideas embracing the whole realm of phenomena" (83), where we are not in time but all time is contained in the mind, and we judge not as an individual but as a species. The formal drive binds us to the internal necessity of reason's laws, and its object is "form, both in the figurative and in the literal sense of this word: a concept which includes all the formal qualities of things and all the relations of these to our thinking faculties" (101).

If we eliminate all the adjectives of Romantic transcendentalism, such as absolute, infinite, and immutable, Schiller's division of human nature into the sensuous drive and the formal drive corresponds to Pater's similar division between sense and intellect, matter and form,

---

8. All page references to the *Aesthetic Education* are to the Wilkinson and Willoughby translation with English and German facing (see n. 1 above).

or the Dionysian impulse and the Apollonian impulse, which are the subjects of later chapters. But equally important to Pater was the manner in which Schiller brought these two drives together.

The play drive combines the *life* of the sense drive with the *form* of the formal drive into "*living form*: a concept serving to designate all the aesthetic qualities of phenomena and, in a word, what in the widest sense of the term we call beauty" (101). Beauty makes human nature whole. With both drives united in the play drive, "man will combine the greatest fullness of existence with the highest autonomy and freedom, and instead of losing himself to the world, will rather draw the latter into himself in all its infinitude of phenomena, and subject it to the unity of his reason" (87–89). Under the play drive the normal laws of the sensuous drive, which bind us to nature, and the laws of the formal drive, which bind us to reason, are suspended, and the spirit operates in a condition of unfettered freedom. This condition is the aesthetic, for Schiller says, "With beauty man shall only play, and it is with beauty only that he shall play." For Schiller this aesthetic condition of play is the highest order of human experience: "Man only plays when he is in the fullest sense of the word a human being, and he is only fully a human being when he plays" (107). Schiller admits that "experience offers us no single example of such perfect reciprocal action" as he describes: "in actuality" no perfect equilibrium is ever achieved, for "we shall always be left with a preponderance of the one element over the other" (111). Nevertheless aesthetic experience closely approximates this ideal condition.

With an aesthetic dualism as his foundation, Schiller explains his conception of the play drive primarily in terms of paradox. He says, for example, that the play drive aims at "annulling time within time" and "reconciling becoming with absolute being"; that it suspends the laws of physical and moral necessity and simultaneously makes the formal and material both contingent and necessary and then abolishes their contingency and necessity (97–99). Thus, he concludes, play is neither contingent nor necessary but a "happy medium between the realm of law and the sphere of physical exigency." "Precisely because it is divided between the two," play is "removed from the constraint of the one as of the other" (105). In play "we find ourselves at one and the same time in a state of utter repose and supreme agitation" (109). The beautiful as play both relaxes and tightens the sensuous and formal impulses simultaneously so that they might be both restrained and energized (111–13). These paradoxes make sense only if we adhere to Schiller's definitions of the three primary drives, in which the laws constraining us under the sensuous and the formal drives, the external necessity of nature and the internal necessity of logic, are both present and suspended in the autonomous realm of play.

Schiller develops his concept of play primarily in the thirteenth through the sixteenth letters of *On the Aesthetic Education of Man*; but in the later letters, particularly eighteen through twenty-seven, the concept of play evolves into a more sophisticated concept of the aesthetic condition, conceived more clearly and consistently in terms of dialectic, a development that indicates Schiller's deepening understanding of Kant. Later Hegel pursued Schiller's original insight into the dialectical method with a thoroughness unmatched in the history of philosophy. Although the concept of the play drive contained the seeds of dialectical thinking, Schiller's analysis of play relied more heavily on the use of paradox; and he never completely reconciled his two different explanations of the aesthetic.[9]

Partly because of their neglect of Hegel, Modernist aesthetics such as New Criticism preferred the paradoxes of play to the dialectics of the aesthetic condition, as did their Romantic ancestors like Coleridge, who had no exposure to Hegel. Pater, however, even though in "Giorgione" he alludes to the importance of play in bringing out the "best powers" of human nature (*Ren.*, 151–52), had a distaste for paradox. Also his assimilation of Hegel made him more receptive to the concept of the aesthetic condition in Schiller's later letters than to the concept of play.

In Schiller's notion of the aesthetic condition beauty is less a union of sense and thought than a mediating condition between them. Thought now reveals itself only in opposition to sense, and the passage from one to the other cannot be made directly. The mind passes "from sensation to thought *via* a middle disposition in which sense and reason are both active at the same time." In this aesthetic middle

---

9. Wilkinson and Willoughby offer an alternative view in their elaborate interpretation that sees dialectic operating throughout the *Aesthetic Education* and no logical inconsistencies between Schiller's different notions of the aesthetic. See especially pp. xlii–cxxxii.

disposition human nature "is subject neither to physical nor to moral constraint, and yet is active in both these ways." It is, like play, a "free disposition" that contains the physical, logical, and moral conditions without being constrained by their laws (141). In this way beauty links sensation and thought without negating their opposition. But unlike the play impulse, which simply fuses the sensuous and the formal impulses in an autonomous state that suspends their normal laws, the aesthetic can contain the other conditions without being constrained by them because, like Kant's transcendental a priori categories, it constitutes the "ground of possibility of them all" (151). In other words, Schiller's concept of the aesthetic condition promotes the aesthetic from the status of a simple fusion to the status of an enabling condition.

By identifying the aesthetic with Kant's a priori categories, Schiller establishes a foundation for the autonomy of art on transcendental grounds, an autonomy that, unlike Kant's, includes rather than excludes understanding and reason. With this strategy Schiller claims that beauty "does not meddle in the business of either thinking or deciding; that it merely imparts the power to do both, but has no say whatsoever in the actual use of that power" (161). Like Kant's transcendental categories, Schiller's aesthetic state does not determine but constitutes "determinability"—in other words, it operates in the infinite, undetermined realm of the possible, not in the finite, determined realm of the actual.

Auden's assertion in his elegy for Yeats that "poetry makes nothing happen" has its roots in Schiller, who says,

> . . . beauty produces no particular result whatsoever, neither for the understanding nor for the will. It accomplishes no particular purpose, neither intellectual nor moral; it discovers no individual truth, helps us to perform no individual duty and is, in short, as unfitted to provide a firm basis for character as to enlighten the understanding. By means of aesthetic culture, therefore, the personal worth of a man, or his dignity, inasmuch as this can depend solely upon himself, remains completely indeterminate; and nothing more is achieved by it than that he is henceforth enabled by the grace of Nature to make of himself what he will—that the freedom to be what he ought to be is completely restored to him. (147)

But if Schiller supports Auden's assertion, he also supports Shelley's view in the "Defence of Poetry" that "the great instrument of moral good is the imagination; and poetry administers to the effect by acting upon the cause." So if aesthetic culture determines nothing, it nevertheless renders all determination possible. This position constitutes a transcendental argument for the cognitive function of art that is often lost in later assertions of the autonomy of art, whether by advocates of art for art's sake or by New Critics.

The third peculiarity of Schiller's borrowed by Pater is the notion of an aesthetic education, what Robert Currie calls a "romantic schema of epistemological history,"[10] a schema that places the aesthetic at the midpoint of an epistemological progression from the physical and the sensuous to the logical and the moral. According to Schiller's notion of an aesthetic education, there are "three different moments or stages of development through which both the individual and the species as a whole must pass, inevitably and in a definite order, if they are to complete the full cycle of their destiny." The first moment is the *physical* condition, where one "merely suffers the dominion of nature"; the second is the *aesthetic* condition, where one "emancipates himself from this dominion"; and the third is the *moral* condition, where one "acquires mastery over it" (171).

In addition to representing "three different epochs . . . of the development of mankind as a whole, or of the whole development of a single individual," these three states are also "to be distinguished in each single act of perception, and are, in a word, the necessary conditions of all knowledge which comes to us through the senses" (183n). In the physical condition, a person's "relation to the world of sense is that of immediate contact"; one perceives oneself and each phenomenon as "single and isolated" (171). In the aesthetic condition, a person integrates the sensuous nature with the rational nature in a state of free contemplation that liberates one from physical necessity and enables one to pass on to the moral condition, which can be developed "only out of the aesthetic, not out of the physical" (165). Schiller says that this "step from the aesthetic to the logical and moral state (i.e., from beauty to truth and duty) is hence infinitely easier than was the

---

10. Currie, p. 100.

step from the physical state to the aesthetic (i.e., from merely blind living to form)" (163). If we try to pass directly from the physical to the logical or moral, according to Schiller, the result is a perverse application of logic and reason—whose only valid realm of operation is the absolute—to the physical realm (175–77). If we extrapolate historically from Schiller's analysis, this metaphysical perversity would characterize all philosophy prior to Kant's epistemological revolution, or what Cassirer calls philosophy of substance, in which the operations of logic and reason are based on ontological premises.

The three main concepts identified here from the *Aesthetic Education of Man*—the play drive, the aesthetic condition of the later essays, and the epistemological schema that constitutes an "aesthetic education"—are not wholly consistent with each other. At times the aesthetic, as the highest order of human experience, synthesizing all other forms of experience, including the sensual, the logical, and the moral, is to be pursued for its own sake. At other points in Schiller's argument, the aesthetic is conceived as the ground of all possible experience. In this view the aesthetic is less a synthesis than the a priori condition of the sensual, the rational, and the moral. The epistemological schema conceives the aesthetic in yet a third way, in which sensuous experience is prior to the aesthetic, and the aesthetic is neither a true synthesis nor an end in itself but an intermediate condition en route from sensation to logical and moral absolutes. The first concept, the play drive, is more poetic than philosophical and derives from an imperfect understanding of Kant. The concept of the aesthetic condition exhibits a more profound understanding of Kant's transcendental grounds and identifies the aesthetic with them. It also signals Schiller's movement toward dialectical thought. The epistemological schema, in which the aesthetic absolute leads to the moral and logical absolutes, anticipates the arguments of Hegel.

Turning to Pater's formulations of aesthetic experience, we find that he not only borrowed the three main concepts of the *Aesthetic Education* but that he also absorbed Schiller's own inconsistencies and contradictions. If we cull the Romantic absolutism out of Schiller's language and place the exercise of aesthetic contemplation in the world of concrete experience, Schiller's views of aesthetic contemplation are very close to Pater's.

Pater's earliest and most influential polemic on art as a privileged condition is his "Conclusion" to *The Renaissance*. In the second half of the "Conclusion," after characterizing a new vision of reality founded on a Humean flux of sensation, Pater proposes art over philosophy and (in the original periodical version) religion as the best means for making the most out of this potentially depressing state of affairs. In such a world as he describes the important question for Pater is, "How shall we pass most swiftly from point to point, and be present always at the focus where the greatest number of vital forces unite in their purest energy?" To achieve this goal Pater proposes that we refine our powers of perception so that we may "discriminate every moment some passionate attitude" and "grasp at any exquisite passion, or any contribution to knowledge that seems by a lifted horizon to set the spirit free for a moment" (*Ren.*, 236–37). Then, having constituted the human organism as a finely tuned perceptual apparatus, and having heaped the entire weight of his emphasis on experience onto the image we form of it in the mind, Pater quite logically chooses art as the best source of our most passionate, brilliant, and finely discriminated images. In our short interval of life art offers us the opportunity to get "as many pulsations as possible into the given time," and it assures that we will get quality as well as quantity, that it will be genuine passion and the "fruit of a quickened, multiplied consciousness." "Of such wisdom," Pater eloquently concludes, "the poetic passion, the desire of beauty, the love of art for its own sake, has most. For art comes to you proposing frankly to give nothing but the highest quality to your moments as they pass, and simply for those moments' sake" (*Ren.*, 238–39).

This formulation of art as a privileged condition had enormous influence on Oscar Wilde and the generation of the nineties in Britain; and its association with the art for art's sake movement (encouraged by Pater's misleading invocation of the phrase) prompted many to ignore Pater's own emphasis on the "moments' sake." The eloquence of the "Conclusion" combined with brevity and imprecision to obscure for many its more profound implications and its roots in Schiller and other German idealists. After the furor of misunderstanding raised at Oxford upon publication of the first edition of *The Renaissance*, Pater spent much of his remaining career spelling out those implications. Although Schiller undoubtedly would not have sanctioned Pater's empirical emphasis on the passing moment (not to mention the emptier notion of art for art's sake), once we allow for Pater's typical strategy of bringing transcendental arguments down to earth, we can see that the "Conclusion" reiterates Schiller's claim for art as the highest form of experience.

Despite the continuing influence of the "Conclusion" and its persistence (usually in misunderstood form) as the view most often associated with Pater's aesthetics, it is not Pater's most comprehensive and sophisticated formulation of the privileged status of art. For that we must turn to his essay on Wordsworth and to *Marius the Epicurean*. In "Wordsworth" and *Marius the Epicurean* the underlying rationale for privileging art over other intellectual disciplines such as philosophy and religion and the source for that rationale in Schiller are much more readily apparent. For example, as Schiller insists in the *Aesthetic Education* that contemplation or reflection "removes its object to a distance" (183), so in "Wordsworth" Pater characterizes aesthetic contemplation as "a certain disposition of the mind" that is detached and distanced from the practical concerns of life, such as teaching lessons, enforcing rules, and motivating people toward noble purposes. For Pater the goal of contemplation, particularly the "impassioned contemplation" afforded by aesthetic experience, is "to withdraw the thoughts for a little while from the mere machinery of life, to fix them, with appropriate emotions, on the spectacle of those great facts in man's existence which no machinery affects." "To witness this spectacle with appropriate emotions," Pater says, "is the aim of all culture" (*App.*, 62–63).

Pater's notion of aesthetic contemplation, then, retains Schiller's emphasis on the aesthetic, on detachment, and on the emotions, but the similarities go even deeper. For Schiller the contemplation of beauty extricates itself from purposeful activity: in the *Aesthetic Education* he says, "Beauty in and for itself alone begins to be an object of [our] striving" as it approaches a freedom of movement "which is at once its own end and its own means" (209–11). For Pater art focuses on "what is desirable in itself" as opposed to "what is desirable only as machinery": aesthetic contemplation is "a type of beholding for the mere joy of beholding"; it is to "treat life in the spirit of art," that is, it makes "life a thing in which means and ends are identified" (*App.*, 62).

For both Pater and Schiller, however, beauty for its own sake does not imply a rejection of cognition or moral purpose. As we have seen, Schiller's concept of the aesthetic condition includes all other faculties. According to his transcendental analysis, truth is contained within beauty (189). Likewise, Pater's view of aesthetic contemplation as an end in itself does not exclude morality because it is prerequisite to it: "That the end of life is not action but contemplation—*being* as distinct from *doing*," Pater says, is "the principle of all the higher morality"; it is an "intangible perfection" like "those *manners* which are, in the deepest as in the simplest sense, *morals*, and without which one cannot so much as offer a cup of water to a poor man without offense." The "true moral significance of art and poetry," according to Pater, is to encourage such aesthetic contemplation (*App.*, 61–62; Pater's emphases).

In *Marius* Pater enlarges his notion of aesthetic contemplation into a *complete aesthetic education* that also echoes Schiller. Marius's "New Cyrenaicism" that aims at a "general completeness of life" as its goal owes as much to Schiller and Hegel as to Aristippus, Epicurus, and Mill. Marius envisions a "true aesthetic culture . . . realisable as a new form of the contemplative life, founding its claim in the intrinsic 'blessedness' of 'vision'—the vision of perfect men and things" (*ME* 1:148). This vision of perfection would be afforded by art: "the products of imagination must themselves be held to present the most perfect forms of life—spirit and matter alike under their purest and most perfect conditions" (*ME* 1:147). Although this notion of perfection derives from the realm of the absolute developed by Schiller and Hegel, Pater did not envision the absolute itself as his final destination; rather, aesthetic culture would function in a finite realm to make the present moment yield its utmost. Like aesthetic contemplation, aesthetic education would treat life in the spirit of art: it would focus on means rather than ends and follow the "maxim of *Life as the end of life*" (*ME* 1:142–43; Pater's emphasis).

Pater's means for accomplishing the goals of an aesthetic education are drawn from Schiller's identification of the aesthetic with Kant's a priori faculties of sense and cognition: as in the "Conclusion," he proposes "refining all the instruments of inward and outward intuition, of developing all their capacities, of testing and exercising one's self in them, till one's whole nature became one complex medium of reception" (*ME* 1:143).

While Pater's notion of aesthetic education, with its focus on the various human faculties, alludes through Schiller to Kant's analysis of those faculties, Pater himself professes to be uninterested in the "origin, and course of development, of man's actually attained faculties and that seemingly divine particle of reason or spirit in him" (*ME* 1:142); he claims that any discoveries along these lines would not affect his "anti-metaphysical metaphysic" (*ME* 1:149). Pater names the thought of Empedocles as such a potential metaphysical discovery Marius would have known, but his allusion to theories about human faculties, particularly to a divine reason or spirit, suggests that he himself had in mind the more modern metaphysical discoveries of Kant, Schiller, and Hegel.

Yet if Pater dismisses the importance of transcendental arguments about the nature and source of the various faculties, he also acknowledges that these theories may on occasion serve a useful purpose: "Such a doctrine, at more leisurable moments, would of course have its precepts to deliver on the embellishment, generally, of what is near at hand, on the adornment of life, till, in a not impracticable rule of conduct, one's existence, from day to day, came to be like a well-executed piece of music; that 'perpetual motion' in things . . . according itself to a kind of cadence or harmony" (*ME* 1:149). So while Pater develops his notion of an aesthetic education out of the transcendental arguments of Kant, Schiller, and Hegel, he is careful to assert that the notion does not depend on them except insofar as they might embellish daily existence lived under such a notion. In other words, Pater would strictly limit transcendental arguments to the functional role of enhancing our experience of the world.

Although Kant's philosophy proscribes the application of pure reason to the world of experience, Pater's argument is sufficiently vague so as not to contradict Kant necessarily. After all, if reason serves as a guide to understanding, does it not serve to embellish and harmonize one's daily existence? On the other hand, Pater's cavalier attitude toward philosophical consistency would certainly allow the misapplications of transcendental arguments that Kant tried to prevent.

In addition to borrowing from Schiller for his notions of aesthetic contemplation and aesthetic education, Pater also adopted his epistemological schema along with its attendant inconsistency with the other two notions. Like Schiller, Pater perceived aesthetic contemplation both as an end in itself, that is, as the highest form of experience including all other forms, and as a halfway house toward moral action. In *Plato and Platonism*, for example, Pater notes, in terms that echo Schiller's epistemological schema, the "close connexion" between aesthetics and ethics in Plato.[11] In Plato's aesthetics, according to Pater, the sensible qualities of phenomena are transformed into formal aesthetic qualities, which are in turn transformed "into terms of ethics, into the sphere of the desires and the will, of the *moral* taste, engendering, nursing there, strictly moral effects" (*PP*, 271–72; Pater's emphasis). While Pater typically has substituted a finite sphere of desire and will for an absolute sphere, Schiller's epistemological scheme is nevertheless evident in the progress from the sensuous through the aesthetic to the ethical and moral, a progression that also characterizes the development of his protagonist Marius, who begins in the predominantly sensuous world of childhood and proceeds through an intermediate aesthetic phase he calls "New Cyrenaicism" to Christianity.

So Pater's notions of aesthetic contemplation and aesthetic education take more than their names from Schiller. Although these notions draw from a number of different sources, their similarities on a number of points to concepts in the *Aesthetic Education of Man* indicate a very prominent role for Schiller in their formation.[12] Schiller's influence is also indicated by the presence of the same inconsistencies between Pater's notions that we find between Schiller's. On the one hand, in its fusion of sense and thought the aesthetic is the highest order of experience containing all the rest, and it is to be pursued for its own sake. In this light the aesthetic becomes the "principle of all the higher morality." Morality, in other words, is a subspecies of art, "one mode of comeliness in things—as it were music, or a kind of artistic order, in life" (*ME* 2:4). Consequently all education, including philosophy and ethics, "will begin and end in 'music,' in the promo-

---

11. For recent analyses of the close connection between aesthetics and ethics in Schiller's thought and the relation of that connection to Kant, see Henrich (especially pp. 244–56) and Schaper (pp. 113–16).

12. Although Schiller's influence on Pater appears to be direct and significant, Pater's notion of aesthetic contemplation was also influenced, as David DeLaura argues convincingly, by Arnold and Newman (*Hebrew and Hellene*, pp. 245, 310 n.7).

tion of qualities to which no truer name can be given than symmetry, aesthetic fitness, tone," in "the sympathetic appreciation of a kind of music in the very nature of things" (*PP*, 268). On the other hand, the cultivation of one's faculties in an aesthetic education both enables and leads to moral actions, which, as part of the "machinery" of life, are not themselves strictly aesthetic.

Pater's inconsistencies notwithstanding, his view on art as a privileged mode of experience provided an important precedent for many Modernists. His influential "Conclusion," though not his most mature and developed position on this issue, reverses Hegel's triad of absolute spirit and sees art, rather than philosophy or religion, as the most effective and powerful means of enhancing our understanding and appreciation of experience. The privileged status of art in Modernist writing derives ultimately from the close association between perception and aesthetic modes of experience in Schiller and other German idealists. In the Modernists this privileged status resulted in a cosmic confidence in the power of art to comprehend and articulate our experience of the world. This confidence, founded ultimately on Kant's transcendental aesthetic, Schiller's concept of the aesthetic condition, and Hegel's placement of art in his triad of absolute spirit, prompted ambitious efforts, even system building at times, in writers like Yeats, Eliot, and Joyce, that rivaled the ambition of epic poetry from Homer to Milton to construct in a work of art a comprehensive vision of its times. Although the Romantics shared with their Modernist descendants this confidence in the artistic imagination and also embarked on epic ventures with varying degrees of success (Blake being perhaps the most successful in completing a system of epic scope), the Romantics tended to ignore Kant's critique of the limits of knowledge and to mythologize the transcendental grounds and logical universals of idealist thought. Modernists, who had more complete exposure to the idealist tradition, particularly its later development in Hegel, Schopenhauer, and Nietzsche, typically followed Pater's strategy of demythologizing the Romantic imagination; and their epic ventures, while retaining a cosmic scope, nevertheless more closely observe the Kantian limits of knowledge.

The privileging of aesthetic experience shows up in a number of different ways in Modernist writers: for example, in Yeats's notion of his wheels and gyres as "stylized arrangements of experience"; in Joyce's view of the artist as "transmuting the daily bread of experience into the radiant body of everliving life"; in Eliot's view of Joyce's "mythical method" as giving shape and significance to contemporary history; in Virginia Woolf's use in *To the Lighthouse* of Lily's painting as a metaphor for the nature and power of art to capture a vision of experience; and in Wallace Stevens's conception of the poetic imagination as a constitutive force in our experience. Two brief illustrations from Yeats and Eliot should suffice to demonstrate the privileging of aesthetic experience as a central tenet in Modernist art.

Yeats was one of the most Romantic of the major Modernists, and his writing as a whole constitutes an important articulation of art as a privileged mode of experience. Yeats claimed art was "a vision of reality,"[13] and like Pater he placed art above religion in its power to lend dignity, harmony, and understanding to our experience.[14] Although many of Pater's disciples in the nineties seized upon his "Conclusion" and took art for art's sake to an extreme by emptying Pater's ideal even of the fleeting moment's experience, Yeats never accepted art as an end in itself. Instead he set himself against his fellow disciples of Pater by arguing for the dependence of "all great art and literature upon conviction and upon heroic life,"[15] a sentiment he would have found confirmed in Pater's essay "Style." Alluding to Pater's "Conclusion," Yeats says, "All art is in the last analysis an endeavour to condense as out of the flying vapour of the world an image of human perfection, and for its own and not for the art's sake."[16]

At times, especially in his earlier writing, Yeats followed the Romantic tradition of mythologizing the vision of the artist. Yeats not only wanted to enhance the actual experience of the moment, as Pater did, but he also wanted to root it in his *anima mundi*, thus endowing it with objectivity and universality. The Neoplatonic, Jungian notion of *anima mundi* gave Yeats's aesthetic philosophy a foundation beyond the individual human mind, and by positing a transcendent

---

13. *The Poems of W. B. Yeats*, p. 161.

14. *Essays and Introductions* (London: Macmillan, 1961), p. 193.

15. *Uncollected Prose by W. B. Yeats*, ed. John P. Frayne (London: Macmillan, 1970), 1:248.

16. *The Variorum Edition of the Poems of W. B. Yeats*, ed. Peter Alt and Russell K. Alspach (New York: Macmillan, 1957), p. 849.

realm Yeats allied himself with a Romantic metaphysics of substance that had not followed through completely, as Pater did, the epistemological shift to a metaphysics of function.

At other times, however, when Yeats's skepticism prevailed, he came much closer to Pater's functionalist perspective on the powers of art. Despite the assurance his transcendent metaphysics provided, Yeats was constantly plagued with epistemological doubt as he vacillated throughout his career between a literal belief in the revelatory power of art and a disturbed skepticism about the possibility of any kind of knowledge. For example, the optimism about the transcendent powers of art expressed in the Byzantium poems and "Lapis Lazuli" is countered by more skeptical poems like "A Dialogue of Self and Soul" and "The Man and the Echo"; and the short, powerful play *Purgatory* is an agon of epistemological doubt. Yeats's vacillation between extremes was a lifelong effort to reconcile somehow his passion for truth with his profound skepticism; and when he did approach reconciliation, he also approached a less mythological, more functionalist view of the cognitive power of art. A good example of this attitude appears at the end of his introduction to the second edition of *A Vision*. Anticipating criticism of his elaborate system of wheels and gyres, Yeats says,

> Some will ask whether I believe in the actual existence of my circuits of sun and moon. . . . To such a question I can but answer that if sometimes, overwhelmed by miracle as all men must be when in the midst of it, I have taken such periods literally, my reason has soon recovered; and now that the system stands out clearly in my imagination I regard them as stylistic arrangements of experience comparable to the cubes in the drawing of Wyndham Lewis and to the ovoids in the sculpture of Brancusi. They have helped me to hold in a single thought reality and justice.[17]

The power of aesthetic contemplation for Yeats is perhaps best illustrated in the poem "Lapis Lazuli,"[18] in which two Chinese men, themselves carved into a work of art like the golden bird in "Sailing to

---

17. *A Vision*, 2d ed. (London: Macmillan, 1937; rev. 1962), pp. 24–25.
18. *The Poems of W. B. Yeats*, pp. 294–95.

Byzantium," contemplate the tragic nature of experience. From a bird's-eye, mountain perspective, "On all the tragic scene they stare," and in their detached contemplation of the scene, they compose it aesthetically to the accompaniment of "mournful melodies." In this metaphoric instance of art aspiring to the condition of music, we have a Hegelian transmutation of experience into tragic gaiety. Because the Chinese men—like the golden bird of Byzantium singing "Of what is past, or passing, or to come"—grasp the cyclical nature of the rise and fall of civilizations and are buoyed by the confidence that "all things run / On that unfashionable gyre again,"[19] they are transformed by their aesthetic vision, just as the suffering of Hamlet and Lear is transfigured in Shakespeare's art.

Even under the moderating influence of his skepticism, Yeats's faith in his "stylistic arrangements of experience" reflects a belief in the power of art that substantially exceeds Pater's heightened consciousness of the fleeting moment. Inspired by a Nietzschean confidence in the mission of the artist, Yeats endowed aesthetic vision and contemplation, as in "Lapis Lazuli," with the power not only to heighten the quality of our experience but also to confer order, harmony, dignity, and understanding on what would otherwise be a merely chaotic flux.

Like Yeats, Eliot and Joyce also attempted to compose the anarchy of experience and the nightmare of history into an aesthetic order. I deal extensively with Joyce in the final chapter. Eliot, however, because of his religious orthodoxy and his explicit rejection of Pater, is a particularly interesting and less obvious case than Yeats or Joyce of a Modernist who perceived art as a privileged mode of experience. Northrop Frye quotes Eliot as saying "a function of all art [is] to give us some perception of an order in life, by imposing an order upon it."[20] In his famous essay on Joyce's *Ulysses* Eliot says much the same thing in different words when he cites Joyce's "mythical method" as "a way of controlling, of ordering, of giving a shape and a significance to the immense panorama of futility and anarchy which is contemporary history."[21] Eliot employed the mythical method himself in *The*

---

19. *The Poems of W. B. Yeats*, p. 293.

20. Northrop Frye, *T. S. Eliot* (London: Oliver and Boyd, 1963), pp. 44–45.

21. *Selected Prose of T. S. Eliot*, ed. Frank Kermode (New York: Harcourt Brace Jovanovich/Farrar, Straus and Giroux, 1975), p. 177.

Waste Land, and both his notion of it and his use of it carry the cognitive power of art beyond the enhanced experience of Pater's privileged moment and almost as far as Yeats's "stylistic arrangements of experience." Unlike Yeats, though, Eliot stops short of granting his early myths divine origins—*The Golden Bough* did not have the status of sacred scripture.

By the time Eliot wrote *Four Quartets*, however, he was employing a myth he believed literally. Whereas earlier, the mythic materials were subordinate to his art, in his late poetry, his art was placed in the service of his religion. Although Eliot's use of art in the service of belief is consistent with his orthodox Christianity, at the same time he still gives art a privileged role in the perception of experience, in the shaping of history, and also, like Yeats, in the perception of divine revelation. But whereas Yeats sometimes endowed art with divine power and Pater balked at the threshold of the supernatural, Eliot retained his dogmatic orthodoxy along with the cognitive function of art by casting his art in an anagogic role, in the Thomist sense. In *Four Quartets* Eliot approaches the divine Word by means of the poetic word. Eliot's art, however, does not lead directly to a transcendent universe as Yeats at times believed his art did, but rather he finds in the formal patterns of sensible things analogues of the divine patterns of spiritual truth:

> The dance along the artery
> The circulation of the lymph
> Are figured in the drift of stars.

For Eliot the discipline of poetry, the struggle to choreograph "undisciplined squads of emotion" into the "complete consort dancing together," becomes the analogue of the divine struggle—the prayer, observance, and discipline, the patience and suffering, the hints and guesses pointing to the divine dance of the Logos.

Although in *Four Quartets* Eliot denies the privileged Paterian moment ("Not the intense moment / Isolated with no before and after") and sees "At best, only a limited value / In the knowledge derived from experience," he does not deviate from the Paterian position on art as a privileged mode of expression and perception. Though Eliot recognized other ways of approaching the Christian Logos, for him art is one way: in *Four Quartets* the incarnate word of poetry mirrors the Incarnation of the Word. In a sense, Eliot canonized Pater's "Conclusion" to *The Renaissance* by converting it to orthodox Christianity. For Eliot the goal of aesthetic contemplation is not the intense, isolated moment of the Paterian gemlike flame, but "a lifetime burning in every moment." What Eliot has done is to move the gemlike flame "Into another intensity / For a further union, a deeper communion." As the pattern of art is the analogue of the divine Logos, the Paterian moment becomes the analogue of the highest moments of spiritual experience "and simply for those moments' sake." Like Yeats, Eliot endows Pater's isolated moment with universal as well as spiritual significance. But it is still art, with its formal patterns and discipline, that brings us to this moment in *Four Quartets*: to experience the unattended moment in and out of time, we must "move in measure, like a dancer."

This belief in the power of art to heighten, organize, or reveal the significance of experience became a distinguishing trait of Modernist writers. Pater was by no means solely responsible for this attitude, but he helped lay the foundations for it, so that when, say, Nietzsche's views on artists made their way to Great Britain, its writers had already been primed by Pater. In contrast to both Romanticism and Modernism, post-Modern writing tends to emphasize epistemological skepticism over other elements inherited from German idealism; the privileging of the aesthetic, cosmic confidence, ambitious epic efforts, and system building consequently all dissolve into various fragmented compartments of the void.

Another literary tradition that can be traced to Schiller through Pater is the Romantic journey of inner growth and discovery, a tradition for which Schiller's notion of an aesthetic education provided one of its most cogent rationales. Because of its universal foundations in the epistemology of German idealism, particularly in Hegel's elaboration of Schiller's insights, this journey took on epic proportions, the journey of one individual becoming the journey of every individual or even the journey of the human race. Sometimes the spiritual journey is conducted in terms of Schiller's dialectic between sense and the rational spirit, as in Blake's *Four Zoas*, Wordsworth's *Prelude*, Pater's *Marius*, Joyce's *Portrait* and *Ulysses*, or the poetry of Yeats or Wallace Stevens; but other kinds of journeys of growth and development also evolved out of this tradition. The influence of Darwin's evolutionary thought, for example, offered scientifically minded empiricists an alternative to the idealist schemes of Schiller and Hegel, as in Butler's *The Way of All Flesh*.[22]

Two prominent fictional genres, the *bildungsroman* and the *künstlerroman*, emerged from this emphasis on inner growth and development. The bildungsroman is usually traced to Goethe's *Wilhelm Meister*; but if *Wilhelm Meister* provided the model for the bildungsroman, Schiller's letters *On the Aesthetic Education of Man* provided its philosophic and aesthetic rationale, a point often overlooked by scholars of the bildungsroman.[23] It was during the years that Goethe was working on *Wilhelm Meister* that he formed a close association with Schiller, and *Wilhelm Meisters Lehrjahre* and Schiller's *Aesthetic Education*, both completed in the early years of that association, were the twin offspring of one of the most fruitful and mutually beneficial literary relationships in history. Insofar as the bildungsroman was a spiritual quest for inner growth and the perfection of all our human faculties, as opposed to, say, the more conventional moral and social growth of Pip in *Great Expectations*, the idealist influence usually predominated; and when the aesthetic became the privileged condition in the education of the protagonist, as in Joyce's *Portrait of the Artist*, the bildungsroman merged with the künstlerroman.

-----

22. For a discussion of Darwin's influence on Butler see Knoepflmacher, pp. 224–95.

23. For detailed discussions of the bildungsroman tradition, its principles, its history, its composition, and its relation to English fiction see Maurice Beebe, *Ivory Towers and Sacred Founts: The Artist as Hero in Fiction from Goethe to Joyce* (New York: New York University Press, 1964); Jerome H. Buckley, *Season of Youth: The Bildungsroman from Dickens to Golding* (Cambridge: Harvard University Press, 1974); Susanne Howe, *Wilhelm Meister and His English Kinsmen* (1930; reprint, New York: AMS Press, 1966); François Jost, "La Tradition Du *Bildungsroman*," *Comparative Literature* 21 (1969): 97–115; Fritz Martini, "Der Bildungsroman: Zur Geschichte des Wortes und der Theorie," *Deutsche Vierteljahrsschrift für Literaturwissenschaft und Geistesgeschichte* 35 (1961): 44–63; Beron Mitchell, "*A Portrait* and the *Bildungsroman* Tradition," in *Approaches to Joyce's Portrait: Ten Essays*, ed. Thomas Staley and Bernard Benstock (Pittsburgh: University of Pittsburgh Press, 1976), pp. 61–76; G. B. Tennyson, "The *Bildungsroman* in Nineteenth-Century English Literature," in *Medieval Epic to the "Epic Theatre" of Brecht*, ed. Rosario P. Armato and John M. Spalek (Los Angeles: University of Southern California Press, 1968), pp. 135–46.

7 / HISTORICAL IDEALISM: HEGEL

IN FORD Madox Ford's *The Good Soldier* the narrator cites the "mental spirituality of Walter Pater" as one of the safe topics of discussion that would not upset the supposedly weak heart of his wife, Florence—safe, that is, in contrast to more controversial topics like "love, poverty, crime, religion, and the rest of it."[1] This ironic but nevertheless shrewd estimate of Pater sharply contradicts his reputation as a priest of sensation; and the figure most responsible for the shape and character of the mental spirituality Ford perceived in Pater is Hegel.

Hegel himself is a crucial figure in the development of both Modernism and post-Modernism; his influence substantially exceeds what was transmitted through Pater. Nevertheless Pater's thought and works constitute the most significant injection of Hegelian ideas into the British aesthetic tradition in the nineteenth century; and consequently, of all the Victorians, Pater provides the most extensive foundation for Anglo-American Modernism, a contribution that accounts for his popularity and influence among the early Modernists. If Coleridge and Carlyle can be said to have brought Kant, Schelling, and Schiller into the British literary tradition, Pater can be identified as the major conduit for Hegel.

Hegel was by far the most important of the German philosophers for Pater. As an undergraduate Pater read in German the *Phenomenol-*

---

1. *The Good Soldier* (New York: Random House, 1955), p. 16.

ogy of Spirit, the *Logic*, and the *History of Philosophy*. Shortly after graduation he added the *Philosophy of Fine Art*.[2] He also may have read other works of Hegel on several visits he made to Germany. In addition to reading Hegel himself, Pater also read widely in his followers, such as Baur and Zeller, and in Hegel's own sources of inspiration, such as Kant, Fichte, Schiller, and Schelling. Moreover, he had close associations with the British Hegelians at Oxford, such as Jowett, Caird, Green, and Nettleship.

It would be no exaggeration to say, as some have, that most of Pater's views on art, philosophy, myth, and religion were informed and inspired to some extent by Hegel and his followers.[3] Critics and scholars, who have devoted more commentary to Pater's relationship to Hegel than to any other German, have already indicated the pervasiveness of Hegel's influence on Pater, an influence that was both general and specific, and they have identified a number of the views and principles Pater adapted from Hegel. At the broadest level, Hegel helped shape the configuration of Pater's thought and sensibility by providing him with an authoritative philosophic sanction for many of his own inclinations and a philosophic vision sufficiently broad and sophisticated to encompass the entire range of his interests. Hegel's example and thought gave Pater confidence in dealing in a highly intellectual manner with the products of culture, particularly aesthetic culture. Although Pater began his career somewhat under the influence of positivism and eighteenth-century rationalism, he was soon converted almost completely to a Hegelian view of the function of intellect in art and culture. After his flirtation with solipsism in the "Conclusion," he came to accept the presence of some kind of universals in our knowledge of experience, particularly under the aegis of Hegel's emphasis on zeitgeist and the evolutionary development of the Idea through history.[4] Pater also absorbed from Hegel the closest thing to what could be called a philosophic foundation or ground for his own weltanschauung—the "idea of Humanity," as Pater calls it in *Marius*, the idea of a "universal commonwealth of mind" (*ME* 2:9), a

---

2. Inman, *Pater's Reading*, pp. 9, 32, 34, 49.

3. Inman, for example, notes that Hegel's *History of Philosophy* "covers almost all of the philosophical subjects that Pater was ever to refer to" (*Pater's Reading*, p. 39).

4. Dale, pp. 228–38; Young, pp. 42–47.

notion that has been linked to Hegel's *Phenomenology* and to his notion of zeitgeist.[5] Pater's view of art as an ideal and privileged condition also owes as much to Hegel as to Schiller;[6] and the same can be said of his observer mentality with its emphasis on seeing, understanding, and knowing, rather than doing. Pater's view of the self-consciousness of art and art criticism was likewise reinforced by Hegel's epistemological goal of a totally self-conscious knowledge.[7]

In addition to shaping the general configuration of Pater's thought, Hegel provided two intellectual methodologies that became part of Pater's own repertoire of mental habits. In general Pater accepted Hegel's phenomenological analysis of experience (though substantially tempered and purged of absolutes) and the dialectical method it entailed. Particularly crucial to Pater's thinking were the dialectic between sense and intellect in art, generated from Hegel's notion of art as the sensuous manifestation of the Idea, and the analysis of form and content that follows from it.[8] Although the phenomenological analysis of experience was available to Pater through other German philosophers, such as Kant, Fichte, and Schelling, Hegel's particular formulation of the dialectic between sense and spirit was, along with Schiller's, the most crucial to Pater's own thought and aesthetic. In Pater's hands Hegelian dialectic became a functional method for both the creation and analysis of all forms of intellectual culture.

The other major methodology Pater adapted from Hegel and his followers was the historical method of criticism with its attendant notions of zeitgeist and the view of history as a cumulative and progressive evolution of intellectual culture.[9] This method informs all Pater's major criticism and culminates in his book-length study of Plato in *Plato and Platonism*. The historical method also provided Pater with the primary structural technique for his fiction, including all the imaginary portraits and his two novels.

---

5. Inman, *Pater's Reading*, p. 33; Ward, pp. 52–55.

6. Dale, pp. 227–28; Inman, *Pater's Reading*, pp. 53, 56; Ward, pp. 67–70.

7. Ward, pp. 70–75.

8. Ruth C. Child, *The Aesthetic of Walter Pater* (1940; reprint, New York: Farrar, Straus and Giroux, 1969), pp. 61–66; Dale, pp. 210, 226, 230–36; Fehr, 302; Inman, *Pater's Reading*, pp. 51, 74–75, 142; Ward, pp. 55, 185–86; Wollheim, pp. 170–71.

9. Dale, pp. 7–8, 200–205; Inman, *Pater's Reading*, p. 33; Knoepflmacher, p. 174; Shuter, "History as Palengenesis in Pater and Hegel," 411–21; Ward, pp. 52–55.

Finally, Pater either adapted or borrowed outright from Hegel his views and analyses of a wide variety of specific aesthetic and philosophic issues. One of the most crucial of these is the notion of "art for art's sake." On this issue Pater, to his credit, adheres more closely to the views of Hegel and Schiller, in which art offers a privileged form of knowledge, than to later French versions that erode the epistemological foundations for the slogan.[10] Even the emphasis on craft and technique, usually associated with the aesthetic movement and often attributed to Gautier and Flaubert, has a precedent in Hegel, who impressed on Pater the importance of technical craftsmanship in art.[11] The privileging of aesthetic experience in Hegel and Schiller also informs Pater's views on tragedy and his identification of music as the ideal art form. Pater's rationale for choosing music, however, is closer to Schiller's than to Hegel's.[12]

Hegel also offered a number of suggestions on the proper conduct of art criticism that Pater adopted in his own theory and practice of criticism, such as the need to disregard abstract theories of art and begin with the work itself and its significance. Following the historical method, the critic would then place the work in the context of its age and nation; but Hegel also advocated placing the work in the context of the artist's own personality. Like Pater, Hegel saw an identification of the artist's entire self with his subject matter and its embodiment; and he saw the artist not as willful and capricious but as one who converts the accidents of his experience into the objectivity of his art.[13] That the artist converts accident into deliberate and objective art was asserted later by both Yeats and Joyce.[14]

Pater adopted whole from Hegel's *Ästhetik* the evolutionary history of art forms from the Symbolic, such as architecture, where the sensuous form distorts the vaguely determined Idea it embodies, through

---

10. Child, pp. 19–26; Germain d'Hangest, *Walter Pater: l'Homme et l'Oeuvre* (Paris: Didier, 1961), 1:351–52 n. 63; Inman, *Pater's Reading*, p. 55.

11. Dale, pp. 227–28; 285–86 n. 40.

12. Inman, *Pater's Reading*, p. 51; Proesler, p. 83.

13. Inman, *Pater's Reading*, pp. 56–57.

14. In Yeats's poem "Lapis Lazuli," "Every discoloration of the stone, / Every accidental crack or dent" is transformed by the carver into "a water-course or an avalanche / Or lofty slope . . ." (*The Poems of W. B. Yeats*, p. 295). Joyce's Stephen Dedalus also insists that the artist transforms the accidents of everyday life into the eternal beauty of art.

the Classical, such as sculpture, where the fusion of sensuous form and the Idea are most perfect, to the Romantic, such as painting, poetry, and music, where the Idea or the context exceeds the adequacy of the sensuous form to contain it.[15] In "Winckelmann" Pater accepts Hegel's judgment that Classical art, particularly Phidian sculpture, represents a perfect fusion of form and Idea,[16] as does the sensuous imagination of the Greeks generally.[17]

On the basis of the frequency of his borrowings and allusions, it appears that of all Hegel's works Pater knew the *Ästhetik* (*The Philosophy of Fine Art*) most thoroughly,[18] and that "Winckelmann" and *Plato and Platonism* are his most thoroughly Hegelian works. In addition to the evolutionary scheme of art forms, "Winckelmann" employs many other details from the *Ästhetik*, and *Plato and Platonism* applies the historic method to the study of Plato and draws from Hegel for its views on dialectic, Pythagoras's "Doctrine of Number," and music as a cosmic principle.[19]

Despite Pater's obvious affinity for Hegel and his periodic immersion in tomes of dialectic, there was a good deal of Hegel Pater could not accept. Pater's encounter with Hegel, as with Plato, was characterized by a profound ambivalence. Pater could never commit himself to one system of thought. He had no patience with metaphysical absolutes or infinities of any kind. Although reason accounted for more in Pater's scheme of things than he cared to admit, he rejected the hegemony of reason over sense in favor of the hegemony of sense over reason. Pater was not a systematic or rigorous thinker; finding himself uncomfortable in the rarefied realms of Hegel's abstractions and absolutes, he simply took whatever he could adapt to his own sensibility. Consequently he rejected Hegel's absolutist doctrines along with their transcendental foundations, while he embraced whatever in Hegel's thought could assist his own understanding of experience, art, and culture. Pater could accept, for example, Hegel's dialectical method

15. Dale, pp. 231–32; DeLaura, *Hebrew and Hellene*, pp. 209–22; Fehr, 302–4; Inman, *Pater's Reading*, pp. 49–51; Proesler, p. 85; Ward, pp. 56–57.

16. Dale, pp. 240–45; Inman, *Pater's Reading*, p. 51; Ward, p. 57.

17. Dale, p. 230; DeLaura, *Hebrew and Hellene*, pp. 210–12.

18. Fehr, 305; Inman, *Pater's Reading*, p. 49; Proesler, p. 85.

19. Knoepflmacher, p. 174; Ward, pp. 185–86.

and his notion of zeitgeist insofar as they applied to experience and cultural history, but he would not pursue dialectical thought or historical evolution into a realm of absolute spirit. So, restrained by his native tendencies toward empiricism, skepticism, and individualism, Pater adopted, as he did with Schiller, the typically British strategy of restricting the application of Hegel's thought to the realm of concrete experience.[20] This strategy dictated most of Pater's deviations from Hegel on specific issues.

Pater's own observations about Socrates' Promethean accomplishment of bringing metaphysics down to earth can be applied to Pater's adaptation of Hegel. Although Pater knew that Hegel's own ultimate goal, even for art, was a realm of pure thought beyond the bounds of the sensuous world, he preferred to view Hegel in the way he viewed Plato—as linking the worlds of thought and sense.[21] What appealed to Pater was not so much Hegel's notion of *Idea*, but his notion of the *Ideal*. In the first version of his essay on Winckelmann Pater says that in Hegel we find the term *Ideal* "attached to a fresh, clear-cut conception! With him the ideal is a *Versinnlichen* [sensible manifestation] of the idea—the idea turned into an object of sense. By the idea, stripped of its technical phraseology, he means man's knowledge about himself and his relation to the world, in its most rectified and concentrated form." [22] For Hegel himself the sensible manifestation of the idea was not his ultimate goal, but Pater nevertheless adopted it as his own. As with Plato, Pater saw Hegel as a promoter of ideals rather than of absolute ideas, ideals that form a philosophic temper—not apodictically but heuristically, by refining and guiding our powers of perception and conception in the appreciation and comprehension of experience, particularly the experience of intellectual culture (*PP*, 195–96).

Pater's typically British strategy of limiting Hegel's philosophy to the realm of concrete experience is well illustrated in his adaptation of Hegel's Classical ideal. Whereas Hegel saw the perfect fusion of sen-

---

20. Dale, p. 229; Fehr, 306; Ward, pp. 45–52; Young, pp. 92, 96–97, 108.
21. d'Hangest, *l'Homme et l'Oeuvre*, 1 : 352–53 n. 71.
22. Hill edition of *The Renaissance*, p. 257.

suous form and Idea in Greek sculpture evolving into the more purely mental forms of Romantic art in painting, music, and poetry, and art itself seeking a realm of pure thought and evolving into religion and philosophy, Pater, like Schiller, saw art as the highest form of intellectual experience precisely because it fused thought and sense. Pater also believed that the perfection of Greek art, which for Hegel represented only an intermediate stage in the evolution of the absolute spirit, could be repeated in later times, that it was an ideal to be sought in every stage of culture, and that it was achieved periodically during periods of great artistic achievement, such as the Renaissance.[23]

A thorough study of Hegel's impact on Pater or Modernism is beyond the scope and purpose of this study. There are several areas, however, where Pater's adaptation of Hegel sheds significant light on the nature and genesis of the Modernist movement. The remainder of this chapter will be devoted to Pater's employment of Hegel's ideas about history and their implications for some of the principal techniques of Modernist literature. The next chapter will be devoted to Pater's transformation of Hegelian dialectic and phenomenology into an idealism that serves strictly as a functional tool for the analysis of finite experience. The following chapters on the unified sensibility and Pater's theory of expression, while not focused specifically on Hegel, reveal Pater's own version of the dialectic between sense and intellect and his adaptation of Hegel's definition of art as the sensuous manifestation of the Idea into an expressive theory of artistic creation.

VIRTUALLY ALL of Pater's work, whether fictional or critical, was informed in one way or another by his adaptation of Hegel's historical method. In *Plato and Platonism* Pater explains that "all true criticism" of intellectual culture "must begin with an historic estimate of the conditions, antecedent and contemporary, which helped to make it precisely what it was." But for Pater, as for Hegel, "a complete criticism does not end there." In addition to the "circumstances of a particular age," the critic must also concern himself with the "inexplicable force of a personality, resistant to, while it is moulded by, them," with "what is unique in the individual genius." To illustrate

---

23. Child, pp. 61–64; Dale, pp. 240–45; Fehr, 306–7; d'Hangest, *l'Homme et l'Oeuvre*, 1:352–53 n. 71; Inman, *Pater's Reading*, pp. 55–56, 139.

what he means by this two-pronged, Hegelian historical method, he describes what he actually does with Plato:

> If in reading Plato, for instance, the philosophic student has to re-construct for himself, as far as possible, the general character of an *age*, he must also, so far as he may, reproduce the portrait of a *per-son*. The Sophists, the Sophistical world, around him; his master, Socrates; the Pre-Socratic philosophies; the mechanic influence, that is to say, of past and present:—of course we can know nothing at all of the Platonic doctrine except so far as we see it in well-ascertained contact with all that; but there is also Plato himself in it. (*PP*, 124–25; Pater's emphases).

Pater's own method in his criticism as well as in his fiction is charac-terized more accurately by this opening paragraph of "The Genius of Plato" than by the better known opening passages in the "Preface" to *The Renaissance*. His general technique is not primarily impression-istic; rather, as Richard Wollheim points out, it "relies most heavily upon the technique of association: the placing of the work firmly in the web of association where it belongs."[24] For Pater a substantial portion of this "web of association" is constituted by the history of the individual and his times—perceived, of course, through the often dis-torting lenses of Pater's own preoccupations and concerns; but Pater's shortcomings as a historian and a scholar do not alter the fundamen-tally historical nature of his technique. Pater applies this technique from his first essay on Coleridge to his last on Pascal; he employs it in his book-length study of Plato; and it constitutes the essence of his fictional strategy in his imaginary portraits and his novels.

At the beginning of *Plato and Platonism* Pater explicitly credits Hegel's "historic method" for inspiring his own attempts to place fig-ures of intellectual culture "in the group of conditions, intellectual, social, material" that actually produced them (9). In his own practice, however, Pater often emphasizes the contributions of individual ge-nius over the general conditions of an age, and when the character of an age does emerge in Pater's works, as in *The Renaissance*, *Marius*, *Gaston de Latour*, or *Plato and Platonism*, it is usually in the form of

---

24. *On Art and the Mind*, p. 171.

a group portrait of individuals. The intellectual character of Rome in *Marius*, for example, is conveyed largely through the individual portraits of Marcus Aurelius, Cornelius Fronto, and Lucian, along with the additional portraits of their intellectual ancestors Epicurus, Aristippus, and Heraclitus.

Closely related to the historical method is Hegel's notion of zeitgeist, which Pater defines in *Plato and Platonism* as "a peculiar *ensemble* of conditions which determines a common character in every product" of an age (9–10). This notion too pervaded all Pater's thinking. The famous passage on the Mona Lisa is a prose ode to the Hegelian zeitgeist; but perhaps the most explicit and eloquent expression of his conception of zeitgeist appears in a section of the "Preface" to *The Renaissance* that is often omitted in selections and anthologies that use the opening, impressionistic paragraphs. For Pater, although all ages have some common character, some ages are more coherent in their articulation of a common spirit, and these are our most productive artistically. "There come," Pater says,

> from time to time, eras of more favourable conditions, in which the thoughts of men draw nearer together than is their wont, and the many interests of the intellectual world combine in one complete type of general culture. The fifteenth century in Italy is one of these happier eras, and what is sometimes said of the age of Pericles is true of that of Lorenzo:—it is an age productive in personalities, many-sided, centralised, complete. Here, artists and philosophers and those whom the action of the world has elevated and made keen, do not live in isolation, but breathe a common air, and catch light and heat from each other's thoughts. There is a spirit of general elevation and enlightenment in which all alike communicate. The unity of this spirit gives unity to all the various products of the Renaissance; and it is to this intimate alliance with mind, this participation in the best thoughts which that age produced, that the art of Italy in the fifteenth century owes much of its grave dignity and influence. (*Ren.*, xiv)

Pater carried the notion of zeitgeist to the point of seeing intellectual and cultural history as Hegel saw it—as cumulative, as each succeeding zeitgeist building on those preceding it. Although Pater did not accept Hegel's ultimate destination for the evolution of the zeitgeist—the realm of absolute spirit—he did accept a notion of perpetual recurrence as well as Hegel's view that all the products of intellect and imagination constituted the cumulative cultural capital of our civilization (*PP*, 159). Defined in this finite sense, the Hegelian notion of progress played an important role in Pater's thought.

In the face of this endorsement of the zeitgeist and its closely allied historical method, it is difficult to maintain, as many critics have, a view of Pater's criticism as purely impressionistic and solipsistic, a view often supported by citations from the first half of the "Preface" to the *Renaissance,* in which Pater emphasizes the necessity of the critic's knowing first his "own impression" of the object before him. Despite his protestations about subjectivity and his emphasis on individual genius, Pater accepted the premise of common intellectual and cultural ground essential to the notion of zeitgeist.

Pater's most ambitious and explicit use of Hegel's historical scheme can be found in *Marius the Epicurean* and *Plato and Platonism,* where Pater links the universal with the particular by retracing "the historic order of human thought" in the "mental pilgrimage" of the individual (*ME* 1:134). This is most explicitly accomplished in the structure of *Plato and Platonism,* where, in addition to setting Plato in the context of the Athens and Sparta of his own times, Pater also charts an ideal, individual, mental pilgrimage for Plato from the thought of Heraclitus through the thought of the Eleatics, Pythagoras, the Sophists, and Socrates to his own doctrines, methods, and aesthetics. After tracing this intellectual journey, Pater completes his Hegelian portrait of Plato with a chapter on the uniqueness of Plato's individual personality and genius.

This same method informs *Marius the Epicurean.* Marius begins his spiritual pilgrimage with his family's religion, the simple, ritualistic "religion of Numa," and from there he passes through the much more rational worlds of Heraclitus, Aristippus of Cyrene, and the Stoic Marcus Aurelius to the all-encompassing vision of early Christianity. Pater leaves Marius at the threshold of Christianity, at the doorway to the most inclusive system of human experience, according to Hegel's historical scheme, that was available to a Roman in the time of Marius. This intellectual pilgrimage constitutes the basic plot of the novel.

Pater repeats the same Hegelian pattern in *Gaston de Latour,* where he sets his protagonist out on a similar pilgrimage: Gaston proceeds from the late-medieval Christianity of Provence, through Ronsard, Montaigne, and Giordano Bruno. Gaston's ultimate destination, however, remains a mystery of the unfinished manuscript.

In the historical schemes governing these major works the earlier positions in the development of Plato, Marius, and Gaston are challenged and negated but never totally dismissed as they are incorporated dialectically into the various succeeding positions until they are all subsumed under the maturity of a fully developed outlook, just as in Hegel's system all earlier manifestations of the zeitgeist are subsumed under the latest manifestation, which for Hegel was represented by his own philosophy.

As Pater's notes indicate, the English protagonist of his projected third novel would begin his intellectual journey with the negations of Kant.[25] Undoubtedly this protagonist would have mirrored an idealized pattern of Pater's own intellectual development. Even though Pater's English novel never proceeded beyond a few preliminary notes, we might speculate, on the basis of the patterns of *Marius, Gaston, Plato and Platonism*, and Pater's own intellectual development, what form that idealized pattern might take in the spiritual pilgrimage of an English youth born in 1839, the year of Pater's own birth. He would begin in the security of a world view composed of the traditional family religious practices and the well-ordered universe of Newtonian mechanics. The security and harmony of his early intellectual environment would be shattered by his reading of Hume and Kant. From Hume and Kant he might proceed to the healing balm of Wordsworth's poetry, and from there to the positive philosophical aestheticism of Schelling and Schiller, who in turn would lead him to the all-encompassing system of Hegel. This English intellectual pilgrim would undoubtedly be restrained by his early exposure to Hume from embracing Hegel's absolutist extremes, but Hegel nevertheless would provide him with a scheme within which he could account for all his various experiences of life and culture. Christianity may figure in the pattern, only it would not be doctrinal and institutional but a form of liturgical, lay Christianity of the kind Pater explores in his later essays, a Christianity perceived from an all-inclusive functionalist perspective as one element in a many-sided intellectual culture.

---

25. Houghton Library MS 31 "[Thistle]."

In effect, then, Pater helped to establish a Hegelian historical paradigm in which the cultural evolution of the race is reflected in microcosm in the intellectual development of the individual, and in which the spirits of the past live on in the present life of that individual. According to this paradigm, history is both cyclical and evolutionary; it proceeds dialectically by assimilating its past into its present, and it often involves the reincarnation of figures from the past in the intellectual and cultural life of the present.

Pater, however, did not have the innovative techniques of Modernist literature available to him; nor did he have the originality to invent them. Rather he forged a shape for his own Hegelian vision of cultural history out of the conventional literary techniques of his time, for example, by drawing his portrait of Aristippus in *Marius* to suggest the more contemporary Hume; but these traditional techniques could do no more than faintly suggest the parallel. If Pater had developed the techniques of Modernist writing, he could have written all three volumes of his projected trilogy (*Marius*, *Gaston*, and "Thistle") as a single work set in contemporary England in which Aristippus, Montaigne, and Hume existed simultaneously in the mind of the protagonist along with Marcus Aurelius, Giordano Bruno, and Hegel. This protagonist would have usurped much of the originality of Joyce's Stephen Dedalus and Eliot's Tiresias, for once we look behind the radically innovative techniques that embody Modernist visions of history, we find that they are very similar to Pater's adaptation of Hegel.

In Modernist writing we often find cosmic visions of history. The later poems and plays of Yeats embody in metaphoric wheels and gyres the elaborate historical scheme laid out in *A Vision*. In *Ulysses* and *Finnegans Wake* Joyce creates intricate historical paradigms that make these books microcosms of Irish and Western cultural traditions. Inspired by Joyce's example in *Ulysses*, T. S. Eliot enunciated in "Tradition and the Individual Talent" his own vision of history as a simultaneous order formed by the present and the past, a vision he also articulates in the structure and techniques of *The Waste Land* and, in a more orthodox Christian version, in *Four Quartets*.[26]

---

26. In "Victorian Compromise and Modern Revolution," *ELH* 26 (1959): 425–44, Jean Sudrann pointed out the use of historical parallels by both Pater and Joyce; and in "The Development of T. S. Eliot's Historical Sense," *Review of English*

Although the historical visions of Yeats, Joyce, and Eliot differ in a number of their particulars, they all have certain features in common, including a focus on cultural history, a privileged role for art in the perception and expression of history, cyclical, dialectical patterns operating on both microcosmic and macrocosmic levels, a concept of reincarnation or metempsychosis, and some notion of development. All of these common features reflect Hegel's historical idealism, with its attendant notions of dialectic, zeitgeist, art as an ideal and privileged condition, and history as a cumulative and progressive evolution of intellectual culture. Of course, the Modernists did not adopt Hegel's Romantic idealism wholesale. By the time Hegel's views had reached them, they had been modified in a more or less consistent manner by the British Hegelians of the late nineteenth century, such as Green, Caird, Pater, and F. H. Bradley, who typically rejected Hegel's absolutism along with its transcendental foundations.

Remarkably enough, the relationship of Modernist visions of history to Pater and Hegel is an inexplicable lacuna in the scholarship of Modernism. Of all the major influences on Modernism, Hegel in particular is one of the least explored. As I mentioned at the outset, however, I am not so much concerned here with direct lines of influence as with cultural confluence. The important point is not whether the Modernists were directly indebted to Pater or Hegel but that the historical ideas embodied in their techniques can be traced to figures like Hegel and can be illuminated by Pater's adaptation of the philosophical thought he absorbed. Whether or not any particular Modernist read Hegel and Hegelians, Pater and Paterians, or simply picked up ideas that were "in the air" and available from a variety of sources, is not crucial to my argument. In other words, I make no claim for the exclusive or direct influence of Pater or Hegel on Modernist views of history. The essential point is that Pater's adaptation of Hegel's historicism formulated a view of history similar to the one typically expressed in Modernist literature. Whether it came from Pater directly or indirectly, or whether the Modernists synthesized their own views from many of the same sources that Pater drew from does not affect the validity of my analysis here. A brief look at the historical visions of

---

Studies 23 (1972): 291–301, P. G. Ellis first noted the connection between Pater and T. S. Eliot's "Tradition and the Individual Talent."

Eliot, Yeats, and Joyce should suffice to demonstrate the relevance of Pater's Hegelian paradigm to Modernist views of history.

TAKEN TOGETHER Eliot's essay "Tradition and the Individual Talent" and its poetic embodiment in *The Waste Land* constitute one of the central expressions of the Modernist view of history. In "Tradition and the Individual Talent" Eliot defines tradition in terms of what he calls "the historical sense," a phrase we find frequently in the writings of Pater and other nineteenth-century sages. For Eliot history is not so much cyclical as in Yeats, or even a matter of metempsychosis as in Joyce, but rather a "simultaneous order." Eliot's simultaneous order, however, seems to merge or include the notions of cycle, metempsychosis, and development as all cycles collapse into a single order. "The historical sense," Eliot says,

> involves a perception, not only of the pastness of the past, but of its presence; the historical sense compels a man to write not merely with his own generation in his bones, but with a feeling that the whole of the literature of Europe from Homer and within it the whole of the literature of his own country has a simultaneous existence and composes a simultaneous order. This historical sense, which is a sense of the timeless as well as of the temporal and of the timeless and of the temporal together, is what makes a writer traditional. And it is at the same time what makes a writer most acutely conscious of his place in time, of his contemporaneity.
>
> No poet, no artist of any art, has his complete meaning alone. His significance, his appreciation is the appreciation of his relation to the dead poets and artists. You cannot value him alone; you must set him, for contrast and comparison, among the dead. I mean this as a principle of aesthetic, not merely historical, criticism. (49)[27]

In this passage the notions of cycle or metempsychosis do not really account for the presence of the past because all the ghosts are present at once with the living; Eliot wants all the spirits present at once and not just spirits of a particular phase or type. In part 2 of "Little Gidding," in the scene set in the moments after a London air raid,

---

27. All page references to "Tradition and the Individual Talent" are from Eliot's *The Sacred Wood* (London: Methuen, 1960).

Eliot creates a memorable metaphor for his view of the relation of a poet to his predecessors. The metaphor is the "familiar compound ghost" who instructs the persona on the "gifts reserved for age." Eliot characterizes this ghost as having the

> . . . look of some dead master
> Whom I had known, forgotten, half recalled
>   Both one and many; in the brown baked features
>   The eyes of a familiar compound ghost
> Both intimate and unidentifiable.

Although the message of the ghost contains echoes of Yeats and Swift and the scene seems like one out of Dante's *Purgatorio*, the ghost represents a composite of all Eliot's predecessors. He is both intimate and unidentifiable because he is the whole of Eliot's literary past as present in his own bones.

Even though Eliot says "art never improves," nevertheless he does maintain some Hegelian notion of an evolutionary zeitgeist. Eliot insists that the poet "must be aware that the mind of Europe—the mind of his own country—a mind which he learns in time to be much more important than his own private mind—is a mind which changes, and that this change is a development which abandons nothing *en route*, which does not superannuate either Shakespeare, or Homer, or the rock drawing of the Magdalenian draughtsmen." Eliot is not willing to claim, however, that this evolutionary accretion is an "improvement" in any sense, but only complication, or perhaps refinement (51–52). Eliot is not willing to say, in other words, that the present stage of Spirit, in Hegel's sense, contains and reconciles all the oppositions of past spirits.

When he explains the relation of the present to the past, the present is no all-inclusive *Geist* but sounds more like the growth of a new branch that changes the shape of a venerable old tree:

> . . . what happens when a new work of art is created is something that happens simultaneously to all the works of art which preceded it. The existing monuments form an ideal order among themselves, which is modified by the introduction of the new (the really new) work of art among them. The existing order is complete before the

new work arrives; for order to persist after the supervention of novelty, the *whole* existing order must be, if ever so slightly, altered; and so the relations, proportions, values of each work of art toward the whole are readjusted. (49–50; Eliot's emphasis)

For Eliot the past is modified "by the present as much as the present is directed by the past" (50); or as he put it in *Four Quartets*,

> Time present and time past
> Are both perhaps present in time future,
> And time future contained in time past.

For Eliot, however, the present is not privileged over the past as with Hegel. The most Eliot will say is that "the difference between the present and the past is that the conscious present is an awareness of the past in a way and to an extent which the past's awareness of itself cannot show" (52). But if Eliot would not accept the superiority of the present in Hegel's scheme, his emphasis on the entire simultaneous order of history and on the present's self-conscious awareness of the past and its relation to it still owes a great deal directly or indirectly to Hegel's analysis of history.

When we turn to *The Waste Land*, we find the principles of "Tradition and the Individual Talent" put into poetic practice. Ancient vegetation myths and the Christian grail legend are all reenacted in a contemporary London setting that becomes a timeless present. The protean character of Tiresias is perhaps the most efficient means Eliot uses to interleave past and present in *The Waste Land*. As the central consciousness of the poem, as both spectator and participant, Tiresias is, as Eliot tells us in one of his infamous notes, "the most important personage in the poem, uniting all the rest. Just as the one-eyed merchant, seller of currants, melts into the Phoenician Sailor, and the latter is not wholly distinct from Ferdinand Prince of Naples, so all the women are one woman, and the two sexes meet in Tiresias. What Tiresias *sees*, in fact, is the substance of the poem" (Eliot's emphasis). Unlike Leopold Bloom, Eliot's Tiresias is not simply a reincarnation of a particular spirit of the past; rather he is more a timeless, universal spirit and his roles in the poem are so numerous as to suggest that they are infinite. Tiresias is literally everyman and everywoman

throughout time and not a symbolic Everyman like Bloom. As a contemporary Londoner, Tiresias assumes the roles of a leisure-class European, a clairvoyant, a sailor, an upper-class husband and wife, a
lower-class husband and wife, a seedy Smyrna merchant, an emotion-
less typist, and her equally indifferent lover. But Tiresias also inhabits
many shapes from the past—Tristan and other grail knights, the Fisher
King, various vegetation gods (Hyacinthus, Adonis, Osiris), Christ,
St. Peter, Queen Elizabeth and her consort Leicester, Phlebas the
Phoenician sailor. In addition to inhabiting bodies past and present,
Tiresias also speaks in voices of the past and present—the Upanishads,
Ezekiel, Virgil, Ovid, St. Paul, Augustine, Dante, Spenser, Shakespeare
and other Elizabethan dramatists, Marvell, Baudelaire, Verlaine,
Nerval, a bawdy Australian song, a contemporary publican, and the
voices of other contemporary personages. Ancient myths, Christian
myths, and history coexist with contemporary life and mutually reflect each other in various ways, always to the detriment of the present
scene. Through the timeless, protean figure of Tiresias, Eliot brings to
bear on contemporary London the wisdom of the Old Testament, of
ancient Greece and Rome, of the Orient, and of the entire culture of
the West built on these ancient cultures. These various cultures, both
ancient and modern, are the pillars of Western civilization Eliot depicts crumbling in *The Waste Land* as a sort of Hegelian version of
"London Bridge Is Falling Down":

> Falling towers
> Jerusalem Athens Alexandria
> Vienna London
> Unreal

In addition to Tiresias, Eliot uses the technique of discontinuous
juxtaposition to interweave scenes from the past with scenes from the
present; at times he fuses the present with the past in the same scene.
He also makes extensive use of allusions to link the present with the
past. The combination of all these techniques creates the impression of
a "simultaneous existence" of past and present, of the "simultaneous
order" of history and literary tradition. In this way Eliot gives a new
shape and significance to what is essentially a Hegelian view of history.
Four Quartets continues to employ Hegelian views of history and

adds the principle of dialectic that was absent in *The Waste Land*. These Hegelian notions, however, are governed in *Four Quartets* by a Christian orthodox vision. The dialectic between flesh and spirit is cast in terms of the Christian opposition between this world and the next, and the progression of history involves a dialectical tension between temporal history and Divine Providence, between time and eternity. Although Hegel himself encouraged the identification of his logical Geist with the orthodox Christian notion of God, history for Eliot does not advance toward a realm of pure spirit in Hegel's sense. In *Four Quartets* history revolves around the Incarnation, the manifestation of the timeless in time, of God in the world of sense, and the central dialectic revolves around the paradoxical mystery of the Word made flesh. Hegel's Geist and Heraclitus's Logos alike become metaphors, or analogies in the Thomist sense, that point to the Divine Mind. The pattern of the entire poem itself is Hegelian. It begins with the mysterious rose-garden scene, and it ends with the metaphor of a rose of fire that elucidates only at the end of the poem the vision in the pool of the rose garden at the beginning. So in true Hegelian fashion the end is seen (but not understood) in the beginning, and we arrive at the end to know the beginning for the first time. Even more so than Pater, Eliot maintains Hegel's emphasis not on the end itself but on the entire process from beginning to end. We are not bid "farewell" toward any particular destination but "fare forward" in a sequence of timeless moments in which the spiritual object of one's contemplation is continuously present. The notion of progression, of course, is implied in the movement of Christian history toward the apocalypse, but Eliot is more interested in personal salvation than in apocalyptic visions; and so from the perspective of the *Four Quartets* history becomes a "pattern / Of timeless moments" that represent both the object of contemplation and the ultimate destination of the individual soul.

Eliot's historical sense, then, with its notions of a simultaneous order of past and present, of the evolution of tradition by accretion, and of the dialectic between the temporal and the timeless, constitutes a variation on Pater's Hegelian paradigm. Like Pater and Hegel, Eliot focuses on cultural history and grants art a privileged role in the perception and comprehension of that history.

Both Yeats and Joyce also employed their art to construct comprehensive visions of cultural history. Since many analyses of Yeats's historical system and the Viconian features of Joyce's work are readily available, I will confine myself here merely to pointing out some of the major structural similarities between their visions of history and Pater's.

Yeats's idiosyncratic vision was drawn from a wide variety of sources, but primarily from sources associated with occult and Neoplatonic traditions. Nevertheless, it contains many of the same essential features as Pater's historical paradigm: it has a strong Hegelian character (Hegel's idealism also contains many Platonic elements); it sees cyclical dialectical patterns operating on both microcosmic and macrocosmic levels; and it involves a doctrine of reincarnation and a notion of development. Yeats also based his historical vision on a system of oppositions that correspond generally to Pater's opposition between the Ionic flux of experience and the Doric impulse to impose a formal order on that flux. As with Pater, the opposition between Classical and Christian is fundamental to the paradigm, although there is no ambivalence in Yeats's preference for the Classical as there is with Pater. Yeats's system also involves a series of phases within each cycle, and, as with Pater and Hegel, the cycles apply to the lives of individuals as well as to the history of civilizations. For Yeats the system applies even to the cycle of an individual thought, and thus he also acknowledges the operation of some form of Hegelian dialectic in each act of perception and conception.

A doctrine of reincarnation provides a link between the various cycles in Yeats's system. The evolutionary element is connected with this notion of reincarnation: an individual or a civilization may progress to a higher order in each successive reincarnation until the final incarnation in an aesthetic realm of pure spirit, which Yeats calls the "Thirteenth Sphere." Of all the Modernists only Yeats pursued Hegel's Romantic ideal of a realm of absolute spirit. In his early stories and essays Yeats predicts the evolution of contemporary civilization into a phase of pure spirit. Although Yeats's notion of evolution follows Hegel's in some respects, it does not see progress as inevitable. Individuals and civilizations can regress from one incarnation to the next depending on how well they achieve their goals. A human, for example, could come back as an ass, the subject of Yeats's play *The Herne's Egg*.

After the turn of the century Yeats vacillated between impulses toward sense and impulses toward an aesthetic realm of pure spirit. *In the Seven Woods* (1904) signaled a return from the "cloud and foam" of his early work to the concrete, quotidian world, but by the time he wrote the *Tower* poems (1928) he was aspiring toward pure spiritual essences again. *The Winding Stair* (1933) returned to earth again, and the later volumes generally maintained a more balanced dialectic between sense and spirit. As Yeats matured, he moved more in the direction of Pater's modification of Hegel toward an ideal fusion of sense and spirit in art. In "News for the Delphic Oracle," for example, Yeats depicts a spiritual realm that is as phenomenal as the physical world, a realm where "nymphs and satyrs / Copulate in the foam."

As Pater had found a unity of spirit in the Renaissance and in the age of Pericles that made them periods of great cultural achievement, so Yeats too conducted a search through history for a time that possessed an ideal "Unity of Being." Yeats found his ideal in sixth-century Byzantium during the reign of Justinian, an age, he says, in which "religious, aesthetic and practical life were one."[28] His Byzantium poems are odes to the perfection of this historical period.

If we turn from Yeats to Joyce, we find many of the same features; for Joyce's views of history, usually associated with Vico, also owe a good deal to the tradition of Pater's Hegelian paradigm, of which Vico was a forerunner. Goethe, in fact, brought Vico's *New Science* to Germany, and from there it found its way to Coleridge and Michelet; and when Hegel's philosophy later found its way to Italy, it was celebrated as the "homecoming of Vico."[29] In the light of this continuous tradition Joyce's attraction to Vico seems less idiosyncratic, since Vico would have reinforced many of the Hegelian crosscurrents of Joyce's own time. Pater too had read Vico's *New Science* as well as Michelet, who had translated it.[30]

Vico's theory, however much it may have differed in particulars from its nineteenth-century counterparts, employs a paradigm similar

---

28. *A Vision*, pp. 279–80.

29. Frederick Copleston, S.J., *Modern Philosophy, Part 1: The French Enlightenment to Kant*, vol. 6 of *A History of Philosophy* (New York: Doubleday, 1964), pp. 188–89.

30. Inman, *Pater's Reading*, pp. 148–57, 166.

in its basic elements to Pater's version of Hegel. Vico says that history repeats itself in cycles according to universal laws that apply both to the history of epochs and to the "histories of individual peoples."[31] The spirit of a given age may also be found embodied in certain individuals of that age. The three ages of each Viconian cycle—the age of the gods, the age of the heroes, and the age of men—anticipate a Hegelian progression from sense to imagination to reason, except that for Vico at the end of each cycle man returns to a barbarian, sensuous state. Vico did not proscribe development from one cycle to another, however; but he did not project history, as Hegel did, toward an ideal rationality.

Although Vico's influence usually has been associated more with *Finnegans Wake* than with *Ulysses*, its operation to some degree in *Ulysses* has been recognized since Stuart Gilbert's ground-breaking study. Gilbert points to the metempsychosis motif in *Ulysses* as the "germ of that ultimate application of the Viconian hypothesis which lies at the root of *Finnegans Wake*."[32] In *Ulysses* Joyce's view of modern Ireland through the matrix of Homeric Greece and his casting of Bloom as the reincarnation of the spirit of Odysseus imply all of the common elements of the Viconian paradigm and Pater's Hegelian paradigm. The cyclical nature of history and the presence of the past through metempsychosis, the manifestation in the present of the spirit of past ages, are all there. The *Odyssey* is not the only paradigm, however; *Hamlet* also functions as an earlier model for Joyce's *Ulysses*, as do the Bible and numerous other works from the past. Dialectic also plays an important role in *Ulysses*, including some of the same dialectical patterns that preoccupied Pater and Yeats, such as the oppositions between sense and intellect, Greek and Christian, Asiatic and European.[33] Some notion of development is certainly implied in "The Oxen of the Sun" episode, in which Joyce traces through parody the evolution of English literary style, but there seems to be little notion of progress toward any ultimate goal. If anything is suggested by the

---

31. Copleston, p. 182.

32. Stuart Gilbert, *James Joyce's Ulysses* (New York: Random House, 1955), p. 41.

33. For a study that emphasizes the dialectical patterns of *Ulysses*, see Richard Ellmann's *Ulysses on the Liffey* (New York: Oxford University Press, 1972).

chaotic, contemporary speech idiom that concludes the episode, it is a Viconian return to an age of barbarism. As with Yeats and Eliot, I am making no special claims here for the direct influence of Pater's Hegelian scheme on Joyce but only wish to point out that his scheme conforms to typical Modernist visions of history.

What this analysis demonstrates is that some of the techniques we typically associate with the Modernist movement are rooted in Hegelian views of history that were modified in a rather consistent manner by British neo-Hegelians like Pater. While preserving the essential elements combined in Pater's historical paradigm, Modernists like Yeats, Joyce, and Eliot forged new techniques in which the present is seen through or in terms of the past, techniques like Joyce's "mythical method" that imposes a Homeric matrix on contemporary Dublin, or the timeless, protean figure of Eliot's Tiresias. The Modernists tended to see the dynamics of history in terms of dialectic and cyclical patterns that often involve a notion of reincarnation or metempsychosis. The emphasis on development, however, is not pronounced. Although Pater's view of progress was considerably more moderate and finite than Hegel's, it was more than most Modernists could grant.

In contrast to the profound historicism of much Modernist art, post-Modern art is just as profoundly ahistorical. Based on a paradigm that privileges the synchronic over the diachronic, the parables of Beckett, for example, are timeless in a different sense from either the Modernists or Hegel: they are founded not on universals that govern time but on universals of semiotic systems that have been cut adrift from the temporal world and its history. Molloy illustrates this in his comic routine over how to carry his sucking stones.[34] His passion for symmetry, balance, and system and the ultimate irrelevance of that passion suggest the unbridgeable Cartesian rift in Beckett's vision between the activities of the mind and the life of the body. There are Modernists who do not have a significant historical vision, such as Wallace Stevens, but no Modernist precludes history as Beckett does.

---

34. *Three Novels* (New York: Grove, 1965), pp. 69–74.

8 / PRAGMATIC IDEALISM

AT THIS point I think we are in a position to appreciate more fully Pater's functionalism, the pragmatic fusion of empiricism and idealism that I have tried to capture in my title phrase *The Sensible Spirit*. This functionalism characterized Pater's approach to all products of the human intellect and imagination, including philosophy, religion, myth, and art. Appearing throughout his career from his early writing to his latest, his functionalism shows up most clearly in his attitude toward philosophic abstractions, which in turn sheds light on his similar attitude toward art, Christianity, and myth. He first expressed his characteristic view of metaphysical speculation as a purely functional guide and stimulant to observation in "Winckelmann" (1867). Although Pater continued his campaign against abstract philosophy in "Winckelmann," he also began to realize, both by using Hegel and other idealists and by reacting against them, how abstract thinking and metaphysical speculation might be much more useful as a servant than a master. In this realization Pater became part of the post-Kantian movement from philosophies of substance to philosophies of function. In choosing within the new orientation, Pater's skeptical temper inclined him more toward accepting Kant's limitations on reason than toward the thrust of German idealism that tried to salvage a dominant role for speculative reason. Because of this skepticism and because he rejected the Romantic transcendentalism that characterized the idealism of Coleridge and Carlyle, he was able to inject the new epistemology into the British literary tradition in a form that would appeal to the Modernist sensibility.

If we look closely at two versions of the "Conclusion" to *The Renaissance*, in which Pater reiterates his position about the proper function of speculative thought stated in "Winckelmann," the role of German philosophy (particularly Hegel's) in his formulation of this position becomes evident, as does Pater's typical modification of his German sources. In the original context of the Morris essay, the intent of the passages that eventually became the "Conclusion" was to "see what modern philosophy . . . really does say about human life and the truth we can attain in it" (309). Although philosophy or any system of ideas remained for Pater always subservient to experience, Pater does not dismiss philosophical thinking altogether. He cites Novalis and Victor Hugo on the vitalizing effect of philosophy,[1] but like many since Kant, he applies philosophy to thought rather than matter: "The service of philosophy," he says, "and of religion and culture as well, to the human spirit, is to startle it into a sharp and eager observation. . . . Theories, religious or philosophical ideas, as points of view, instruments of criticism, may help us gather up what might otherwise pass unregarded by us" (311–12). The allusion to religion as an instrumental theory, after appearing in the Morris essay and the first (1873) edition of *The Renaissance*, was deleted in the 1888 and subsequent editions.[2] The revision, however, still included religious thought, but in an Hegelian disguise that was less likely to offend the orthodox pieties of his contemporaries as the earlier version had. In the revised version all explicit mention of religion was deleted and the phrase "The service of philosophy, and of religion and culture" becomes "The service of philosophy, of speculative culture." The term "speculative culture" alludes to the Hegelian triad in the realm of absolute spirit that includes religion along with art and philosophy as the highest products of the human spirit. Pater clearly had this Hegelian cultural triad in mind in the original version, and in its revision he simply substituted the Hegelian term "speculative culture" for "religion and culture."

---

1. Billie Inman points out that Pater cites Novalis and Hugo out of context and alters their original meanings to suit his own purposes (*Pater's Reading*, pp. 184–86, 188).

2. For the different versions of this passage, see Hill's edition of *The Renaissance*, pp. 188–89, 273–74. The entire "Conclusion" was omitted in the second edition (1877).

Pater's use of Hegel in the "Conclusion" is typical of his adaptation of German idealism. As we saw in the previous chapter, whereas Hegel placed philosophy and religion above art in his triad because they were less tied to the senses, Pater concluded that art would best conduct him to his goal. In the "Conclusion" art is superior to philosophy and religion because it does not sully unalloyed experience with the impurities of abstract systems or dogmas. While for Hegel the forms of knowledge achieved in the realm of his absolute spirit are ends in themselves, for Pater (his invocation of art for art's sake notwithstanding) art, as well as philosophy and religion, is a strictly functional means of heightening and enhancing experience. In his characteristic manner Pater limits Hegel's triad of absolute spirit to its application in a finite, phenomenal world. At one point Pater appears to allude to the freedom the human spirit experiences in Hegel's realm of the absolute: he says that the kind of heightened experience he describes may be fulfilled by "any contribution to knowledge that seems by a lifted horizon to set the spirit free for a moment" (*Ren.*, 237). The tentativeness of this allusion to the untrammeled spirit, however, evokes only a pale and finite shadow of the freedom that characterizes Hegel's notion of absolute knowledge.

Pater's first comprehensive exploration of his functionalist weltanschauung and its implications is conducted under a fictional guise in *Marius the Epicurean*. Here Marius quite deliberately and systematically works out his philosophic position and then applies it to his artistic vocation and to his engagement with Christianity. The functionalist perspective is not as boldly stated in *Marius* as it was in "Winckelmann" or the "Conclusion," because Pater chiseled his thoughts much more carefully to forestall the kind of controversy precipitated by the first publication of *The Renaissance*. Despite careful rewording, *Marius* nevertheless maintains essentially the same pragmatic orientation of the "Conclusion" toward all forms of speculative culture. The main differences are the modulated tone, the depth of the discussion, and the detailed extension of his position beyond philosophy and art to a form of Christian humanism. The bold polemical announcements of the earlier essays are subdued in the exploratory prose of *Marius*, as Pater extends them into careful and qualified examinations of how a philosophic functionalism might be conducive to a full and honorable life—not just a self-serving hedonism, as many took his "Conclusion" to be advocating, but a life of intellectual, ethical, and moral integrity and of genuine Christian sympathy.

Marius first encounters a functionalist attitude toward philosophic speculation in the pragmatic wisdom of Aristippus, whose thought Pater portrays as an early form of critical philosophy. Aware of the subjectivity of all knowledge and of the distorting effects of our instruments of cognition, but without abandoning philosophy for mere unphilosophical common sense or for religious faith, Aristippus's position entails for Marius "a strict limitation, almost the renunciation, of metaphysical enquiry itself." Under the influence of Aristippus Marius readily dismisses Greek Theoria—"that vision of a wholly reasonable world" with all its " 'doubtful disputations' concerning 'being' and 'not-being,' knowledge and appearance." This reaction against an older metaphysics of substance came for Marius (as for Hume, Kant, and Pater) as "a sort of suicide . . . by which a great metaphysical *acumen* was devoted to the function of proving metaphysical speculation impossible, or useless" (Pater's emphasis). Pater then combines this critical attitude with tenets from the empirical positions of Locke and Bacon, who limit the function of abstract theory to clearing the mind of prejudice, superstition, and presuppositions, thus leaving it an "absolutely virgin" tabula rasa to the impressions of concrete experience (*ME* 1:140–41).

In place of a "metaphysical system" Marius would cultivate a "metaphysic skill" that would send him back, sooner or later "to the world of concrete impressions, to things as they may be seen, heard, felt by him; but with a wonderful machinery of observation, and free from the tyranny of mere theories" (*ME* 1:141–42).

The intellectual position Pater attributes to Aristippus here is a pastiche synthesized from elements of German idealism and British empiricism, and the various elements of the pastiche are not wholly compatible. Insofar as the critique of metaphysics is concerned, Pater's language encompasses the very different skeptical premises of Bacon, Hume, and Kant and opposes them to the equally divergent absolutisms of Berkeley and Hegel. Pater's proposal that the purpose of this critique is to establish a tabula rasa of our sensory apparatus is drawn from Locke. We might defend Pater by noting that he never accepted the transcendental categories of German idealism that conflict with Locke's notion of a tabula rasa; but Pater also could not be satisfied by

the assumptions underlying the view of the mind as a tabula rasa—
that strict adherence of Locke and Hume to sensation and the relatively simple ideas that could be derived from it. His polemics about
the primacy of sensation notwithstanding, Pater's primary allegiance
was not to sensory perception but to a much more complex and
highly integrated intellectual culture. As in the "Conclusion," so in
Marius the Hegelian triad of absolute spirit—art, religion, and philosophy—tamed and limited to a finite realm, informs Pater's rhetoric
and constitutes the essence of cultural perfection, a perfection whose
complexity lies beyond the analytic powers of the sensationism of
Locke or Hume.

A philosophic program based on aesthetic culture would focus not
on doctrine or dogma but on refining the powers of perception. The
purpose of such a limited, finite philosophy of the "here and now," of
an ideal present with a pragmatic orientation, might seem to evolve
naturally into some form of action. But on the contrary, its adherents
would pursue no hedonistic or even utilitarian pleasure, but rather a
"fulness of life, and 'insight' as conducting to that fulness," a fullness
achieved not through action but contemplation. Pater characterizes
this mode of contemplation in his typically pragmatic fashion as a vocation governed by "a very narrowly practical design"—"to understand the various forms of ancient art and thought, the various forms
of actual human feeling . . . to satisfy, with a kind of scrupulous equity,
the claims of these concrete and actual objects on his sympathy, his
intelligence, his senses" (*ME* 1:151–52). This is the program most
readers associate with Pater, the program of the aesthetic observer, detached, solipsistic perhaps ("Could he but arrest, for others also, certain clauses of experience," Marius wonders [*ME* 1:155]), subor-
dinating philosophy and religion to art and culture in the cultivation
of a complete aesthetic experience, an experience that does not deny
philosophy, religion, and morality, but subsumes them under it.

Despite the considerable advantages of the perspective of a detached observer, Marius nevertheless becomes aware that this "narrow perfection" overlooks something: he realizes that there exists all
around him a "venerable system of sentiment and idea, widely ex-
tended in time and place," a "wonderful order, actually in possession
of human life" (*ME* 2:26–27). This venerable system of wonderful
order is the Christianity of the early Church.

Marius has often been considered a major turning point in Pater's career, especially with respect to his softened attitude toward Christianity and the modification of his early views, as exemplified in the "Conclusion." This view of *Marius* is accurate to some extent, for Pater's rhetoric on Christianity did undergo a significant shift in tone and orientation. This shift, however, took place much earlier than *Marius*; it is detectable even in the later essays written for *The Renaissance*, such as "Pico della Mirandola" (1871) and "The Poetry of Michelangelo" (1871). *Marius* is probably more important, not for its differences from earlier writings, but for the deepening and extension of Pater's earlier positions. The rapprochement with Christianity in *Marius* is less a new element in Pater's thinking than an expansion of his earlier position, for Marius's approach to Christianity is conducted in the same functional manner that characterizes his (and Pater's) earlier attitude toward philosophy and art.

If we look at two of Pater's earlier statements about Christianity, it becomes clear that Marius's attitude does not indicate a significant change in Pater's thinking. In "Pico della Mirandola" Pater engages in a Hegelian speculation on how a "modern scholar" might view religion as a historical and cultural product of the human mind. Confronted with the "question of the reconciliation of the religion of antiquity with the religion of Christ," such a scholar, according to Pater,

> might observe that all religions may be regarded as natural products, that, at least in their origin, their growth, and decay, they have common laws, and are not to be isolated from the other movements of the human mind in the periods in which they respectively prevailed; that they arise spontaneously out of the human mind, as expressions of the varying phases of its sentiment concerning the unseen world; that every intellectual product must be judged from the point of view of the age and the people in which it was produced. He might go on to observe that each has contributed something to the development of the religious sense, and ranging them as so many stages in the gradual education of the human mind, justify the existence of each. The basis of the reconciliation of the religions of the world would thus be the inexhaustible activity and creativeness of the human mind itself, in which all religions alike have their root, and in which all alike are reconciled. (*Ren.*, 33–34)

One of the modern scholars Pater had in mind, as Billie Inman notes,[3] was probably Renan, whose positions on Christianity influenced Pater's considerably. For Renan, as for Hegel, Christianity was a historical product of human nature rather than of divine revelation; and Renan, like Pater, stopped short of Hegelian absolutes as well. The important point here for the purposes of understanding Pater's attitude toward Christianity is that he effected his rapprochement, with the help of thinkers like Hegel and Renan, through the strictly pragmatic and secular means of viewing religion, like philosophy and art, as one mode of intellectual culture.

Pater's functionalist view of Christianity, attributed to a "modern scholar" in "Pico della Mirandola," is reiterated in "The Child in the House" (1878), where religion again is viewed as a version of human experience rather than of divine truth. Religion contributes not to the honor and glory of God but to the nobility and dignity of man. What Pater says of Florian Deleal in his youth applies equally to himself: "His way of conceiving religion came then to be in effect what it ever afterwards remained—a sacred history indeed, but still more a sacred ideal, a transcendent version or representation, under intenser and more expressive light and shade, of human life and its familiar or exceptional incidents, birth, death, marriage, youth, age, tears, joy, rest, sleep, waking" (MS, 193–94). Pater uses the word transcendent here, as describing a "scheme of some higher and more consistent harmony," in a strategically vague manner so that it could be taken to imply either a truly religious vision or a transcendental critical philosophy like Kant's or Hegel's.

So by the time he wrote Marius, Pater had abandoned his earlier strident opposition to Christianity. He also believed that it represented a possibility that could not effectively be dismissed; and yet he still considered it only as a "workable hypothesis" (Ltrs., 94) and not as a system of doctrine and dogma to be accepted as literal truth. But since this "hypothesis" also happened to be the prevailing philosophic and religious system, Pater, like Marius, was willing to accept "some curtailment of his liberty" by accommodating himself to it, otherwise "some drops of the great cup would fall to the ground." For Marius

---

3. Inman, Pater's Reading, p. 236.

the system he found in early Christianity was "rich in the world's experience; so that, in attaching oneself to it, one lets in a great tide of that experience, and makes, as it were with a single step, a great experience of one's own, and with great consequent increase to one's sense of colour, variety, and relief, in the spectacle of men and things." The sense of belonging to such a system "has, in itself, the expanding power of a great experience," an experience comparable to being admitted into citizenship in the Roman state or, in more modern times, to being "admitted from narrower sects into the communion of the catholic church." So the system might be a religion, a state, or perhaps even a widely shared philosophical perspective. Whatever its nature, accepting such a system would open up a world of cultural riches (*ME* 2:26–28).

Pater even goes so far as to compare the acceptance of a religious system to learning a foreign language. Pater's narrator notes that the acceptance of a religion or a philosophy for Marius is similar to "what the coming into possession of a very widely spoken language might be, with a great literature, which is also the speech of the people we have to live among" (*ME* 2:26–27). In other words, the acceptance of Christianity, like the learning of a new language, gives his Marius access to the riches of an entire new culture. But the comparison of philosophy and religion to language obviates the necessity for literal belief. One does not *believe in* a language. This analogy of religious systems with learning a language as a means of entry into a broadly spread world of highly developed cultural experiences emphatically underscores that Marius's acceptance of such a system is strictly pragmatic, entered into for the sake of the experiences and the understanding of one's experiences such a system might offer. There is no commitment on the part of Marius, or Pater, to belief in the substance or absolute value of the system.

Although Pater's revisions to *Marius* suggest that he tried to align his protagonist's views as much as possible with the requirements of his consciously adopted religious system,[4] Pater is careful to point out that Marius's acceptance of Christianity would not compromise his intellectual integrity and that his entrance into the Church would de-

---

4. Edmund Chandler, *Pater on Style, Anglistica*, vol. 11 (Copenhagen: Rosenkilde and Bagger, 1958): 65–68.

fine "not so much a change of practice, as of sympathy—a new departure, an expansion, of sympathy" (*ME* 2:27). As in Hegel's dialectical progression of philosophy in history, the earlier views are not discarded but are incorporated into a larger whole. Marius realizes that, although embracing any system would involve some curtailment of his liberty, "if he did not make that concession," if he remained with the narrow perfection of his aesthetic detachment, he would be an "inconsistent Cyrenaic" and a faulty economist of life, for he would deprive himself of a whole range of great experiences (*ME* 2:28). With this rationale Marius proceeds to the threshold of Christianity as the expansive system of new and great experiences opening up to him just then. Although he never accepts the dogma of Christianity, he concludes that as a coherent and widely held interpretation of human experience, it is the richest available.

For Pater as for Marius, then, the function of religion, like that of philosophy or political systems, was a matter of maximizing the "economy of life." All such systems were to be judged not in terms of any absolute claim they might have to truth but in terms of their usefulness in granting us access to the greatest possible range of experience. This cultural relativism expressed in *Marius* is not fundamentally at variance with the philosophic and aesthetic relativism of the "Conclusion" to *The Renaissance*, where art, rather than philosophy or religion, elicits the "quickened, multiplied consciousness" of experience.

Pater maintained throughout his later writings the fundamental approach to Christianity articulated in "Pico della Mirandola," "The Child in the House," and *Marius*. In "Amiel's 'Journal Intime,'" published the year after *Marius*, he faults Amiel for "shrinking" from his natural destiny in the "actual," "concrete" "Church of history," and for failing to see the equally probable evidence for belief as for disbelief. But Pater characterizes belief as he does the absolutes of Plato or Hegel and similar to the way Kant viewed the products of pure reason—as useful ideals in charting the "direction of men's hopes," and in complementing intellectual judgments by bringing them harmoniously "into connection with the facts, the venerable institutions of the past" (*EG*, 33). As vague as this sounds, it is clear that the *facts* in question here are not absolute, spiritual facts, but the facts of temporal history, and more specifically of the institutional history of the

Church. Amiel's failure to arrive at belief, according to Pater, was a failure not of his faith but of his "historic sense," the same failure that twenty years earlier Pater saw leading Coleridge into Christian belief.

In two late essays on Dante and Raphael, both published in 1892, Pater continues to maintain his unorthodox attitude toward Christianity. In the Dante essay he characterizes medieval Christianity as "the theoretic construction which catholicism puts on the facts of nature and history" (*UE*, 147), and in "Raphael" as "a scheme of the world as it should be, as we should be glad to find it" and which was "still welcome" to the heart and imagination of the Renaissance (*MS*, 58).

All of these statements Pater makes about Christianity and belief are carefully worded both to preserve his intellectual integrity and to disguise from the casual reader the unorthodox means by which his own reconciliation with Christianity is achieved. His views of Christianity do not violate essentially any of his positions established thus far—the subjectivity and relativity of knowledge, the primacy of sensory experience, skepticism, and the functional nature of all thought. From childhood, Pater was temperamentally inclined toward Christianity, especially its sensuous ritual form, and for him it always remained, not a system of dogma, but one version or interpretation of human experience. It succeeded in the face of other versions by virtue of the systematic comprehensiveness of its vision, not by virtue of its absolute truth; and it may be succeeded in turn by an even more comprehensive vision. Its ultimate validity derives not from any metaphysical source but from its temporal history. As Pater had used Hegelian critics of Christianity such as Renan and Baur to support his early attacks on the Church, he also used a Hegelian rationale to effect his later rapprochement.

Pater's functionalist attitude also applied to myth, where his views were typically Victorian in that they were inspired by the Germans and did not accept the positivistic dismissals of myth. Like other Victorians, Pater followed Grote's *History of Greece* in emphasizing the literary and evolutionary nature of myth;[5] and rather than viewing myth positivistically as inferior to modern science, Pater makes Hegelian claims for the cognitive function of myth as the representa-

---

5. James Kissane, "Victorian Mythology," *Victorian Studies* 6 (1962): 5–28.

tion of the inner vision of a people. According to Pater, early Greek myth was a "continuous act of conception" that primitive minds employed instead of metaphysical concepts to represent to themselves "in sensibly realised images, all they knew, felt, or fancied, of the natural world about them" (GS, 97).

Pater's conception of the cognitive function of myth is particularly evident in "A Study of Dionysus: The Spiritual Form of Fire and Dew" (1876), in which Pater describes the cult of Dionysus as "a complete religion, a sacred representation or interpretation of the whole human experience" (GS, 10). This is essentially how he characterizes the Catholic Mass in Marius (2:128–40). The figure of Dionysus is the "outward body of flesh presented to the senses, and comprehending, as its animating soul, a whole world of thoughts, surmises, greater and less experiences" (GS, 10). He is the "*spiritual form* [Pater's emphasis] of Arcadia": the representation of "the ways of human life there; the reflexion, in sacred image or ideal, of its flocks, and orchards, and wild honey; the dangers of its hunters; its weariness in noonday heat; its children, agile as the goats they tend, who run, in their picturesque rags, across the solitary wanderer's path, to startle him, in the unfamiliar upper places; its one adornment and solace being the dance to the homely shepherd's pipe, cut by Pan first from the sedges of the brook Molpeia" (GS, 15). The image of Dionysus, in other words, like the shield of Achilles or the image of Christ, evokes a vision of a world order. Dionysus is the "projected expression of the ways and dreams" of a people, a unifying power, harmonized by the imagination, linking body and soul and the whole range of human experience, physical and spiritual (GS, 29). Consequently such myths appealed to the entire human organism as an idealization of itself—sense and bodily qualities, ethical qualities, the inner vision (GS, 36). These mythic conceptions, projected finally in drama or sculpture, are the names, the identities, the spiritual forms of its given matter (GS, 37). For Pater, then, the validity of myth lay, not in its correspondence to external facts of nature or history, but in its correspondence to an internal vision of nature and its relation to man, the same expressive criterion he applies to art.

The cognitive function of myth, however, is not limited to the historical situation that produced it. As a form of poetry, the edifying power of myth can still operate on the modern mind. Once admitted into the general cultural consciousness, myths, "long after the earlier and simpler races of their worshippers have passed away . . . may be a pledge to us of the place in our culture, at once legitimate and possible, of the associations, the conceptions, the imagery, of Greek religious poetry in general, of the poetry of all religions" (GS, 151). So myths and their artistic embodiments as expressions of humanistic ideals still possess a certain power over the imagination, which, in Hegelian fashion, has not been superseded but has been assimilated by successive states of intellectual development.

Pater's analysis of myth recognizes the simultaneous existence and operation in the modern mind of mythical, literary, religious, and scientific consciousnesses. But he himself does not make the logical neo-Kantian shift to move the scientific mode inward as well, from a mode of thought operating on "an observed sequence of outward phenomena" (Greek myth, after all, sought to explain outward phenomena too) to another internal version of nature and its relation to man. Although Pater does not push his analysis this far, his logic intimates this conclusion. He also did not take the step of perceiving the various modes of knowing as complementary to each other and not necessarily conflicting, if they are all taken symbolically rather than literally. Seen in this way, they become alternative symbolic systems, each with certain inherent characteristics, strengths, and limitations. These fuller implications of Pater's functionalist attitude remained for twentieth-century minds, such as Cassirer, Joyce, and Nelson Goodman, to realize.

Although Pater's pragmatic idealism toward the various forms of intellectual culture emerges from time to time in the course of his criticism and fiction (as in his essay on Winckelmann, in the "Conclusion," in his studies of Greek myth, and in his portrait of Florian Deleal), his only other thorough discussion of this attitude besides the one in Marius appears in Plato and Platonism in the first section of his chapter on "The Doctrine of Plato." Entitled "The Theory of Ideas," this section contains both a theoretical exposition and a lucid parable that articulate Pater's view of abstract universals, an articulation that clearly demonstrates the balance between empiricism and idealism in Pater's mature philosophic outlook and the extent to which Hegel and other German thinkers informed it. The parable also provides a concise microcosm of Pater's mature weltanschauung that can be used to establish his position in relation to Modernist and post-Modernist thought.

Despite its shortcomings as a piece of systematic thinking, Pater's theoretical exposition helps create the philosophical context for his pragmatic approach to speculative thought by explicitly distinguishing between the older ontological orientations and the post-Kantian epistemological orientation he accepts for himself. Plato's form of transcendental realism, according to Pater, has lost its claim on the intellect and has passed "into a phase of poetic thought" (155). By realism Pater means a philosophy of substance, the positing of the actual existence of universals "independent of the particular instances which come into and pass out of it, as also of the particular mind which entertains it" (151). This philosophic orientation, according to Pater, has been found by many to be a "fantastic and unintelligible habit of thought" (153).

In place of an untenable philosophic realism, Pater calls for a "common sense" view of "logical 'universals'" (152). His appeal to common sense is somewhat misleading, however, for in *Marius* Pater disparages philosophers who employ "'common,' but unphilosophical, sense" (1:138). Pater's position on logical universals derives primarily from Hegel. As with Plato's transcendentalism, Pater tempers Hegel in his typical manner by ignoring the realm of absolute spirit and by applying dialectical thought only to the mind's engagement of the phenomenal world. This pragmatic adaptation of Hegel constitutes Pater's "common sense" approach to logical universals. Pater's appeal to common sense also serves perhaps as a rhetorical strategy that enables him to put forth a position on logical universals and, at the same time, evade being called to account for it as a systematic philosopher.

Explaining his position somewhat vaguely, Pater says that "our own [modern] stand on this matter" of logical universals is "somewhere between the realist and the conceptualist." He says that there is a "general consciousness, a permanent common sense" that is independent of the individual, but with which the individual is in communication. Common or general ideas reside in this consciousness to which everyone has access. Giving due recognition to nominalism, Pater says that these "abstract or common notions come to the individual mind through language, through common or general names, *Animal, Jus-*

tice, Equality, into which one's individual experience, little by little, drop by drop, conveys their full meaning or content" (Pater's emphasis). These terms mediate "between general and particular, between our individual experience and the common experience of our kind," and through their instrumentality "we come to understand each other, and to assist each other's thoughts, as in a common mental atmosphere, an 'intellectual world'" (151–52). Pater's description of this "modern view" of logical universals, concocted from empirical, idealistic, and other philosophic sources, is too vague to be satisfying; however, it is sufficiently explicit to contradict the charge of solipsism so frequently associated with his reputation.

In *Plato and Platonism* Pater has moved well beyond the limitations of strict Humean empiricism. Here Pater posits two worlds. One is the "mental world we actually live in, where classification, the reduction of all things to common types, has come so far, and where the particular, to a great extent, is known only as the member of a class." The other world is the phenomenal world, in which experience is intuition, "life a continuous surprise, and every object unique," and where all knowledge is of the concrete and particular (156). The world we share with others, according to this analysis, is the mental world, and what we experience solipsistically is the individual and the concrete. Pater typically does not distinguish between logical or necessary truths and empirical or contingent truths, a distinction that pervaded the philosophical thinking he was absorbing on all sides; but this distinction nevertheless seems to lie beneath his division of experience into the mental and the phenomenal.

Although Pater accepts both worlds as part of his philosophic outlook, he is still nostalgic about our intuitive experience of the phenomenal world—"a world," he says, "we might describe as being under Homeric [as opposed to Platonic] conditions, such as we picture to ourselves with regret." He also considers the concrete to be more natural than the abstract and intuition more natural than intellect. Nevertheless he recognizes that the abstractions of the mental world make what we actually perceive with the senses "more interesting than ever," and that the concrete gains "immeasurably in richness and compass, in fineness, and interest" through abstraction. So while still insisting on the primacy of the concrete, the sensuous, and the particular, and still holding to it "last as first" as the "one vital and lively thing, really worth our while in a short life," he is anxious to acknowledge what generalization and abstraction do for the particular and what their "proper service is to a mind" in search of "concrete and intuitive knowledge" (155–57). So the concrete remains for Pater, in theory at least, the end of knowledge, and the abstract remains subordinate and in service to the concrete; but this position does not stop him from grafting Hegel's powerful mode of dialectical thought onto his empirical base.

In contrast to his unsatisfying theoretical explanation of the role of logical universals in modern thought, the dialectical nature of Pater's view on this matter emerges with eloquent clarity in his parable of the shell, which is well worth considering in toto, since it provides an important counterargument not only to the view of Pater as a priest of sensation but also to a lot of misconceptions about the relations between the concrete and the abstract in Modernist aesthetics and criticism. Pater's parable is as follows:

> Think, for a moment, of the difference, as regards mental attitude, between the naturalist who deals with things through ideas, and the layman (so to call him) in picking up a shell on the seashore; what it is that the subsumption of the individual into the species, its subsequent alliance to and co-ordination with other species, really does for the furnishing of the mind of the former. The layman, though we need not suppose him inattentive, or unapt to retain impressions, is in fact still but a child; and the shell, its colours and convolution, no more than a dainty, very easily destructible toy to him. Let him become a schoolboy about it, so to speak. The toy he puts aside; his mind is drilled perforce, to learn *about* it; and thereby is exercised, he may think, with everything except just the thing itself, as he cares for it; with other shells, with some general laws of life, and for a while it might seem that, turning away his eyes from the "vanity" of the particular, he has been made to sacrifice the concrete, the real and living product of nature, to a mere dry and abstract product of the mind. But when he comes out of school, and on the sea-shore again finds a fellow to his toy, perhaps a finer specimen of it, he may see what the service of that converse with the general has really been towards the concrete, towards what he sees— in regard to the particular thing he actually sees. By its juxtaposition and co-ordination with what is ever more and more not *it*, by

contrast of its very imperfection, at this point or that, with its own proper and perfect type, this concrete and particular thing has, in fact, been enriched by the whole colour and expression of the whole circumjacent world, concentrated upon, or as it were at focus in, it. By a kind of short-hand now, and as if in a single moment of vision, all that, which only a long experience, moving patiently from part to part, could exhaust, its manifold alliance with the entire world of nature, is legible upon it, as it lies there in one's hand. (157–58; Pater's emphases)

What applies to the physical world, Pater says, also applies to the moral and emotional world. "Generalisation," he says, "is a method, not of obliterating the concrete phenomenon, but of enriching it, with the joint perspective, the significance, the expressiveness, of all other things beside"; it taps "the accumulative capital of the whole experience of humanity." The scholar, as opposed to the layman, "not only sees, but understands (thereby only seeing the more)" (159).

Although Pater renders the parable of the shell in ordinary language, the pattern of Hegel's dialectical thought lies beneath the surface simplicity. The shell as perceived by the uninformed layman corresponds to the first step in the dialectical process, a simple notion of raw, unreflecting sense, an unmediated perception of the object's familiar concrete form. The object is perceived with the unreflecting and uncomprehending enthusiasm of the child. Pater's sending his layman to school corresponds to the second step in the dialectical process (Hegel also uses the metaphor of a boy educating himself). This state is characterized by the analysis and determination of the object by the reflective, mediated thought of the understanding. This stage negates the first, and in it the object is dismembered by analysis, differentiated by the implicit assertion and renumeration of all that is not itself to the extent that it becomes other than what it is; it becomes all that it is differentiated from. It is also subsumed and absorbed into the forms of thought of the perceiving subject, just as the subject, immersed in and operating on the object, losing itself in the object, becomes its other—the object dismembered. This is a state of estrangement or alienation of both the object from itself and the subject from itself, each being immersed in the other and becoming the other. At school in this second stage Pater's layman finds himself, so he thinks, preoccupied with everything except the thing itself; the concrete object appears to be sacrificed "by its juxtaposition and co-ordination with what is ever more and more not *it*" to "a mere dry and abstract product of the mind" (Pate's emphasis). Both the initial immediate intuition and the subsequent analytical discriminations that enable it to become an object of knowledge are considered by Hegel to be abstract stages because they are incomplete.

The third and final dialectic step, represented in Pater's parable by the layman's return to the seashore after his schooling, is the return of both object and subject from alienation and estrangement. It is a re-union of the initial perception in its concrete wholeness with the rational process involved in comprehending it. This final stage is that of Hegel's concrete universal, the object's true concept or absolute idea, which is the individual concrete object understood. It is a self-conscious awareness of the object in its concrete form, of the subject's knowledge of the object, and of the union of the two. In Hegelian terms, it is a knowledge of the object in itself and for itself. Pater does not accept the notion of an absolute, even in the logocentric Hegelian sense, but he does agree with Hegel that the mind provides the most perfect forms of life; or, as he puts it in his parable, the result of the dialectical process provides the concrete particular with "its own proper and perfect type." And like Hegel, Pater brings the whole process full circle, at the phenomenological level of analysis at least, to arrive at the end to know the object at the beginning for the first time. By a kind of shorthand the manifold alliance of the shell with the entire world of nature becomes legible as it lies in one's hand, as if in a single moment of vision.

Pater, however, diverges significantly from Hegel in his focus and emphasis. Hegel focuses on the entire dialectical movement as a dynamic process never resting at a fixed point. No one stage of the process is given priority over another; the final goal is not arrival at the absolute idea in the end but the dynamic movement through the whole process itself. Pater's empirical bent, on the other hand, still insists on the primacy of the intuitive sensation; the dialectical process focuses on the original concrete phenomenon and is in service to it. Although Hegel's emphasis on the whole process could be adapted to Pater's emphasis on experience for its own sake, Pater missed this logi-

cal parallel because of his continued insistence on the priority of concrete sensation.

The significance of Pater's attitude toward abstract universals and
its place in Modernist thought can be illustrated by comparing it
to two other attitudes, one post-Modern and the other Modernist.
The first is exemplified in a parable from Beckett's *Molloy* in which
Molloy steals an object from a woman named Lousse, who provided
for his needs while he stayed at her home for a while. Since Beckett's
parable also focuses on a single object and its relation to abstract
thought, it serves as an excellent contrast to Pater's shell parable. Here
is Beckett's version:

> I had stolen from Lousse a little silver, oh nothing much, massive
> teaspoons for the most part, and other small objects whose utility I
> did not grasp but which seemed as if they might have some value.
> Among these latter there was one which haunts me still, from time
> to time. It consisted of two crosses, joined, at their points of inter-
> section, by a bar, and resembled a tiny sawing-horse, with this dif-
> ference however, that the crosses of the true sawing-horse are not
> perfect crosses, but truncated at the top, whereas the crosses of the
> little object I am referring to were perfect, that is to say composed
> each of two identical V's, one upper with its opening above, like all
> V's for that matter, and the other lower with its opening below, or
> more precisely of four rigorously identical V's, the two I have just
> named and then two more, one on the right hand, the other on
> the left, having their openings on the right and left respectively. But
> perhaps it is out of place to speak here of right and left, of upper
> and lower. For this little object did not seem to have any base prop-
> erly so-called, but stood with equal stability on any one of its four
> bases, and without any change of appearance, which is not true of
> the sawing-horse. This strange instrument I think I still have some-
> where, for I could never bring myself to sell it, even in my worst
> need, for I could never understand what possible purpose it could
> serve, nor even contrive the faintest hypothesis on the subject. And
> from time to time I took it from my pocket and gazed upon it, with
> an astonished and affectionate gaze, if I had not been incapable of
> affection. But for a certain time I think it inspired me with a kind of
> veneration, for there was no doubt in my mind that it was not an

object of virtu, but that it had a most specific function always to be hidden from me. I could therefore puzzle over it endlessly without the least risk. For to know nothing is nothing, not to want to know anything likewise, but to be beyond knowing anything, to know you are beyond knowing anything, that is when peace enters in, to the soul of the incurious seeker.[6]

In Beckett's parable the object Molloy has filched from Lousse is a silver knife rest or fork rest. Molloy never identifies the object; in fact, he never learns what it is. The reader knows, or surmises, its identity from the details of the theft (that Molloy stole it along with some other silver pieces) and the physical description of the object. Molloy's experience with the fork rest is the antithesis of the experience of Pater's aspiring naturalist with the shell. Beckett frustrates the cognitive process at every point by maintaining the Cartesian split between mind and matter that he first enunciated in *Murphy*. These two realms do not commingle in any systematic way, nor do they exist in dialectical opposition to each other. They remain forever alienated from each other and incomprehensible to each other. The object of sense and the object dismembered in the mind have no meaningful relationship to each other. If they have a relationship at all, it can only be said to be arbitrary.

Yet at the same time the object retains some kind of mysterious power over Molloy—it haunts him occasionally and inspires veneration. He knows that the object had a specific function, but he also knows that this function will always remain hidden from him. So Molloy knows neither the name nor the function of his pilfered object, which he describes mostly in terms of its geometric shape. He often uses the term *crosses*, however, to characterize the shape, and although Beckett suppresses any overt allusion to the many connotations of that word, those connotations nevertheless remain submerged in the narrative, like the object struck by the Patna in *Lord Jim*, haunting and dogging the existence of the uncomprehending quester. Beckett purports to discourage the connotative associations of the word, but in calling attention to its lack of signification, he heightens our interest in it. Molloy's fascination with the object, its hidden func-

---

6. *Three Novels*, pp. 63–64.

tion, and its source of power all point to the absent connotations, as well as to the fact that they are absent.

Although Beckett casts his parable in a positive light as leading to peace, it is the peace of nihilism. There is no reference point whatsoever to orient the object or to establish a perspective on it. The issues of relativism and functionalism are moot. The best Molloy can do is a rather arbitrary comparison to a sawhorse and an inept, pointless description of its geometric form. The comparison with the sawhorse is mimetic—an attempt to relate the object to other things in the outer world; while the inefficient, though very accurate, description of its shape attempts to relate the object to ideal forms in the mind of the subject. Neither attempt amounts to much, although Molloy's mind seems attracted to its own passion for symmetry reflected in the object.

The marked contrast between Beckett's parable of the fork rest and Pater's parable of the shell illustrates the magnitude of the gulf between the Modernist and the post-Modernist temperament. Molloy's encounter with his nameless object represents a genuine despair of knowledge of the type Pater rejects in "Prosper Mérimée." The solipsistic isolation in the prison of the self is total and consistent in Beckett. There are no chinks in the prison wall. The self is totally cut off from other selves and the world outside. By comparison even Pater's "Conclusion" seems rather optimistic and cheerful. For Beckett there is no resolution, dialectic or otherwise, to the unbridgeable gap between the objects of the world and the abstractions of the mind. Molloy invents his own abstractions, and their relation to the object of contemplation is at best arbitrary. For Pater, on the other hand, the abstractions of the second stage of the dialectical process, in which the object is dismembered by analysis and determined by its relations to all it is not, are a positive enrichment of the original concrete phenomenon, an enrichment by means of the joint perspectives, significance, and expressiveness "of all other things beside." This condition of alienation and estrangement is only a temporary phase en route to a final moment of cognition in which the object of sensuous intuition is united in harmony with the ordering structures of the perceiving subject, a unity of the object sensed and the object understood. Such a unity is totally alien to Beckett's world.

A second alternative attitude toward abstraction, as negative as

Beckett's but on different grounds, is located within the Modernist movement, and it is founded on the cult of the concrete. Since I have already discussed this view in some detail in chapter 4, I will only summarize it briefly here. This view—expressed notably by Bergson, T. E. Hulme, Pound, the Imagists, William Carlos Williams, and New Critics like John Crowe Ransom—seeks direct, unmediated contact with reality and the "primordial freshness" of raw experience. Abstractions of all kinds consequently are suspect and considered to be "predatory" and destructive of the uniqueness and individuality of concrete things.

Pater's attitude toward abstraction as expressed in the shell parable is equally distanced from a highly rational post-Modern temperament and from the empirically oriented cult of the concrete. When Pater says in his essay on Browning (1887) that "only the intellectual poet . . . can be adequate to modern demands" (EG, 47), he is recognizing a world far more complex than that of Hulme or Ransom; but he is hardly willing to sacrifice the world of sensation to the hermetically sealed Cartesian mind of Beckett. Pater struck his balance between concrete sensation and intellectual abstraction by grafting post-Kantian German thought, especially Hegel's, onto the native British empirical tradition. This middle road between empiricism and rationalism, similar to the compromise Cassirer and the American pragmatic philosphers tried to work out, is perhaps Pater's most significant contribution to the development of Modernism. Although Pater himself backed away from the full implications of his functionalist and relativist weltanschauung, he was instrumental in naturalizing it into the pragmatic, empirical Anglo-American literary tradition, and he prepared the way for writers like Joyce and Wallace Stevens, who accepted totally the functionalist attitude toward all constructs of the human intellect and imagination.

Pater's shell parable represents an alternative version of the Paterian privileged moment to the one expressed in the "Conclusion." The shell parable is much less solipsistic, and it reflects Pater's increasing assimilation of German idealism as his career progressed. The parable also further refines and clarifies the goal of aesthetic education expressed in Marius—the cultivation of a finely tuned perceptual apparatus: if one is to observe the precept of culture by being perfect with regard to the here and now, one must employ a highly developed sensory apparatus, which is for the most part subjective and individual, in conjunction with a learned capacity for abstract thought, which transcends and enriches individual experience by bringing to bear on it the collective experience of humanity. This version of the privileged moment, represented by the shell parable, containing both an individual and a universal component, is closer to the Joycean epiphany than to the privileged moment of the "Conclusion"; it is also closer to the balance between concrete experience and abstract systems that characterizes a central core of Modernist literature composed of the work of Yeats, Eliot, Joyce, and Wallace Stevens.

One might legitimately ask at this point why, if the shell parable is more representative of Modernist thought, it is so much less a part of Pater's reputation than the "Conclusion." There are several explanations to such a question. First of all, Pater's reputation was well established before *Plato and Platonism* appeared, and it was based primarily on *The Renaissance* and *Marius*. In the early 1890s, Pater's influence was at its peak among writers such as Oscar Wilde, George Moore, Lionel Johnson, Ernest Dowson, Arthur Symons, and Yeats. Wilde, moreover, was one of Pater's most outspoken advocates. After his trial in 1895 (two years after *Plato and Platonism* was published) and the scandal associated with it, Pater's aesthetic philosophy was linked to the misfortune of Wilde and other writers who never survived the nineties.

Another reason for the influence of the "Conclusion" was that it supported the cult of the concrete propagated by the polemics of Bergson, Hulme, and Pound that prevailed in the first two decades of the twentieth century. These polemics heavily influenced the aesthetics of the New Critics, who, along with their students, edited most of the anthologies of criticism that have perpetuated the views of the "Conclusion." These critics have also misconstrued the emphases of other commonly anthologized pieces like "Style" and the opening passages of "The School of Giorgione" by reading into them their own preoccupations with formalism.

Pater himself was partly responsible for obscuring the balanced dialectic of his later works with his own polemics in favor of the primacy of sensation. His continuing emphasis on sensation, even as he assimilated more and more from the Germans, led him into inconsistency and aesthetic dualism. His own relativism begat a certain casualness in his attitude toward the stability of philosophic thought generally. In *Plato and Platonism*, for example, Pater says that as the Platonic doctrine of "the Many and the One" has ceased to interest the modern speculative mind, so the pressing questions of his own day were destined to become in turn "lifeless and unendurable" (154). This relativism fostered a certain license in his own philosophic speculations.

Pater's stance in the shell parable on the role of intellectual abstraction hardly had to wait until a succeeding age to be supplanted by another view, for he supplants it himself in the second half of the same chapter, in the section entitled "Dialectic," which expounds the skeptical theory of dialectic discussed in chapter 3. This version of dialectic is at odds with the Hegelian version underlying the shell parable, and it comes very close to returning to the solipsism of the "Conclusion." Citing Plato's concern about the falsification of truth by the temperament of the receiver, Pater says, "The proposition which embodies [truth] very imperfectly, may not look to him, in those dark chambers of his individuality, of himself, into which none but he can ever get, to test the matter, what it looks to me, or to you. We may not even be thinking of, not looking at, the same thing, when we talk of Beauty, and the like" (*PP*, 189–90). Here Pater argues that beauty and "the like" are matters of immediate intuition or vision and therefore unanalyzable and "incommunicable by words." Although Pater attributes this state of affairs to Platonists, he clearly accepts it for himself too, as he draws his own skeptical conclusion from this supposedly Platonist premise: "Place, then, must be left to the last in any legitimate dialetical process for possible after-thoughts; for the introduction, so to speak, of yet another interlocutor in the dialogue, which has, in fact, no necessary conclusion, and leaves off only because time is up." "Another turn in the endless road," Pater adds, "may change the whole character of the perspective" (190). In the second half of "The Doctrine of Plato" Pater in effect becomes his own interlocutor who takes a turn in the road and sees the intellectual landscape before him from a new vantage point. We ourselves might view "The Doctrine of Plato" not as inconsistent but as we view a cubist painting that presents us with multiple, simultaneous perspectives of the same subject.

However we perceive the multiple perspectives of Pater's philosophic position, one of those perspectives maintained in most of his writing held in some kind of balance the relations between concrete experience and abstract thought. His skepticism did not so much confute his functional approach to logical universals as allow the possibility of another perspective, and it reflected a sanguine rather than a pessimistic attitude toward the possibilities of knowledge as relative, contingent, and functional. Pater's intellectual affinities as a whole remain close to the cluster of ideas, principles, and sensibilities that inform a tradition in Modernism that took abstraction as seriously as concrete experience. The polemics of sensation notwithstanding, Pater's truly dialectical vision anticipated Modernists with similar intellectual inclinations, such as Yeats, Joyce, Eliot, and Stevens.

9 / THE UNIFIED SENSIBILITY

IN AN 1889 review of Flaubert's correspondence Pater cites the following passage as one of the most striking he found there:

> Materialists and spiritualists, in about equal degree, prevent the knowledge of matter and spirit alike, because they sever one from the other. The one party make man an angel, the other a swine. (*UE*, 113)

Flaubert's statement formulates an issue that became a central preoccupation of the Modernist movement. Eliot's lament in "The Metaphysical Poets" about a "dissociation of sensibility" that had set into Western culture since the Renaissance and his proposal of a reintegrated sensibility capable of "direct sensuous apprehension of thought," of feeling "thought as immediately as the odour of a rose,"[1] closely parallels Flaubert's sentiment and formulates for his own generation the quest for a unified sensibility that runs all through Modernist literature. Yeats's struggle for Unity of Being and his insistence on the "flow of flesh under the impulse of passionate thought,"[2] Joyce's ineluctable commingling of actual and ideal in all his works, Virginia Woolf's reconciliation and balancing of the intellectual and the emo-

---

1. *Selected Essays*, pp. 246–47.
2. *Essays and Introductions*, p. 354.

tional, Wallace Stevens's continual manipulation of the dialectic between concrete and abstract—all reflect the Modernist pursuit of a unified sensibility.

The movement toward the integration of sense, emotion, and intellect was part of the Romantic reaction to a long tradition in Western culture of fragmenting these faculties. Eliot at first identified Milton as responsible for this cultural lapse in literature, but he later retracted this oversimplified accusation. Pater blamed medieval Christianity at first, but he later tempered his judgment to include only certain forms of Christianity, mainly the scholasticism of the late Middle Ages. Pater was aware, however, that scholasticism and rationalism went back through Aristotle and Plato to the pre-Socratic philosophers and that they were permanent traditions in Western thought.

By the end of the eighteenth century, however, there was a special urgency in the efforts of philosophy to reestablish an integrated view of human nature in which emotion, sense, and intellect operated harmoniously. Centuries of Christianity had disparaged sense and emotion and placed them under the hegemony of reason. Then the rise of a scientific world view abstracted and fragmented the human faculties, and philosophies of reason desiccated them. The empiricism of Locke, Berkeley, and Hume contended with the rationalism of Descartes, Spinoza, and Leibniz; between them they parceled out the faculties of perception and understanding. The emotions were neglected by both sides. Kant and Hegel tried to reconcile the empirical and rationalist traditions with a new epistemology, which, despite the rationalism of its authors, laid the foundations for an integrated vision of humanity, a vision that would attempt to redeem human nature from both the desiccation of metaphysics and the disintegration of materialist and empiricist philosophies.

In the realm of aesthetics the concept of organicism arose as a counterpart to the general philosophic reaction against dividing the world between Cartesian abstraction and Humean sensation. Organicism, which passed into the English aesthetic tradition from Schelling through Coleridge, rejected the rationalism and analytical methods of the Enlightenment in favor of a more "natural" and holistic response to experience. Metaphors from Newton's mechanical world were suppressed in favor of metaphors from nature. The creative process was seen to resemble more the unconscious growth of an oak from an acorn than the conscious construction of some artificial, mechanical contraption. From Coleridge to the New Critics, with few exceptions, organic was better.

One of these exceptions, in part at least, was Pater. As we have seen, Pater was not as responsive to Schelling's form of transcendentalism as he was to the critical idealism of Kant or Hegel. Also, although he later began to use the term *organic* as a positive attribute of art, in "Coleridge's Writing" he opposed organicism as a form of determinism, and he himself never attempted to develop the concept. Instead Pater developed the parallel concept of a unified sensibility, a concept he designated variously as the "imaginative reason," the "imaginative intellect," or the "sensuous intellect." Whatever term he used, they all referred to the same faculty—that "complex faculty for which every thought and feeling is twin-born with its sensible analogue or symbol" (*Ren.*, 138).

If the organicism of Schelling and Coleridge had little appeal to Pater, there were other formulators of a unified sensibility he could readily turn to. His notion of the "imaginative reason" has been associated with Kant and Hegel, as well as with Matthew Arnold,[3] but among Pater's predecessors the most eloquent pleader for a unified sensibility in a formulation that pleased him was Schiller. Like Pater, Schiller combined a philosophic with a poetic temperament, and with Goethe as his model he constructed out of the new epistemological orientation an ideal aesthetic temperament that conceived human nature as an integrated organism of sense, emotion, and intellect.

Schiller develops his notion of the unified sensibility particularly in his letters *On the Aesthetic Education of Man*. According to Schiller, primitive man responded to his experience almost exclusively with his senses. Progress in civilization necessarily demanded that he desert the realm of nature and sensory experience for the realm of abstract reason. But for Schiller, a person in either state is incomplete: "Man can be at odds with himself in two ways," he says, "either as savage, when feeling predominates over principle; or as barbarian, when

---

3. d'Hangest, *l'Homme et l'Oeuvre*, 1 : 350 n. 24; DeLaura, *Hebrew and Hellene*, pp. 212, 262.

principle destroys feeling" (21).[4] Like Winckelmann, Schiller saw ancient Greece as the only civilization to achieve a harmony of sense and
intellect. From there he charted the fall into division that culminated
for him, as for Wordsworth and many other Romantics, in the French
Revolution:

> Once the increase of empirical knowledge, and more exact modes of
> thought, made sharper divisions between the sciences inevitable,
> and once the increasingly complex machinery of State necessitated a
> more rigorous separation of ranks and occupations, then the inner
> unity of human nature was severed too, and a disastrous conflict set
> its harmonious powers at variance. The intuitive and the speculative
> understanding now withdrew in hostility to take up positions in
> their respective fields, whose frontiers they now began to guard
> with jealous mistrust. (33)

The hostility Schiller notes here is still evident in the relations between
the arts and sciences, and his description of his own time is still apt
for our even more fragmented society today:

> State and Church, laws and customs, were now torn asunder; enjoy-
> ment was divorced from labour, the means from the end, the effort
> from the reward. Everlastingly chained to a single little fragment of
> the Whole, man himself develops into nothing but a fragment; ever-
> lastingly in his ear the monotonous sound of the wheel that he
> turns, he never develops the harmony of his being, and instead of
> putting the stamp of humanity upon his own nature, he becomes
> nothing more than the imprint of his occupation or of his special-
> ized knowledge. (35)

At the level of the individual, according to Schiller, all forms of perception except the aesthetic divide man "because they are founded
exclusively either upon the sensuous or upon the spiritual part of his
being; only the aesthetic mode of perception makes of him a whole,

---

4. Page references to Schiller's *Aesthetic Education* are indicated in parentheses
in the text.

because both his natures must be in harmony if he is to achieve it" (215). "By means of beauty," Schiller says, "sensuous man is led to form and thought; by means of beauty spiritual man is brought back to matter and restored to the world of sense" (123). As we saw in chapter 6, after dividing human nature into the *sensuous* impulse, the impulse toward the finite, contingent, physical matter of external nature, and the *formal* impulse, the impulse toward the infinite, unconditioned abstractions of pure reason, Schiller reconciles them in the *play* impulse, an aesthetic mode in which the human spirit operates in disinterested freedom over the realms of both sense and reason. Schiller concludes that human nature is complete only at play, play conceived very broadly as an aesthetic state or activity where both sensuous and formal impulses are operating in harmony.

Inspired by Schiller, Hegel, and others, Pater devoted much of his writing career to developing his own understanding of what must constitute a unified sensibility in the modern world. Like many before and after him, Pater never wholly escaped from the rhetoric of dualism, but he nevertheless declared himself a monist by emphatically denying the opposition between spirit and matter. He cites this "false contrast" as an artificial contrivance of schoolmen: "In our actual concrete experience," he insists, "the two trains of phenomena which the words *matter* and *spirit* do but roughly distinguish, play inextricably into each other" (*App.*, 212; Pater's emphases). Like Yeats and Eliot, Pater found his unified ideal in Dante. In Dante's work, Pater says, "the material and the spiritual are fused and blent: if the spiritual attains the definite visibility of a crystal, what is material loses its earthiness and impurity" (*App.*, 212). Writers like Dante conceive of no realm of the spirit that is not also sensuous or material (*App.*, 213).

Many of Pater's own fictional characters either strive for this ideal unity or illustrate the consequences of failing to strive for it. Pater's clearly autobiographical creations (Florian Deleal, Marius, and Gaston de Latour) all embrace the unified sensibility as their personal ideal. In "The Child in the House" (1878), while stressing his preference for the sensuous over the ideal, Florian acknowledges his immersion in "philosophies which occupied him much in the estimate of the proportion of the sensuous and the ideal elements in human knowledge" (*MS*, 186). The title itself suggests the fusion or interpenetra-

tion of the thinking child with his physical habitat, "inward and outward being woven," as the narrator tells us, "through and through
each other into one inextricable texture—half, tint and trace and accident of homely colour and form, from the wood and bricks; half,
mere soul-stuff, floated thither from who knows how far" (*MS*, 173).
Marius's nature is also composed of both "instincts almost physical"
and "slowly accumulated intellectual judgments" (*ME* 2:75). Gaston
de Latour likewise consciously strives for a harmony of body and
soul, of the outer and the inner worlds.

One passage in particular from *Gaston* states Pater's unified ideal
in a form that anticipates Joyce's notion of epiphany, a concept that
also has its foundation in a fusion of sense and spirit. In Ronsard's
odes Gaston discovers a secular embodiment of the unified sensibility
that up to this point in his life had been effectively embodied only in
the medieval religion of Chartres. Ronsard's poetry exposed Gaston to
a "new world of seemingly boundless intellectual resources, and yet
with a special closeness to visible or sensuous things" (50); it was
"faithful to the precise texture of things," yet it seemed even more real
"just because soul had come to its surface":

> Here was a poetry which boldly assumed the dress, the words, the
> habits, the very trick, of contemporary life, and turned them into
> gold. It took possession of the lily in one's hand, and projecting it
> into a visionary distance, shed upon the body of the flower the soul
> of its beauty. Things were become at once more deeply sensuous and
> more deeply ideal. (54)[5]

Joyce's passion for extracting spiritual significance from the precisely
detailed texture of characterization or from a piece of Dublin street

---

5. The ideal expressed here contains significant echoes, given important modifications, of Browning's aesthetic ideal in "Fra Lippo Lippi," where the rakish painter
desires to make "flesh liker" and "soul more like" through faithful rendering of realistic detail. Lippi asks, "Can't I take breath and try to add life's flash, / And then add
soul and heighten them threefold?" For a comprehensive discussion of the aesthetics of
"Fra Lippo Lippi," see David J. DeLaura's "The Context of Browning's Painter Poems:
Aesthetics, Polemics, Historics," *PMLA* 95 (1980): 367–88.

furniture achieves in its most extreme form the dialectical poles of the aesthetic ideal Gaston finds in Ronsard's poetry.[6] In the Joycean epiphany, "the most delicate and evanescent of moments" which it is the artist's duty to record with "extreme care," "we recognize that it is *that* thing which it is. Its soul, its whatness, leaps to us from the vestment of its appearance" (Joyce's emphasis).[7]

The new secular poetry, of which Ronsard's was but the prime example, seemed to transform Gaston's "whole nature into half-sensuous imagination" (70), so that when he later came under the tutelage of Montaigne, his entire being resonated with the master's words on the unity of the human organism: "There is nothing in us either purely corporeal, or purely spiritual. 'Tis an inhuman wisdom that would have us despise and hate the culture of the body. 'Tis not a soul, 'tis not a body, we are training up, but a man; and we ought not to divide him" (111). Gaston's experience upon hearing these words of Montaigne must have resembled Pater's own response upon reading Flaubert's denunciation of materialists and spiritualists alike for rending the unity of the human organism.

Despite his embrace of the unified sensibility and his embodiment of it in his fictional characters, Pater's lifelong effort to achieve this ideal for himself was as problematic for him as it was for some of his Modernist successors, such as Yeats. Like Yeats, Pater vacillated between the poles of sense and spirit; notwithstanding his polemic emphasis on sensation, Pater portrays in his writing a sensibility that exists on a level of rarefied contemplation several times removed from concrete, sensuous experience. Although he began his quest for a unified sensibility in "Winckelmann" by concentrating on the sensuous component, his own predilection for detached contemplation soon led him into more and more intellectualized formulations of it.

Even Pater's fictional characters, such as Marius or Gaston, who supposedly exemplify a balance of sense and intellect, engage life as an intellectual pilgrimage and work out their destinies primarily through intellectual means. They are primarily intellectual portraits,

---

6. For another view of Pater's influence on the Joycean epiphany, see Robert M. Scotto, "'Visions' and 'Epiphanies': Fictional Technique in Pater's *Marius* and Joyce's *Portrait*," *James Joyce Quarterly* 11 (1973): 41–50.

7. *Stephen Hero* (New York: New Directions, 1963), pp. 211–13.

like Marius, or embodiments of ideas, like Denys L'Auxerrois; and Pater's method is much like what he describes in Plato's dialogues: knowledge in Plato, according to Pater, becomes like knowing a living person—"the absolute Temperance, in the person of the youthful Charmides; the absolute Righteousness, in the person of the dying Socrates" (*PP*, 146). Pater's emphasis here is revealing—the "living person" we come to know is the embodiment of an abstract virtue or idea; and all Pater's fictional characters suffer from his attempt to emulate this Platonic ideal. Also, because Pater's technique was not equal to his desire, instead of embodying the intellect in the flesh, as many of his Modernist successors were able to do, his characters remain, for the most part, ideas masquerading as living persons. His characters are marionettes of the mind and not living artistic forms; the bodily eye is strictly subordinate to the intellect and only imperfectly fused with it. When Pater did succeed in fusing sense and intellect, it was usually as a sensuous response to ideas and not as an effective artistic embodiment of ideas in concrete, sensuous forms. The characters of Shaw's plays, who often embody intellectual positions, are much more successful realizations of Pater's Platonic ideal than Pater's own characters.

Pater's preference for the intellectual component of the unified sensibility is also evident in the choice of "sensualists" he admires as exemplars of this ideal temperament: they include Plato and the Renaissance Platonists Pico della Mirandola and Giordano Bruno. Pater also found the unified sensibility of Michelangelo, not in the sensuous grandeur of his painting and sculpture, but in the meditative calm of his Platonic poetry. Pater always tried to root his favorite Platonists in the sensuous world, to discover, or even invent, the corrective to their tendency toward abstract ideals. In the case of Plato, for example, Pater says that he carried "an elaborate cultivation of the bodily senses, of eye and ear . . . into the world of intellectual abstractions" (*PP*, 139–40). Consequently Plato was a sensuous lover of the unseen, who gave visible form to what only the eye of the mind perceived (*PP*, 143).

Despite his attempts to root these Platonists in the sensible world, Pater's preference for them indicates his inability to live in a Humean world composed of sensations and of ideas that are like sensations. Pater's visual sense is informed instead by a Kantian model of the mind; it is an inward-looking vision rather than an outward-looking vision. Nevertheless Pater's struggle to formulate an ideal for an integrated human organism, an ideal synthesized from conflicting philosophical and cultural forces swirling about him, created a model sensibility that became central to the Modernist movement and for which Pater's disciples in the twentieth century developed the appropriate literary vehicles.

Published the year after the Coleridge essay, "Winckelmann," with its emphasis on the sensuous component, is Pater's first formulation of an ideally unified sensibility. In contrast to Coleridge's agonizing over his abstractions, Pater found Winckelmann's ideas much more congenial. He agreed with Hegel's judgment that Winckelmann had discovered " 'a new organ for the human spirit' "—the sensuous intellect (*Ren.*, 177). Pater claims that, with a "sense of exhilaration almost physical" (*Ren.*, 178), a "power of re-enforcing the purer emotions of the intellect with an almost physical excitement" (*Ren.*, 191), Winckelmann rediscovered Greek art for eighteenth-century Germany. "With the sensuous element in Greek art," Pater tells us, "he deals in the pagan manner"; that is, with a sensuousness that "does not fever the blood,"[8] that is "shameless and childlike." Free from any guilt induced by Christian asceticism, Winckelmann "fingers those pagan marbles with unsinged hands, with no sense of shame or loss" (*Ren.*, 221–22).

For Pater, Winckelmann, like an artist, "gradually sunk his intellectual and spiritual ideas in sensuous form," and his soul became "more and more immersed in sense, until nothing which [lacked] the appeal to sense [had] interest for him" (*Ren.*, 221). With the sensuous intellect, Winckelmann was able to recover "the earlier sentiment of the Renaissance" (*Ren.*, 184) and literally make "himself a pagan for the purpose of penetrating antiquity" (*Ren.*, 190). Consequently he provided his age with the "key to the understanding of the Greek spirit" because he had made it part of his own nature (*Ren.*, 220).

For Winckelmann, Hegel, and Pater (at least at this stage of his development), the supreme embodiment of this sensuous intellect was Greek sculpture. According to Pater's Hegelian analysis, Greek reli-

---

8. In the 1893 and the 1910 editions of *The Renaissance*, the word *blood* is replaced by the word *conscience* (Hill edition of *The Renaissance*, pp. 177, 264).

gion, unlike Christianity, was able to manifest itself in an art that contained the "two conditions of an artistic ideal"—the fusion of reflection with "the perfect animal nature of the Greeks." Greek art, in other words, is a perfect fusion of reflection and sense "in which the thought does not outstrip or lie beyond the proper range of its sensible embodiment." This expression of the unified ideal could have come from any one of a number of Modernists. Drawing from Hegel's analysis of the evolution of art, Pater says that a work of Greek art "is in no sense a symbol, a suggestion, of anything beyond its own victorious fairness. The mind begins and ends with the finite image, yet loses no part of the spiritual motive. That motive is not lightly and loosely attached to the sensuous form, as its meaning to an allegory, but saturates and is identical with it" (*Ren.*, 205–7). Pater's expression of this Greek ideal, as beginning and ending with the finite image without losing the spiritual motive, does not vary essentially from his Hegelian shell parable twenty-five years later in *Plato and Platonism*.

In "Winckelmann" Pater was trying to reestablish the legitimacy of the senses in culture, in art, and in the functioning of the entire human organism; and thus his polemics focus on Winckelmann's introduction of the sensuous component into the study of Greek art. Once he had established that legitimacy for himself, however, Pater began to readjust his balance between sense and intellect. This readjustment began almost immediately in the essay that followed "Winckelmann," "Poems by William Morris" (1868). Except for a brief period between the publication of *The Renaissance* (1873) and *Marius* (1885), Pater never really returned to the heavy emphasis on sense found in "Winckelmann." Although Pater continued with his polemics in favor of sense and the concrete, polemics that many disciples and critics took at face value and propagated along with his reputation as a priest of sensation, from the Morris essay on Pater's formulation of the unified sensibility migrated persistently, if not consistently, in the direction of idealism of various sorts.

"Poems by William Morris" clearly continues to develop Pater's interest in the sensuous intellect, but in this essay Pater begins to develop the intellectual side of the sensuous intellect. Moreover, he achieves a formulation of it that characterizes his own work more appropriately than the formulation in "Winckelmann." Pater found Morris, like Winckelmann, to be another example of a cultural phenomenon that had been taking place since the Renaissance—the "return from the overwrought spiritualities of the middle age to the earlier, more ancient life of the senses" (307).[9] Pater calls Morris a "Hellenist of the middle age" (305), and his review dwells upon the shading of religion "into sensuous love, and sensuous love into religion" evident in the passing between the "mystic passion" of medieval religion and the "rebellious flesh" of the great romantic lovers, such as Lancelot and Abelard (301). This tension resulted in a "beautiful disease or disorder of the senses," which Pater captures in his characterization of typical lovers of the Middle Ages: "Here, under this strange complex of conditions, as in some medicated air, exotic flowers of sentiment expand, among people of a remote and unaccustomed beauty, somnambulistic, frail, androgynous, the light almost shining through them, as the flame of a little taper shows through the Host. Such loves were too fragile and adventurous to last more than for a moment" (302). This passage, fragile, precious, exotic, rarefied, and ritualistic itself, expresses a great deal of the Paterian temperament. This rarefied sensibility, a sensuousness that is almost drained of its blood, diaphanous as it were, so that a taper's flame would shine through it, is an important quality of Pater's own sensibility.

Although Pater pronounces Morris free from this disorder of the senses, he nevertheless characterizes the spirit of Morris's "aesthetic poetry" in terms that resemble the characterization of his rarefied medieval lovers:

> Greek poetry, medieval or modern poetry, projects above the realities of its time a world in which the forms of things are transfigured. Of that world this new poetry takes possession, and sublimates beyond it another still fainter and more spectral, which is literally an artificial or "earthly paradise." It is a finer ideal, extracted from what in relation to any actual world is already an ideal. (300)

This rarefied level on which Morris's aesthetic poetry operates, described by Pater in terms that suggest Hegel's characterization of poetry in the realm of absolute spirit, is twice removed from the actual

---

9. All page references to "Poems by William Morris" are to the *Westminster Review* 90 (1868).

world: it abstracts from an already existent idealized abstraction of the world. This is the same level on which Pater's own prose typically operates. The highly refined, sensuous intellect Pater characterizes in Morris's poetry is very much Pater's own. Even though he implies that he prefers Morris's sensuous simplicity to the "sought-out simplicity" of Wordsworth, whose desire is not "towards the body of nature for its own sake," but "because a soul is divined through it" (306), Pater's own affinities are with Wordsworth; that is, he is less concerned with sense for its own sake than with the "soul divined through it."

An excellent illustration of the rarefied level of Pater's own prose is his famous description of the Mona Lisa, a description whose passages haunted the aesthetic imaginations of the 1890s. (Yeats set part of it in vers libre as the first modern "poem" in his 1936 collection of *The Oxford Book of Modern Verse*.) Pater claims to have discovered in Leonardo another manifestation of the unified sensibility because his painting "pleases the eye while it satisfies the soul" (*Ren.*, 114). A close examination of his passages on Leonardo's masterpiece, however, reveals very few eye-pleasing details and a very generous portion of soul-satisfying speculation. In Pater's analysis, the "remote beauty" of Leonardo's art resembles Morris's aesthetic poetry in being two removes from the actual world: according to Pater, this beauty "may be apprehended only by those who have sought it carefully; who, starting with acknowledged types of beauty, have refined far upon these, as these refine upon the world of common forms" (*Ren.*, 105). In addition to possessing a sensibility similar to that of Morris, Leonardo also becomes, in Pater's view, a world-weary aesthete and a Hegelian.

In the description itself Pater quickly dispenses with the visuals in one sentence: "We all know the face and hands of the figure, set in its marble chair, in that circle of fantastic rocks, as in some faint light under sea." To be fair to Pater, he also mentions "the unfathomable smile, always with a touch of something sinister in it"; however, this smile is not unique to Lady Lisa, but "plays over all Leonardo's work" (*Ren.*, 123–24). In any case, the words *unfathomable* and *sinister* are already leading us from the eye to the soul, which is the real focus of Pater's interest.

What fascinates Pater about this portrait are not concrete sensuous details, but a spectre in the consciousness of Leonardo and, ultimately, in the consciousness of Western civilization. More with the mind's eye than the visual eye, Pater sees the Mona Lisa as an image, gemlike no doubt, that from Leonardo's childhood was "defining itself on the fabric of his dreams." This image resembles closely the notion of the image in the "Conclusion"—"that clear, perpetual outline of face and limb"—but it seems less a design wrought in the web of experience than in the tapestry of the soul.

"What was the relationship of a living Florentine to this creature of his thought?" asks Pater rhetorically. "By what strange affinities had the dream and the person grown up thus apart, and yet so closely together?" (*Ren.*, 124). For Pater, Leonardo was one of the fortunate who found an object of the senses that answered to his dream. He found her in the person of Francesco del Giocondo's third wife, Lisa, who served as his model: "Present from the first," explains Pater, "incorporeally in Leonardo's brain, dimly traced in the designs of Verrocchio,[10] she is found present at last in *Il Giocondo's* house" (*Ren.*, 124).

So far everything cited above from the Leonardo essay only leads up to the famous passage on the painting which is, as Pater says of Morris's poetry, a "finer ideal, extracted from what in relation to any actual world is already an ideal." Still fainter and more spectral than the original, it sublimates it into a more highly artificial and rarefied atmosphere. What Pater finds in Leonardo's "ideal lady" is not a woman but an essence or an abstraction of the ages. In a Hegelian passage in the Morris essay that anticipates T. S. Eliot's views on history in "Tradition and the Individual Talent," Pater says, "The composite experience of all ages is part of each one of us" (307); and for Pater, Leonardo's portrait was a composite of the ages. The famous passage on the Mona Lisa begins, "The presence that rose thus so strangely beside the waters, is expressive of what in the ways of a thousand years men had come to desire. Hers is the head upon which all 'the ends of the world are come,' and the eyelids are a little weary." A few lines later he adds, "All the thoughts and experience of the world have etched and moulded there . . . the animalism of Greece, the lust of Rome, the mysticism of the middle age with its spiritual ambition and imaginative loves, the return of the Pagan world, the

---

10. Leonardo's master.

sins of the Borgias. She is older than the rocks among which she sits."
Pater's fascination with spiritual pathology is also read into the portrait: this troubled beauty, "into which the soul with all its maladies
has passed," is "like the vampire"—"she has been dead many times,
and learned the secrets of the grave; and has been a diver in deep seas,
and keeps their fallen day about her; and trafficked for strange webs
with Eastern merchants: and, as Leda, was the mother of Helen of
Troy, and, as Saint Anne, the mother of Mary." This woman—elegant,
languorous, dripping with corruption and weariness—became the
dream lady of 1890s aesthetes. Like the typical art of the nineties, she
transcended all her tainted experience by composing it, like the Chinese men in Yeats's "Lapis Lazuli," into a work of art: "All this has
been to her," continues Pater, "but as the sound of lyres and flutes,
and lives only in the delicacy with which it has moulded the changing
lineaments, and tinged the eyelids and the hands" (*Ren.*, 124–25).

Certainly this passage deals almost exclusively with Pater's ideas of
Leonardo's lady, with the intellectual side of the sensuous intellect,
except in so far as the seductive rhythms of Pater's prose appeal to
the auditory sense. Otherwise, there is very little that appeals to the
senses in the passage. Pater talks about "a beauty wrought out from
within upon the flesh" (*Ren.*, 125); but the beauty here is inward, intellectual, and spiritual—it is weighted with "the meaning of nature
and purpose of humanity" (*Ren.*, 103). Certainly Pater mentions visual objects—head, eyelids, Greece, Rome, the Borgias, vampires, a
diver in deep seas, Eastern merchants, Leda, St. Anne—but these objects are not endowed with any substantial physicality or appeal to
sense; they are not fleshed out as, say, in the poetry of Yeats or Eliot;
rather they are intellectual ciphers, guideposts for the mind, not for
sense and emotion. Pater appropriately concludes his reverie by de-
picting the Mona Lisa as the epitome of the Hegelian philosophical
ideal: "The fancy of a perpetual life, sweeping together ten thousand
experiences, is an old one; and modern philosophy [meaning Hegel]
has conceived the idea of humanity as wrought upon by, and summing
up in itself, all modes of thought and life. Certainly Lady Lisa might
stand as the embodiment of the old fancy, the symbol of the modern
idea" (*Ren.*, 125–26).

So the Mona Lisa in the end symbolizes an idea, "wrought out
from within upon the flesh" to be sure, but nevertheless an idea in

essence. Pater's own passage, like the Mona Lisa itself, is a perfect example of what he means by burning with a "hard, gemlike flame": it is a concurrence of forces that momentarily produce "that clear, perpetual outline," a design in the web of his experience, his "own dream of a world." The different threads of Pater's own experience come together in this passage, including Hegel, his studies of Hellenism, Christianity, and the Renaissance, and his own brooding Romanticism—the languorous fascination for pathology, for the solitary and remote, for the strange and bizarre, for the odor of death, for the aesthetically rarefied experience. The passage is infused with Pater's intellect and temperament; it is eminently soul-satisfying, for which his disciples in the nineties cherished it. But it has little appeal to the senses.

For all Pater's rhetoric about the senses and the concrete, especially the visual sense, the visual quality of his own writing, fictional or critical, is very unremarkable. For example, in his description of Botticelli's Birth of Venus, there are many more physical details, especially in the characterization of light, than in the Mona Lisa passage; but the passion and aesthetic impact of Pater's writing on the Birth of Venus pale beside his reverie over Leonardo's masterpiece. What is missing in the former is the intellectual passion Leonardo's lady aroused in him. In the Botticelli essay Pater's passion emerges when he deals with matters of the human spirit pressing for expression from the subtlest recesses of the artist's consciousness. Purely sensuous and concrete detail, however, is not what motivates Pater's most famous and moving passages.

He is not sensuous in the usual sense of the word. Rather he is a devotee and master of the sensuous response to intellectual stimuli, complex stimuli that involve both intellect and sense, but often more intellect than sense. For example, when he describes a person in either his criticism or fiction, it is seldom in terms of physical appearance, but overwhelmingly in terms of the person's intellectual and spiritual character. In describing a work of art, as in the Mona Lisa passage, he most typically emphasizes its intellectual and spiritual life, its soul, over its appeal to sense. Like his own characterization of Plato, Pater himself is a sensuous lover of the unseen.

Although Pater could be fascinated with a certain amount of spiritual pathology, there were limits to how close his overwrought sensibility could actually approach some of the more grossly sensual aspects of human experience. He distances himself from the sordid sensual indulgence of Wilde's *Dorian Gray*, [11] and it is hard to imagine Pater embracing the "slightly soiled" ideal that Molly Bloom represented for Joyce, or agreeing with the insight of Yeats's Crazy Jane that "Love has pitched his mansion in / The place of excrement." [12] This limitation on Pater's part, his reluctance to see, as his Modernist disciples did, the necessity of Stein's Nietzschean dictum in *Lord Jim*, "In the destructive element immerse," inhibited Pater from developing in his own work a unified sensibility that ran the gamut, in Eliot's words, from "garlic and sapphires in the mud" to their reconciliation among the stars. [13] Unlike the Joycean artist, Pater could not devote himself to the "disorder, the misrule and confusion of his father's house and the stagnation of vegetable life"; nor could he pitch himself periodically, as Yeats did, into the "frog-spawn of a blind man's ditch,"

> Or into that most fecund ditch of all,
> The folly that man does
> Or must suffer, if he woos
> A proud woman not kindred of his soul. [14]

For all his appreciation of things sensuous, Pater usually operated on a level with ideals we might well call Platonic. In contrast to Joyce's or Yeats's recognition of the necessity for immersion even in the sordid elements of sensory experience in order to realize a totally unified sensibility, Pater's preference was for a more sanitized ideal, an ideal in a realm where, as Auden put it in "In Praise of Limestone," everything is like music, "Which can be made anywhere, is invisible, / And does not smell." Out of all the racy and macabre satires of Apuleius's

---

11. According to d'Hangest's description in *l'Homme et l'Oeuvre* of the unpublished sections of *Gaston de Latour*, Pater did explore there in some detail the sordid consequences of sensual indulgence that prevailed in the court of Henry III of France (2:116–26).

12. *Ulysses* (New York: Random House, 1961), p. 653; *The Poems of W. B. Yeats*, pp. 259–60.

13. Joseph Conrad, *Lord Jim*, ed. Thomas C. Moser, Norton Critical Editions (New York: W. W. Norton, 1968), p. 131; T. S. Eliot, *The Complete Poems and Plays: 1909–1950* (New York: Harcourt, Brace and World, 1962), pp. 118–19.

14. *A Portrait of the Artist as a Young Man* (New York: Penguin, 1976), p. 162; *The Poems of W. B. Yeats*, p. 236.

The Golden Ass, with what Pater termed their "almost insane pre-occupation with the materialities of our mouldering flesh, that luxury of disgust in gazing on corruption," Marius chose "The Story of Cupid and Psyche," the anomaly, the "true gem" amid the other coarse mock-eries and "burlesque horrors"; and even then he bowdlerized it consid-erably in accordance with his aesthetic ideal. While acknowledging the "genuine humanity" of the other tales, Marius was temperamen-tally drawn to the "gentle idealism" of "Cupid and Psyche" (*ME* 1:60–61). For Marius this story represented "the *hiddenness* of per-fect things" (Pater's emphasis), "an ideal of a perfect imaginative love, centered upon a type of beauty entirely flawless and clean." This story made "men's actual loves" seem by comparison "somewhat mean and sordid" (*ME* 1:92–93). A little later on Marius resolves, quite consis-tently with his reaction to "Cupid and Psyche," to remain aloof from personal relations, "that pre-occupation with other persons, which had so often perturbed his spirit," and to express his passions "not as the longing for love—to be with Cynthia, or Aspasia—but as a thirst for existence in exquisite places" (*ME* 1:157). In other words Marius would reserve his passion not for women but for the idealized perfec-tion of art.

Pater's mature formulation of the unified sensibility is best illus-trated by his essay on Wordsworth. With the exception of Goethe per-haps, Wordsworth was the most pervasive literary influence of the nineteenth century on Pater's imagination, and, along with Goethe, he remained throughout Pater's career his touchstone for the ideal liter-ary sensibility and for the ideal fusion of sense and intellect. Pater bor-rows from him extensively, especially on the relations between the inner and outer worlds, between the world of the mind and the world of nature. Wordsworth was also for Pater the native English embodi-ment of Winckelmann's sensuous intellect. What is interesting about Pater's view of Wordsworth is that even when he was professing more interest in the sensuous element of the sensuous intellect, he still pre-ferred the relatively more abstract imagination of Wordsworth, whom he called "the most philosophic of English poets" (*EG*, 91–92), to the more richly sensual imagination of Keats, whom he rarely men-tions in his writings.

In his essay "Wordsworth," published in 1874, Pater maintains his inclination toward the intellectual pole of the unified sensibility that

evolved during the composition of the *Renaissance* essays. Wordsworth's poetry has special appeal, according to Pater, "for those who
feel the fascination of bold speculative ideas, who are really capable of
rising upon them to conditions of poetical thought" (*App.*, 56). Although Pater claims that in contrast to Coleridge, who languished in
philosophic abstraction, Wordsworth was always aware "of the limits
within which alone philosophical imaginings have any place in true
poetry," still what he most admired in Wordsworth were the "majestic
forms of philosophic imagination" that evoked Shelley's notion of " 'a
sort of thought in sense' " (*App.*, 48, 56–57). In "The Genius of
Plato" Pater even compares the "speculative poetry" of Wordsworth
to Plato's dialogues. In Wordsworth's poetry, Pater says, "we may observe that a great metaphysical force has come into language which is
by no means purely technical or scholastic; what a help such language
is to the understanding, to a real hold over the things, the thoughts,
the mental processes, those words denote; a vocabulary to which
thought freely commits itself, trained, stimulated, raised, thereby, towards a high level of abstract conception, surely to the increase of our
general intellectual powers" (*PP*, 141–42). In the end Wordsworth's
poetry was for Pater less a true fusion of sense and intellect than
a means of raising the imagination to an edifying level of abstract
conception.

Pater's attraction to Platonists as embodiments of the unified sensibility strikes one as a paradox; Pater himself must have sensed this,
for in his essay on Michelangelo's poetry (1871), he wrestles with
"two great traditional types" in the pursuit of the ideal, one represented by Dante and the other by Plato:

> Dante's belief in the resurrection of the body, through which, even
> in heaven, Beatrice loses for him no tinge of flesh-colour, or fold of
> raiment even; and the Platonic dream of the passage of the soul
> through one form of life after another, with its passionate haste to
> escape from the burden of bodily form altogether; are, for all effects
> of art or poetry, principles diametrically opposite. (*Ren.*, 86)

From the Winckelmann essay one would think that Pater's allegiance would lie firmly with the tradition of Dante; but subsequent
essays make it clear that he is more fascinated by the struggles of fig-

ures from the Platonic tradition, such as Pico, Bruno, and Plato himself, and by artists with a strong intellectual component. Indeed, Pater's Platonic Wordsworth serves as a corrective to Pater's rhetoric about the senses and to views of Pater that emphasize the flux of sensation over the equally, if not more important, element of intellectual abstraction in his sensibility.

Pater's vacillation between the poles of sense and intellect in his formulation of the unified sensibility was repeated in the next generation in the career of Yeats. Although Yeats's sensibility was capable of much closer contact with the sensual world, as with Pater, Yeats's vision had a strong component of Platonism; it was informed by a Hegelian dialectic, and it never escaped from the dualism implicit in both Plato's and Hegel's thought. Some of Yeats's poems, such as "The Stolen Child," "The Song of Wandering Aengus," and "Sailing to Byzantium," clearly aspire to a realm of pure spirit, while others, like "Adam's Curse," "A Dialogue of Self and Soul," and "The Circus Animals' Desertion," embrace the "sensual music" of "mire and blood," flesh and bone. Even when flying to these extremes, however, Yeats was always ambivalent and could not sacrifice one world to the other for long. Still other poems, such as "The Double Vision of Michael Robartes," "Among School Children," "Lapis Lazuli," "News for the Delphic Oracle," and the Crazy Jane poems, tried, with varying degrees of success, to articulate a unified vision of both worlds. Regardless of their vacillation, however, both Pater and Yeats devoted much of their energy to forging an ideal sensibility that would not slight our experience of either sense or spirit.

So despite Pater's emphasis on the intellectual side of the "sensuous intellect," his postulation and career-long exploration of an ideally unified sensibility helped to lay the foundations for the Modernist experiments in form and technique that more capably realized the ideal than Pater did. Modernist expressions of this ideal ranged from Imagism to Symbolism, and Pater's position, regardless of its particular formulation, falls between these two extremes. It contrasts with the symbolist ideal which, as in the early poetry of Yeats, uses the symbol as a springboard into an ineffable beyond. This form of symbolism, derived from a form of Romanticism, had not yet given up a metaphysics of substance for one of function. In his concept of the *anima mundi*, for example, Yeats still held to a Platonic notion of an independent reality for symbols and ideas. Pater's position also contrasts with Imagism, which would resist any attempt to look beyond the image to a "spiritual motive" or ideational content.

Of the Modernists with a tendency toward intellectual abstraction similar to Pater's, perhaps Wallace Stevens best illustrates how one might successfully embody a "sensuous intellect" in poetic technique. One stanza in particular from "The Idea of Order at Key West" appears to possess the quality of "thought in sense" Pater admired in Wordsworth, a quality capable, according to Pater, of "enlarging so strangely the bounds" of the visible world and of "breaking such a wild light" over it (*App.*, 57):

> Ramon Fernandez, tell me, if you know,
> Why, when the singing ended and we turned
> Toward the town, tell why the glassy lights,
> The lights in the fishing boats at anchor there,
> As the night descended, tilting in the air,
> Mastered the night and portioned out the sea,
> Fixing emblazoned zones and fiery poles,
> Arranging, deepening, enchanting night.[15]

In contrast to Pater's writing in which, more often than not, sense is sacrificed to intellect, in Stevens's stanza, as in his poetry generally, the boundaries of the visible world expand imperceptibly into the world of imagination, and in that "wild light" sense and intellect are as truly indistinguishable in fact as they are in theory. Stevens's poetry, in other words, embodies more successfully than Pater's own prose a sensibility in which "every thought and feeling is twin-born with its sensible analogue or symbol."

---

15. *The Collected Poems of Wallace Stevens* (New York: Knopf, 1968), p. 130.

10 / THEORY OF EXPRESSION

ONE LOGICAL consequence of the new epistemology, whether empirical or idealist, was the plunge of the arts into the depths of the self and the attendant rise of aesthetic theories of expression. Both Hume's and Berkeley's emphasis on the psychology of sensation and Kant's emphasis on the structures of the mind itself helped to redirect the focus of philosophy from an external to an internal world. Whether the emphasis was on the rational interior of the human psyche, as in Hume or Hegel, or on the irrational, as in Schopenhauer or Freud, this shift has permanently altered the direction of Western thought. At first, inward-looking metaphysics contended with science as its chief antagonist, since science continued to emphasize a more positivistic, external, or objective reality. But by the twentieth century even science was brought more and more into the inner universe of functional metaphysics, Cassirer's philosophy being one of the most ambitious attempts to reconcile neo-Kantian philosophy with scientific empiricism. By the time of the Modernist revolution in the arts, neo-Kantian philosophy, which had spawned a cult of spontaneity and subjectivity among the Romantics, had become more objective by absorbing scientific thought into its own premises, a movement Pater fostered when he shifted the emphasis of expressive theories from the personal emotions of the artist to the artist's inner scheme of the world. The increasing objectification, however, did not reverse the revolutionary shift of thought from its focus on an outer world to an inner world.

The movement of thought inward resulted in the emphasis on the inner world of the artist, an inner world that could be rational, emotional, instinctual, conscious, unconscious, or any combination of these. It also prompted the development of new techniques appropriate to rendering the inner vision; and it lent an authority to individual, subjective visions that triggered the autobiographical impulse that has dominated nineteenth- and twentieth-century literature. As a result of directing their focus inward, artists became self-conscious and self-reflective. Like Montaigne, they took themselves as their subject matter and trusted that each self constituted a microcosm of humanity. The artist became both the subject matter and the hero/protagonist, even to the point of the writer writing about the writer writing: "Mirror on mirror mirrored is all the show," says Yeats in "The Statues"; and Escher depicts the hand of the artist drawing itself.

Pater has often been depicted as a precursor to the formalist aesthetics of the twentieth century; but because of their emphasis on formal criteria, most critics of Pater and of Modernism have failed to perceive that a continuing tradition of expressionist theory weaves nineteenth- and twentieth-century aesthetics together and that Pater was a crucial link in the evolution of this tradition. Pater did play a role in the development of formalist aesthetics, but that role has been misunderstood and exaggerated because it has been perceived outside the context of an expressive theory that dominates it. For Pater the "essence of all good style" is "expressiveness," the justice or precision "with which words balance or match their meaning, and their writer succeeds in saying what he *wills*" (*MS*, 67; Pater's emphasis), or, more concisely, the writer's "exact expression of his mind" (*App.*, 126). Pater considered this quality of expressiveness to be the one "which alone makes works in the imaginative [and moral] [1] order really worth having at all" (*Ren.*, 71–72).

Pater's expressive orientation conforms generally to the "central tendency" of Romantic aesthetics characterized by M. H. Abrams:

---

1. The phrase in brackets was included in the first three editions of *The Renaissance* (1873, 1877, and 1888), but it was deleted in the 1893 edition (Hill edition of *The Renaissance*, p. 222).

A work of art is essentially the internal made external, resulting from a creative process operating under the impulse of feeling, and embodying the combined product of the poet's perceptions, thought, and feelings. The primary source and subject matter of a poem, therefore, are the attributes and actions of the poet's own mind; or if aspects of the external world, then these only as they are converted from fact to poetry by the feelings and operations of the poet's mind.[2]

Expressive theories of art, however, were not peculiar to the Romantics or to the nineteenth century. Abrams traces them back to Longinus and even to elements in Horace, but, more important for our purposes here, they persist into the twentieth century as well. Despite polemics about objectivity and impersonality, in practice many major writers of the twentieth century operate according to a theory of expression that perceives truth, as Pater did, as an absolute fidelity to an inner vision and the precise accommodation of language to that vision.

Benedetto Croce's aesthetics provide one of the most fully articulated theories of expressionism in the twentieth century; but Croce's expressionism is in many ways more Romantic and less modern than Pater's. Although Croce articulated some of the major concerns of Modernist writers and critics, the Plotinian idealism of his emphasis on the image in the artist's mind, his exclusive emphasis on intuition over intellect in aesthetic experience, and his neglect of craftsmanship and technique in handling the sensuous materials of the various arts make his theory of expression more idiosyncratic and less central to the Modernist tradition than Pater's.

Pater's formulation of an expressive theory, on the other hand, altered some of the typical features of Romantic expressiveness in ways that made it more tenable for twentieth-century minds and sensibilities: he shifted the Romantic emphasis on the expression of personal emotion in art to an emphasis on the expression of a more intellectualized inner vision or scheme of the world; the nineteenth-century cult of sincerity and moral integrity became in Pater's hands intellectual and artistic integrity with a concomitant emphasis on aesthetic craftsmanship; and, apparently without being wholly successful or

---

2. *The Mirror and the Lamp* (New York: Oxford University Press, 1953), p. 22.

aware of what he was doing, Pater tried to fuse with his expressive emphasis a new objective orientation (in Abrams's sense) that he had found in Flaubert, a fusion his successors accomplished more successfully by focusing on the expressiveness of the work itself, rather than of the mind of the artist.

Like Croce, Pater derived his theory of expression primarily from Hegel. By defining art as the sensuous manifestation of the absolute Idea, Hegel privileged both the expressive function and the intellectual content of art, emphases that also characterize Pater's aesthetics. According to Hegel, art is a "mode and form through which the *Divine*, the profoundest interests of mankind, and spiritual truths of widest range, are brought home to consciousness and expressed" (9; Hegel's emphasis).[3] For Hegel, then, the essence of art is intellectual while its expression is sensuous: Hegel says that the region of absolute mind "artistically presented to sensuous vision and emotion forms the center of the entire world of art" (111), and art imparts to phenomena "a reality of more exalted rank born of mind" (10). To put it another way, Hegel says that in art man "imprints the seal of his inner life" upon the external world (42). For Hegel the *content* of art is the intellectual element, the absolute Idea, while the *form* lies in "the configuration of the sensuous or plastic image" (95). But the sensuous form, "which is essentially impressed with a content that is open to mind," is ultimately addressed not to the senses but "to the inward conscious life"; the external shape exists "exclusively for the soul and mind of man" (97).

Hegel's emphasis on mind and inner being, however, does not ignore the sensuous form. He recognizes the importance of craftsmanship in art, the artist's technical mastery of his sensuous medium (36–37), and he evaluates art according to "the correspondence and unity of the two aspects, that is the Idea and its sensuous shape" (98). But although the excellence of art depends on the degree of unity with which the Idea is fused to its sensuous shape, this correspondence is not "mere correctness," the mere precision of form to import; rather,

---

3. The page references in this chapter to quotations from Hegel are to F. P. B. Osmaston's translation of *The Philosophy of Fine Art*, by G. W. F. Hegel (London: G. Bell and Sons, 1920), vol. 1.

the Idea rendered in sensuous shape must both be appropriate to such rendering and relate to the most profound and universal of human interests (55, 95–96). In Hegel's view only an Idea that is truly both concrete and universal will be able to generate a sensuous form absolutely appropriate to itself (102).

Despite his emphasis on what is conscious and rational in art, Hegel does not neglect the roles of instinct and feeling; rather, he represents art as a unified totality of intellect, sense, and emotion. "The creative imagination of an artist," he says, "is the imagination of a great mind and a big heart; it is the grasp and excogitation of ideas and shapes, and, in fact, nothing less than this grasp of the profoundest and most embracing human interests in the wholly definite presentation of imagery borrowed from objective experience" (55).

In adapting Hegel's aesthetics Pater typically ignored the emphasis on absolute truth, and he limited art to expressing the individual mind of the artist. Also, as we have seen, Pater could not accept Hegel's evolutionary scheme of the arts, which privileged those forms of art, such as painting, music, and poetry, which, according to Hegel, led away from the sensuous world toward the more purely intellectual regions of religion and philosophy. But otherwise Pater accepted Hegel's aesthetic orientation and most of its essential features, including its expressive thrust, its analysis of form and content, its emphasis on the intellectual component, and its concern with technical craftsmanship, a concern later reinforced by Flaubert.

Pater's adaptation of Hegel's aesthetics was not without its difficulties, however. Although the orientation Pater drew from Hegel early in his career remained primarily expressive, his later exposure to Flaubert introduced objective elements into his aesthetics that were never fully reconciled with his Hegelian theory of expression. Partly because of his confusion of these two orientations, Pater was never consistent in his formulations of the relations between sense and intellect in art. Nevertheless, compared to Croce's aesthetics, Pater's adaptation of Hegel was more faithful to the original; and if we view Pater's aesthetics as essentially Hegelian, many of the so-called impressionistic and formalist elements in them appear in a new light. Moreover, through Pater, Hegel's aesthetics emerge as central to the Modernist tradition.

Pater began to develop his theory of expression somewhat haltingly in his earliest essays, particularly in "Diaphaneitè," written to be read before the Old Mortality Society at Oxford in 1864,[4] and in the Coleridge essay (1866). After a hiatus of several years spent wrestling with problems of philosophy and religion and their relation to art, Pater developed the theory in earnest in some of the later essays written for *The Renaissance*, especially "Sandro Botticelli" (1870) and "Luca della Robbia" (1873). This development continued in "Wordsworth" (1874) and "The School of Giorgione" (1877), and culminated with a fully formulated articulation in "Style" (1888). These last three essays are among the most important and influential in Pater's canon.

In "Diaphaneitè" and "Coleridge's Writings" Pater first articulates an ideally expressive nature as a type of transparency, a transparency that operates in two directions, one mostly passive and the other active. The passive transparency is a form of ideal receptivity, a "clear crystal nature," that, like Shelley's sensitive plant, absorbs "unconsciously all that is really lifegiving in the established order of things" (*MS*, 251, 253). Pater calls this receptive capacity the "element of genius" in the "artistic gift," and it anticipates the Bergsonian view of the uniqueness of the artist's vision, his ability to break through the conventions of ordinary perception because of a "natural susceptibility to moments of strange excitement, in which the colours freshen upon our threadbare world, and the routine of things about us is broken by a novel and happier synthesis" ("CW," 123).

This type of crystal-clear transparency is not far removed from the classic and neoclassic notion of mimesis with its attendant metaphor of the mirror; nevertheless, it has begun to break down the mimetic view of art, founded on the orientation of philosophies of substance, by means of a Hegelian correspondence between the inner and outer worlds. The transparent nature, according to Pater, "detects without difficulty all sorts of affinities between its own elements, and the nobler elements in [the established] order" (*MS*, 251).

Although Pater has not completely broken with philosophies of substance with his notion of a passive transparency between the mind

---

4. Gerald Monsman, "Pater, Hopkins, and Fichte's Ideal Student," *South Atlantic Quarterly* 70 (1971): 365–76; reprinted in *Walter Pater*, Twayne's English Authors Series (Boston: Twayne, 1977), pp. 26–35. As mentioned in chap. 6, n. 1, the incorrect accent mark on *diaphanéité* is Pater's, and I have retained it throughout.

and the "established order of things" that the mind of the artist unconsciously absorbs, his second element of the "artistic gift," the "talent of projection," completes the transition, charted by Abrams in *The Mirror and the Lamp*, from the mimetic mirror to the expressive light of inner vision. The "talent of projection" is the active capacity in the crystal nature, and it operates in the opposite direction from the passive, receptive capacity. Its function is to reveal without hindrance the vision of the artist's inner world, to project that vision in Hegelian fashion "into an external concrete form" ("CW," 123).

Pater's diaphanous ideal, then, applies both to exquisitely refined and purified powers of reception and to equally refined powers of expression: "The artist and he who has treated life in the spirit of art," says Pater, "desires only to be shown to the world as he really is; as he comes nearer and nearer to perfection, the veil of an outer life not simply expressive of the inward becomes thinner and thinner" (*MS*, 249).

Another quality of the crystal temperament is that it is highly intellectual. Although Pater claims that its operations are largely unconscious, paradoxically he perceives language and expression primarily as functions of intellect. Heavily influenced by Hegel's *Ästhetik*, Pater cites art as the "highest product of intellect"; and his ideal, composed mostly, he says, of "intellectual, moral and spiritual elements," exhibits simplicity in "the repose of perfect intellectual culture," and represents one of the "higher forms of inward life"—"a mind of taste lighted up by some spiritual ray within" (*MS*, 249–50).

Pater's theory of expression remained embryonic in the essays immediately following "Coleridge's Writings," but several years later in his essays on Botticelli and Luca della Robbia he elaborated on his dualistic distinction between an inner and an outer world. In his study of Botticelli Pater is concerned with the "transmutation of ideas into images," which he also discussed in his essay on Leonardo the year before. In the Leonardo essay Pater used the term *idea* in two senses that parallel the receptive and projective capacities of his diaphanous ideal: idea in the abstract, outward-directed sense of "the meaning of nature and purpose of humanity," and idea in the sense of the artist's inner vision, his own "secret wisdom" or "scheme of the world" pressing for expression from the "subtlest retreats" of his consciousness (*Ren.*, 99, 103–4). In "Botticelli" Pater begins to focus almost exclusively on the latter sense of *idea*.

Pater's preference for this sense of idea is articulated more clearly, however, in "Luca della Robbia," where his contrast between the sculpture of ancient Greece and that of Michelangelo illustrates his distinction between an outward-looking and an inward-looking vision. Greek sculpture, according to Pater, looked outward and was characterized by *Allgemeinheit*—breadth, generality, universality, as defined in "Winckelmann." Like Samuel Johnson's Shakespeare, the Greek sculptors sought "the type in the individual" and endeavored to "abstract and express only what is structural and permanent, to purge from the individual all that belongs only to him, all the accidents, the feelings and actions of the special moment." "In this way," Pater continues, "their works came to be like some subtle extract or essence, or almost like pure thoughts or ideas: and hence the breadth of humanity in them, that detachment from the conditions of a particular place or people, which has carried their influence far beyond the age which produced them, and insured them universal acceptance" (*Ren.*, 66).

But for Pater the Greek solution "involved to a certain degree the sacrifice of what we call *expression*," the sense that "some spirit in the thing seems always on the point of breaking out" (Pater's emphasis). Michelangelo's work, on the other hand, epitomized the highest degree of "individuality and intensity of expression." Attributing a Hegelian inwardness to Christianity, Pater says that Michelangelo's genius, "spiritualized by the reverie of the middle age, penetrated by its spirit of inwardness and introspection," living "a life full of intimate experiences, sorrows, consolations," could not be satisfied by a "mere outward life like the Greek," or any "system which sacrificed so much of what was inward and unseen." To him any work "which did not bring what was inward to the surface, which was not concerned with individual expression, with individual character and feeling, the special history of the special soul, was not worth doing at all" (*Ren.*, 66–67). What Pater admired in Renaissance artists like Michelangelo and Botticelli was that they were not merely mimetic transcribers of an external world, but rather they usurped the data before them "as the exponent of ideas, moods, visions" of their own (*Ren.*, 53).

The writer who best illustrates this diaphanous ideal for Pater is Wordsworth, and his characterization of him in the essay "Wordsworth" elucidates that ideal much more successfully than the abstractions of "Diaphaneitè." According to Pater, Wordsworth possessed transparency both of perception and of expression. Part of Wordsworth's genius was an "unusual sensibility, really innate in him, to the sights and sounds of the natural world," an "exceptional susceptibility to the impressions of eye and ear" and to the sensuous side of things generally. This resulted in an "intimate consciousness of the expression of natural things": to Wordsworth "every natural object seemed to possess more or less of a moral or spiritual life, to be capable of a companionship with man, full of expression, of inexplicable affinities and delicacies of intercourse." There was, in other words, a Hegelian correspondence between the structures of the mind and the rationality of nature; and "by raising nature to the level of human thought," Wordsworth gave it "power and expression" and exposed "the soul of apparently little or familiar things" (*App.*, 43–49). With this extraordinary sensitivity to the influences of nature Wordsworth, in his highest, most impassioned moods, combined "faultless expression":

> In him, when the really poetical motive worked at all, it united, with absolute justice, the word and the idea; each, in the imaginative flame, becoming inseparably one with the other, by that fusion of matter and form, which is the characteristic of the highest poetical expression. His words are themselves thought and feeling; not eloquent, or musical words merely, but that sort of creative language which carries the reality of what it depicts, directly, to the consciousness. (*App.*, 57–58)

In his use of the "real language of men," Wordsworth was "pleading indirectly for that sincerity, that perfect fidelity to one's own inward presentations, to the precise features of the picture within, without which any profound poetry is impossible" (*App.*, 51).

In "Wordsworth" Pater's aesthetics of expression convert the Victorian passion for sincerity from a moral to an aesthetic virtue, the writer's "absolute sincerity of feeling and diction" (*App.*, 64). Sincerity and transparency, then, amount to the same thing for Pater. In his essay on Rossetti he defines "transparency of language" as "the control of a style which did but obediently shift and shape itself to the mental motion" (*App.*, 206). Transparency, in other words, is the precise molding of language to the inner vision of the artist. This transparency Pater claims is "the secret of all genuine style, of all such style as can truly belong to one man and not to another" (*App.*, 207).

By the time Pater had completed the essays written for *The Renaissance* and "Wordsworth," the various features of his theory of expression were well formed: the ideal literary artist was a highly intellectualized, transparent receptor and reflector, who combined a highly refined, exquisitely tuned perceptual apparatus with a highly disciplined, subtle, precise instrument of language, with which he projected with absolute fidelity and sincerity his own private vision of the world, a vision composed of elements judiciously selected from the world without and fused with the coloring and preoccupations of his own individual temperament. Works by such artists exhibit the rare and desirable quality of the "intimate impress of an indwelling soul" (*Ren.*, 63).

The figures of both Pater's fiction and his criticism often exhibit either a highly refined perceptual apparatus or superb faculties for rendering the inner vision in external form with precision and integrity. Sometimes both the powers of reception and the powers of expression are found in the same individual, and these are our great artists. In addition to Wordsworth and the figures he examines in *The Renaissance*, Pater finds models of expressiveness in a number of writers, including Plato, Pascal, Sir Thomas Browne, Cardinal Newman, Flaubert, and D. G. Rossetti.

In *Marius the Epicurean* Pater endows his protagonist with his own expressive theory. In the chapter entitled "Euphuism," devoted to a discussion of style, Marius's friend Flavian explores the secrets of expression "through which alone any intellectual or spiritual power within one can actually take effect upon others." As a Latin Wordsworth, Flavian desired to promote the "colloquial idiom" in serious literature in order to reestablish "the natural and direct relationship between thought and expression, between the sensation and the term, and restore to words their primitive power," that is, their ideal transparency (*ME* 1:94–96). Later Marius adapted Flavian's stylistic insights for his own aesthetic and philosophical needs under a "New Cyrenaicism." In his attempt to arrest momentarily "something to hold by amid the 'perpetual flux'" of experience, he adopted as his goal, "To create, to live, perhaps, a little while beyond the allotted hours, if it were but in a fragment of perfect expression"; and to frame such perfect expression he would employ "the word, the phrase, valuable in exact proportion to the transparency with which it conveyed to others the apprehension, the emotion, the mood, so vividly real within himself." As a consequence of such an ideal, "a true understanding of one's self" would become the "first condition of genuine style" (*ME* 1:155), as it was the "first condition" of Pater's ideal critic in his "Preface" to *The Renaissance*.

The dualism of Pater's theory of expression and its emphasis on the inner vision of the artist reflect the movement of philosophy generally from pre-Kantian metaphysics of substance, which looked outward, or at least beyond the human mind, for its subject matter, to post-Kantian metaphysics of function, which turned philosophy inward to contemplate the mind itself. In this post-Kantian, relativistic world, the integrity of one's own personal vision had a new meaning and a new status. With a philosophy that located the structures of reality in the human mind and perceptual apparatus, Kant's Copernican revolution in epistemology had, among other things, opened the floodgates of introspection. This new orientation precipitated and fostered the growth of expressive theories throughout nineteenth-century Europe.

Pater's theory of expression informed all his writings, and in one form or another it has continued to inform much of modern literature. Many twentieth-century scholars and critics mistakenly have discounted expressive theories as belonging primarily to the nineteenth century and have emphasized Pater's contribution, in essays like "The School of Giorgione" and "Style," to the development of the more objective orientation of Modernist aesthetics. While Pater did move toward an objective orientation in his later essays, like his Modernist successors he never abandoned his expressive orientation. By focusing on Pater's theory of expression in "Giorgione" and "Style," important light can be shed on problems in these two influential essays, problems which have been largely misunderstood and which have persisted in their misconceived forms in Modernist aesthetics.

Along with the "Conclusion" and "Style" the opening of "The

School of Giorgione" (1877) is one of the most frequently anthologized pieces of Pater's writing, and it has become a major document of Modernist aesthetics, especially in its emphasis on technique, on the identity of form and matter (mentioned only briefly in "Wordsworth"), and on the tendency of all arts to aspire to the "condition of music." Upon closer inspection, however, it turns out that in "Giorgione" Pater's emphasis on technique is misleading, his discussion of the relations of form and matter is confused and inconsistent, and the real focus of these paragraphs is the continuing evolution of his Hegelian theory of expression.

Pater opens the essay by objecting to criticism like Ruskin's that deals only with what art addresses to the intellect to the neglect of the sensuous material of each art form. "All true aesthetic criticism," according to Pater, recognizes "that the sensuous material of each art brings with it a special phase or quality of beauty, untranslatable into the forms of any other." "Each art," he says, "has its own special mode of reaching the imagination, its own special responsibilities to its material." The criticism of painting, for example, requires attention to "inventive or creative handling of pure line and colour," what Pater calls "essential pictorial qualities" that appeal first of all to the senses. In this "primary aspect," Pater says, "a great picture has no more definite message for us than an accidental play of sunlight and shadow for a few moments on the wall or floor" (*Ren.*, 130–33). After defending the untranslatability of the sensuous materials of each of the arts, however, Pater then reverses himself when he says, "But although each art has thus its own specific order of impressions, and an untranslatable charm . . . yet it is noticeable that, in its special mode of handling its given material, each art may be observed to pass into the condition of some other art"; and particularly, "*all art constantly aspires towards the condition of music*" (Pater's emphasis) in its effort to obliterate the distinction between form and matter. The "mere matter" is "nothing without the form, the spirit, of the handling," which "should become an end in itself" (*Ren.*, 133–35).

If the essay stopped at this point, despite his inconsistency, there might have been less confusion, and Pater could have been declared more unequivocally the apostle of technique. But then Pater introduces a concrete illustration: "This abstract language becomes clear enough," he says, "if we think of actual examples." Pater's examples, however, only contradict his arguments about the primary sensuous materials of the various arts and obscure the issue of form and matter. "In an actual landscape," Pater begins his illustration,

> we see a long white road, lost suddenly on the hill-verge. That is the matter of one of the etchings of M. Alphonse Legros:[5] only, in this etching, it is informed by an indwelling solemnity of expression, seen upon it or half-seen, within the limits of an exceptional moment, or caught from his own mood perhaps, but which he maintains as the very essence of the thing, throughout his work. (*Ren.*, 135)

Notice that the focus here is not on the handling of sensuous materials, but on the "indwelling solemnity of expression." Pater mentions a particular effect of light, "a momentary tint of stormy light," but he is interested in it not because it appeals to sense, but because it has "a character which might well have been drawn from the deep places of the imagination" (*Ren.*, 135–36). Pater has little interest here in the formal mode of handling for its own sake; instead he would be, like Leonardo's Lady, a "diver in deep seas" who plumbs the depths of consciousness.

In "The Beginnings of Greek Sculpture" (1880) Pater is much more consistently interested in the sensuous materials, the ivory and gold ornamentations of early Greek craftsmanship, yet again not for their own sake but for the sake of "tracing what we call expression to its sources" (*GS*, 221).[6] As a Greek craftsman strove to "record what his soul conceived" in the sensuous forms and subject matter of his art (*GS*, 235), so the Venetian school of Giorgione presented only the spiritual essence of a landscape, "a country of the pure reason or half-imaginative memory" (*Ren.*, 137). Pater even preferred picturesque paintings of French riversides and Swiss valleys because the "mere topography, the simple material, counts for so little," and effects of light and shade can easily modulate it into "one dominant tone" expressive of the artist's mood and vision (*Ren.*, 136). The ideal elaborated here is not so much the fusion of form and matter as the transparent ex-

---

5. A contemporary of Pater and Slade Professor of Art in London.

6. Wollheim also recognizes that Pater was interested in the "surface qualities" of art works only insofar as they were expressive (167–69).

pression of the indwelling spirit of the artist, whose imagination provides, in Wordsworthian fashion, the "one dominant tone" for his landscape.

So when Pater says, "in the subordination of mere subject to pictorial design, to the main purpose of a picture, [Giorgione] is typical of that aspiration of all the arts towards music, which I have endeavoured to explain,—towards the perfect identification of matter and form" (*Ren.*, 142), he is misleading; for he has explained nothing of the sort. He has not discussed in his examples the interpenetration of subject matter with its organizing vision. What he has emphasized is the *subordination* of subject matter to the inner vision of the artist to the extent that the inner vision is transparently conveyed through the artist's handling of details of subject and technique; although precisely how this is done is never explained.

Since the opening paragraphs of "Giorgione" dwell on the technical handling of each art's sensuous materials, one would expect Pater to focus on this aspect in his own criticism of painting that follows—but he doesn't. Instead he mires himself in a discussion of the relations of form and matter in art, a discussion in which what he means by either form or matter is not readily apparent. One would expect *matter* to refer to the primary sensuous materials of the respective arts—but it doesn't. Instead, in a painting it refers, for example, to the particular scene of a landscape—"a long white road, lost suddenly on the hill-verge"—or in a poem, to the words addressed to the intelligence and dealing "with a definite subject or situation." In other words by *matter*, he means the subject matter, the "given incidents or situation" of a painting or poem "addressed to the mere intelligence," and not the sensuous raw material of the particular art form, such as line, color, or verbal rhythm. The word *form* is used in two different senses: first, as technique, the "mode of handling" that "should penetrate every part of the matter"; and second, as the "informing, artistic spirit," which also should penetrate the subject matter (*Ren.*, 135–37).

Pater's theoretical problems in "Giorgione" stem from his entanglement of expressive and formalist aesthetic criteria. He expounds a Romantic theory of expression based on Hegel's view of art as the sensuous manifestation of the Idea. Pater individualizes the Hegelian Idea and eliminates its absolute status by converting it to the artist's own inner vision or "scheme of the world." Then he makes this vision the formal element of art, the organizing force of the subject matter. This Hegelian intellectual element, and not technique, is what he means by "the form, the spirit, of the handling," which becomes, as it does with Hegel, "an end in itself." His analysis of the Legros landscape confirms this orientation. So from the point of view of Pater's expressive orientation, the artist's inner vision—not sense—is primary, while all the other elements infused with this vision are secondary. Form and matter do not "completely saturate each other," but form subsumes matter; and when Pater says art strives "to become a matter of pure perception," he does not mean sense perception but the intuitive perception of the artist's inner vision acting through the agency of the "imaginative reason." To put it another way, art becomes a matter of pure perception when it expresses with absolute transparency the indwelling spirit of the artist.

By identifying form with the underlying intellectual vision and content with the subject matter (the scene or incident), Pater has inverted Hegel's definition of content and form. For Hegel the absolute Idea provides the content and its sensible embodiment the form. Pater also has substituted subject matter for the sensuous mediums of the various arts. Nevertheless, in other respects, Pater's Hegelian orientation remains intact. As Hegel insists that "the sensuous aspect of a work of art has a right to determinate existence only in so far as it exists for the human mind" (48), so with Pater, despite his assertions to the contrary, the intellectual element remains primary. His analysis of the Legros landscape conforms exactly to Hegel's emphasis on the indwelling spirit of art, and the subordinate sensuous elements are important only insofar as they express that spirit. Hegel himself claims that a landscape painting is a work of art only by "virtue of the emotion and insight" of which it is a manifestation and that what makes something a work of art is the presence of mind. Pater's analysis of subject matter, in fact, may have come directly from the introduction to *The Philosophy of Fine Art*, in which Hegel says that in art the spiritual value of a human interest must attach itself to something like an incident, a character, or a plot and its resolution. This interest, according to Hegel, is exhibited "with greater purity and clarity" in art than in nature (39).

At the same time that Pater propounds an Hegelian expressive orientation by asserting the formal intellectual element, the inner vision of the artist, as "an end in itself," he continues to claim that the sensuous element in art is primary. But to focus on the sensuous elements themselves and their "creative handling," whether these elements are at the level of "pure line and colour" or at the level of subject matter, is to focus on the work itself and the technical arrangement and design of those sensuous materials. This orientation is not expressive, but objective in its emphasis on the work itself, and this is the orientation that most of Pater's twentieth-century readers have read into the Giorgione essay. Pater invites this reading by emphasizing the technical handling of the sensuous materials of art in his opening paragraphs, but Pater himself does not follow up on the implications of his language for an objective orientation; rather, he continues to expound his Romantic theory of expression, but partly in terms of a nascent, more objective theory. It is only in terms of his expressive orientation and its Hegelian bias, however, that "Giorgione" can be properly understood.

Pater's confusion over form and matter in art is not unique to the Giorgione essay. Nowhere does he contradict himself more than on this issue. The problem is not Pater's alone, however: the polemics of form and matter pervade Modernist aesthetics and are seldom satisfactorily expressed. Because we got into the mental habit of discussing form and matter as separate attributes of a single thing, we began to think that they were two different things. John Crowe Ransom's analogy of a poem to a house that has a logical structure separable from a local texture is a good illustration of this habit. Pater and his Modernist successors generally understood that form and matter were inextricably bound up with each other and that they could be separated only by the incomplete logic of language. Nevertheless, despite awareness of the inseparability of form and matter, in persistently trying to discuss them separately, Pater kept getting tangled up in the issue. Modernist writers and critics just as persistently entangled themselves in paradox and then solved the problem mainly by making paradox a virtue. Pater was prevented from a consistent articulation of the relations between form and matter partly because he confused two orientations on the issue and partly because, like Hegel, he never escaped the language of Platonic dualism.

Despite its theoretical shortcomings, "Giorgione" had a substantial impact on Pater's Modernist successors. His emphasis on technical skill and his own reputation for meticulous craftsmanship affected the next generation of English writers in the 1890s. Yeats has remarked on the impact of Pater's aesthetic philosophy on his friends in the Rhymers' Club and their consequent obsession with technique, even to the exclusion of intellectual content.[7] In their early works Yeats and Joyce both drew on Pater's stylistic experiments; and by the early decades of the twentieth century, Pater, along with other self-conscious aesthetic craftsmen like Flaubert and Mallarmé, had helped make the obsession with technique almost universal. In addition to Yeats and Joyce, such writers as Pound and Eliot continued to develop the objective orientation nascent in "Giorgione" by immersing themselves more fully than Pater in technical matters involving the sensuous materials of the various arts and by exploring in practice as well as theory the possibilities of transferring formal principles from one art to another.

So notwithstanding Pater's own limitations and confusion, "Giorgione" fostered some of the more successful Modernist experiments. For example, in "Giorgione," Pater took music, the expressive ideal of earlier German critics, modernized it by making its ideality rest on the more objective criterion of the fusion of form and matter rather than as the ideal vehicle for emotions, as the Germans saw it, and enthroned it as the perfect art form. Subsequently the "condition of music" as an aesthetic ideal inspired a number of attempts to apply formal musical principles to language and literature and even to imitate the effects of music in literature. The "Sirens" episode of Joyce's *Ulysses* is an extreme example of the latter, but the efforts of writers to find musical forms and principles to replace the worn-out, ill-fitting literary forms of previous centuries pervaded twentieth-century literature. Eliot, one of the most inveterate explorers of what music had to offer poetry, concluded that "the properties in which music concerns the poet most nearly, are the sense of rhythm and the sense of structure."[8] More generally, in advocating the ideal fusion of form and matter, Pater's "Giorgione" was one of the most important formulations of an aesthetic principle that resulted in virtually endless experi-

---

7. *Autobiographies*, pp. 302–4; *Essays and Introductions*, pp. 352–54; *The Oxford Book of Modern Verse*, pp. viii–xi; *Uncollected Prose*, 1:248–49, 266.

8. *On Poetry and Poets* (London: Faber and Faber, 1957), p. 38.

mentation and innovation to develop the unique, precisely appropriate formal structures to fit each subject matter to be expressed.

If Pater was not consistent on the issue of form and matter in
"Giorgione," he was at least faithful to his aesthetics of expression,
and he continued to develop them in his subsequent work, even to the
extent of broadening their application beyond the vision of an individual artist. Pater says in "Giorgione" that the principles enunciated
there apply to "all things that partake in any degree of artistic qualities, of the furniture of our houses, and of dress, for instance, of life
itself, of gesture and speech, and the details of daily intercourse"
(*Ren.*, 138). In "The Beginnings of Greek Sculpture" he attributes the
expressive function of art to myth. Instead of expressing the inner vision of an individual, myth expresses the vision of a people, who in
their myths "can but work outward what is within them" (*GS*, 212).
In *Plato and Platonism* philosophy is linked with art as the "eternal
definition of the finite" on the "infinite, the indefinite, formless, brute
matter, of our experience" (59–60). As with Hegel, so with Pater
both myth and philosophy express in their respective forms an indwelling spirit that is analogous to the cohesive and informing vision
an artist renders in the concrete matter of his art.

Pater's theory of expression culminates in his essay "Style" (1888).
Here Pater restates with more confidence and precision the expressive
ideal articulated eleven years earlier in "The School of Giorgione."
Like "Giorgione," however, "Style," with its invocation of Flaubert's
ideals of *le mot juste* and impersonality in art, has been considered a
major polemic in the cause of aesthetic formalism. Critics who have
insisted on the formalism of "Style," however, consistently have failed
to detect its primary expressive orientation, and they have been
puzzled by the emphasis of its well-known conclusion on matter over
form as the determining factor of great art. But if we view "Style" as
the climax and clearest exposition of Pater's expressive theory, these
difficulties evaporate, and Pater's alliance with Flaubert becomes more
the problem to be explained.

By the time he wrote "Style," Pater had equated beauty with truth
through his aesthetics of expression. "All beauty is in the long run,"
he says, "only *fineness* of truth, or what we call expression, the finer
accommodation of speech to that vision within" (*App.*, 10; Pater's emphasis). Pater supports this contention by drawing a distinction be-

tween positivistic, scientific fact and a post-Kantian *sense of fact*, by which he means a Wordsworthian representation of fact "as connected with soul, of a specific personality, in its preferences, its volition and power" (*App.*, 10). In this contrast between truth "as accuracy" and truth "as expression," the latter for Pater is the "finest and most intimate form of truth, the *vraie vérité*" (*App.*, 34).

To guard against the potential solipsism of truth as an expressive sense of fact, Pater offers a twofold check, one drawn from Hegel and the other from Flaubert. He insists that style is not a matter of "the subjectivity, the mere caprice, of the individual" (*App.*, 36) and that both the receptive capacity of the artist and his "talent of projection" can be judged against standards external to the individual mind. On one hand, the accuracy or justice of the artist's inner vision with respect to the world of experience he inhabits is somehow gauged by virtue of an innate, Hegelian correspondence between the structures of perception and the structures of what is perceived. On the other hand, Flaubert's ideal of *le mot juste* ensures the precisely transparent expression of that vision: Pater says, "The problem of style was there!— the unique word, phrase, sentence, paragraph, essay, or song, absolutely proper to the single mental presentation or vision within" (*App.*, 29). This precise mesh of terms to import is not a judgment of the writer alone; that a word "fits with absolute justice," says Pater, "will be a judgment of immediate sense in the appreciative reader" (*App.*, 33–34). Rigor is not a quality of Pater's logic in his analysis of these Hegelian and Flaubertian checks against solipsism, and his vagueness begs a number of crucial and complex questions; nevertheless, his concern with these checks serves as another illustration that he was far from the solipsism often associated with him.

Flaubert's notion of the impersonality of the artist, which Pater raises in "Style," appears to contradict the central thrust of Pater's theory of expression. If "style is the man," the expression of the most intimate recesses of his soul, it would seem that style is very personal. Not so, according to Pater: "If the style be the man," he says, "in all the colour and intensity of a veritable apprehension, it will be in a real sense 'impersonal'" (*App.*, 37). Pater derives this conclusion, however, from a passage on Flaubert he quotes from Guy de Maupassant, a passage that is somewhat at variance with his own theory of expression.

Styles (says Flaubert's commentator[9]), *Styles*, as so many peculiar moulds, each of which bears the mark of a particular writer, who is to pour into it the whole content of his ideas, were no part of his theory. What he believed in was *Style*: that is to say, a certain absolute and unique manner of expressing a thing, in all its intensity and colour. For him the *form* was the work itself. As in living creatures, the blood, nourishing the body, determines its very contour and external aspect, just so, to his mind, the *matter*, the basis, in a work of art, imposed, necessarily, the unique, the just expression, the measure, the rhythm—the *form* in all its characteristics. (*App.*, 36–37; Pater's emphases)

The definition of style in this passage as "a certain absolute and unique manner of expressing a thing" is consistent with Pater's aesthetics of expression, but the formulation of an organic relationship between form and matter shifts the orientation of Pater's theory: the form is no longer the artist's inner vision molding the matter of his perception but the form of the work as a whole that has structured and organized the matter of which it is composed. Whether the matter comes from the artist's inner vision or the external world or both is not clear. In any case, de Maupassant's passage does not substantiate Pater's statement about the impersonality of style in the sense that Pater has defined style, that is, as the expression of the inner vision of the artist. As in "Giorgione," Pater gets tangled in the shift of aesthetic orientations from the Romantic emphasis on the mind of the poet to the Modernist emphasis on the form of the work. Even though he helped pass on the new orientation to his successors, Pater was apparently unaware, as he used de Maupassant's passage to support his own expressive theory, that the ground had shifted under him.

Pater's lack of total awareness of the shifting aesthetic grounds and his inconsistent accommodation of Flaubert's objective orientation into his expressive theory were not necessarily disastrous to Pater or to the history of aesthetics. The adamant illusions of Modernist theorists and critics about objectivity, impersonality, and formalistic au-

---

9. Guy de Maupassant, in his "Gustave Flaubert: A Study."

tonomy were more pernicious. Pater's inconsistencies, on the other hand, had several advantages that restrained him from some of the excesses and rigidities of Modernist theory. First of all, Pater was much more sensible about the issue of impersonality in art than many of its later polemicists. Second, his inability to sacrifice successfully a Romantic emphasis on expression for a purely formal and objective orientation was intellectually more honest than the attempts of some of his Modernist successors to camouflage their own neo-Romantic aesthetics of expression with polemics about objectivity and impersonality. Finally, although he vacillated on the issue of form and matter (or perhaps because he vacillated on it), Pater did not in the end embrace a pure formalism that discounted the importance of the matter in aesthetic judgments.

Pater felt that total impersonality in art was no more possible than pure realism. Consistent with his expressive theory, he says, "The artist *will* be felt; his subjectivity must and will colour the incidents, as his very bodily eye *selects* the aspects of things" (*UE*, 108; Pater's emphases). This perceptive insight was ignored for a long time in the Modernist polemics of impersonality. While the author may disappear in his more obvious manifestations, such as an omniscient narrative voice, he is still omnipresent, even in his guise of a thoroughly distanced persona, in the less obtrusive authorial tasks of selecting, arranging, and coloring details and incidents.[10] Pater observed that even in *Madame Bovary* Flaubert did not manage to make himself disappear: "The author might be thought to have been completely hidden out of sight in his work," says Pater in his 1889 review of Flaubert's correspondence. "Yet even here he transpires, clearly enough, from time to time; and the morbid sense of life, everywhere impressed in the very atmosphere of that sombre history, came certainly of the writer himself. The cruelty of the ways of things—that is a conviction of which the development is partly traceable in these letters" (*UE*, 108). A few years later in his review of Prosper Mérimée's work, he quotes Flaubert's own awareness of the impossibility of total self-effacement in art: "It has always been my rule to put nothing of myself

---

10. For an extensive and complex discussion of impersonality in fiction, see Wayne Booth's *The Rhetoric of Fiction* (Chicago: University of Chicago Press, 1961).

into my works," he quotes Flaubert as saying, "yet I have put much of myself into them" (*MS*, 36). Even with very realistic art like Leonardo's or Raphael's, Pater maintains his Romantic emphasis by insisting that the artist will assert himself in a "transcript" of the "veritable data" of the world around him in accordance with the "embodiment of the creative form within him" (*MS*, 50).

The conflict between Pater's Romantic emphasis on expression and the more objective emphasis he assimilated from Flaubert has broad implications for the relations between nineteenth- and twentieth-century aesthetics. Notwithstanding Pater's inconsistent accommodation of Flaubert's objective orientation, that orientation does not in itself contradict Pater's expressive emphasis; it merely looks at the issue of form and matter from a different perspective. Likewise, the general shift in the focus of aesthetics from the mind of the artist to the work itelf does not deny the expressive theory, as the polemics of Modernists like Eliot might suggest, but simply looks at the whole artistic process from a different point of view. Thus the objective orientation of Pater's successors in the twentieth century did not reverse the Romantic aesthetic of expression but merely masked it with the new polemics of objectivity and impersonality. Joyce recognized the coexistence of these two orientations by practicing both in the extreme: the ideal of the artist standing aside from his work, "invisible, refined out of existence, indifferent, paring his fingernails," coexists with the autobiographical ideal enunciated by Stephen in his parable about Shakespeare in "Scylla and Charybdis." [11]

On the issue of form and matter Pater was never a strict formalist. In addition to his vacillation over the relative importance of form and matter, his emphasis on the artist's inner vision necessarily involves considerations other than formal, a necessity that led him, as well as some of his critics, into some confusion of formal and expressive criteria. At the end of "Style," for example, Pater's criteria for great art depend more on matter than on form: good art may be determined by the ideal fusion of form and matter represented by music, but the

---

11. *Portrait*, p. 215; the implications of "Scylla and Charybdis" for an autobiographical theory of art are discussed in my essay "*Ulysses* and the Pragmatic Semiotics of Modernism," *Comparative Literature Studies* 19 (1982): 164–74.

greatness of art, especially literary art, depends on "the matter it informs or controls, its compass, its variety, its alliance to great ends, or the depth of the note of revolt, or the largeness of hope in it." Given that the art is good, that is, characterized by "the absolute correspondence of the term to its import," it will be great art if it also contributes "to the increase of men's happiness, to the redemption of the oppressed, or the enlargement of our sympathies with each other, or to such presentment of new or old truth about ourselves and our relation to the world as may ennoble and fortify us in our sojourn here, or immediately, as with Dante, to the glory of God." A work will be great art if, in addition to expressing the artist's individual vision of a world in its precisely appropriate form, "it has something of the soul of humanity in it, and finds its logical, its architectural place, in the great structure of human life" (*App.*, 37–38).

Critics have claimed that this conclusion to "Style" contradicts the rest of the essay and the formalist implications of Pater's aesthetics generally.[12] It is not a contradiction, however, if we see the main thrust of Pater's aesthetics as expressive rather than formalist. The conclusion to "Style" continues to follow Hegel closely. As Hegel would evaluate art not solely on the "mere correctness" of the correspondence of its Idea to its sensuous manifestation but also according to the profound and universal human interests contained in the Idea, so Pater claims that great art expresses not just the inner vision of the artist in its precisely appropriate form, but the inner vision of a people or a civilization; it expresses a zeitgeist or the "soul of humanity."

---

12. Typical examples of this view are Harold Bloom, *Selected Writings of Walter Pater*, p. 125 n. 34, and René Wellek, *A History of Modern Criticism: 1750–1950*, (New Haven: Yale University Press, 1965), 4:395. The blindness of ardent formalists to Pater's expressive orientation is well illustrated by Wellek's comments on the concluding passages of "Style":

> There could not be a fuller and more explicit revocation of Pater's earlier aestheticism. It is a recantation at the expense of any unified, coherent view of art. It gives up the earlier insight into the unity of matter and form, divides and distinguishes them again, and either introduces a double standard of judgment or shifts the burden of criticism to the subject matter. Pater ends in a dichotomy destructive of his own insights into the nature of art.

In general Pater's formulation of an expressive theory has more in common with his twentieth-century successors than simply the continuation of the expressive orientation. Pater helped in several ways to make Romantic theories of expression more palatable for Modernist writers and critics. Despite his own inconsistencies on the relations of form and matter, he helped to shift the focus of expressive theories from the Romantic emphasis on the emotions of the artist to a more intellectualized inner vision of the artist. With the shift in orientation from expressive to objective, the scheme of a world, as well as aesthetic form, was sought in the work of art rather than in the mind of the artist; but the expressive function of art remains in either case.

This shift from personal emotion to individual visions of the world can also be traced at the philosophical level. Kant's *Critique of Judgment* associated art almost exclusively with the subjective faculties, an emphasis that encouraged the Romantic focus on pleasure and emotion. As the implications of post-Kantian philosophy were drawn out, however, art became less exclusively associated with pleasure and the emotions and more important as a valid mode of cognition, comprehending as well as apprehending experience and the world around us. Hegel placed art, along with philosophy and religion, in his realm of absolute spirit; Nietzsche made the artist over into a culture hero; Cassirer and the Marburg school elevated art to a valid mode of cognition, though still limited to intuitions of forms; and Nelson Goodman dissolved even these limitations, as art became a major mode of cognition, employing all the faculties of an integrated human organism. Joyce, especially in *Ulysses*, arrived at Goodman's position much earlier, as did a number of other artists inspired by Joyce's example and the age's evolving zeitgeist.

Three Modernist manifestos that reflect this shift in the expressive orientation between the nineteenth and twentieth centuries, a shift from an emphasis on the personal emotions of the artist to the artist's vision of experience and to the impersonal emotions in the work, are Conrad's Preface to *The Nigger of the "Narcissus"* (1897), Virginia Woolf's "Modern Fiction" (1919),[13] and Eliot's "Tradition and the In-

---

13. Although written in 1919, "Modern Fiction" was not published until 1925.

dividual Talent" (1919). Of the three, Conrad's Preface is the most Romantic in that it has shifted less toward the Modernist version of expressiveness than the other two, while Eliot's essay exhibits the most extensive movement of the three toward "objectivity."

In contrast to the outward-looking tendencies of Western thought before Berkeley, Hume, and Kant, Conrad's Preface accords with the dictates of post-Kantian and post-Romantic thought. It insists that "the artist descends within himself," that his truth is not the truth of philosophers and scientists who appeal to ideas and facts, but the "more permanently enduring" truth of intuition that appeals to temperament, emotion, and sense; "to our capacity for delight and wonder, to the sense of mystery surrounding our lives; to our sense of pity, and beauty, and pain." [14] So far this sounds solidly Romantic, with its emphasis on emotion and sublimity, as if it could have come from Wordsworth's Preface to *Lyrical Ballads*;[15] but there are some new emphases in Conrad's Preface that we do not find in Wordsworth's Preface. First, the emotions Conrad appeals to are not the personal emotions of the artist but the capacity for feeling in the reader. Art for Conrad is not the spontaneous overflow of powerful feelings but a crafted piece of work calculated to make the reader *see* by means of his temperament, emotions, and senses. Second, although art appeals, in Kantian fashion, to the capacities for pleasure and pain, its primary object is not pleasure, as it was for Coleridge, but truth: "art itself," says Conrad, "may be defined as a single-minded attempt to render the highest kind of justice to the visible universe, by bringing to light the truth, manifold and one, underlying its every aspect." This is the same kind of truth advocated by Yeats's attempt to capture in his metaphors "reality and justice." Such truth as this is much more appropriately achieved not by a Wordsworthian fountain of feelings but

---

14. All quotes and summaries of Conrad's Preface are taken from *The Nigger of the "Narcissus,"* ed. Robert Kimbrough, Norton Critical Editions (New York: W. W. Norton, 1979), pp. 145–48.

15. Ian Watt's detailed analysis, "Conrad's Preface to *The Nigger of the "Narcissus," Novel: A Forum on Fiction* 8 (1974): 101–15, reprinted in the Norton Critical Edition of *The Nigger of the "Narcissus,"* pp. 151–67, comments on the Wordsworthian analogy, as well as the Paterian echoes and other issues I deal with here.

through a Paterian emphasis on the writer's personal scheme of the world. To be fair to Wordsworth, he offered his own scheme of a world, and he recognized in his Preface that the mind of man was the fairest mirror of nature; but the preponderance of his polemical emphasis was on the personal feelings of the artist, an emphasis totally absent from Conrad's Preface.

A third new concern in Conrad's Preface is a preoccupation with form, craftsmanship, and the sensuous materials of the various arts, interests that Conrad expresses in terms closely resembling Pater's in his essay on Giorgione. In its effort to appeal to the senses, Conrad contends, art "must strenuously aspire to the plasticity of sculpture, to the colour of painting, and to the magic suggestiveness of music—which is the art of arts. And it is only through complete, unswerving devotion to the perfect blending of form and substance; it is only through an unremitting, never-discouraged care for the shape and ring of sentences, that an approach can be made to plasticity, to colour; and the light of magic suggestiveness may be brought to play for an evanescent instant over the commonplace surface of words." Although Conrad appears to borrow from "The School of Giorgione," he avoids the contradictions Pater entangled himself in: Conrad does not desert the sensuous materials of art for an intellectual, inner vision, nor does he expound on the inevitable paradoxes of form and matter. Conrad may have saved himself from contradiction only by the "magic suggestiveness" of brevity, which often conceals a multitude of a writer's confusions; but in any case, in both his Preface and in the practice of his early fiction particularly, he adhered closely to the principles of Pater's Modernist aesthetics.

Conrad's proximity to Pater's aesthetics is particularly evident in the passage that concludes his Preface, a passage that contains strong echoes of Pater's "Conclusion":

> To arrest, for the space of a breath, the hands busy about the work of the earth, and compel men entranced by the sight of distant goals to glance for a moment at the surrounding vision of form and colour, of sunshine and shadows; to make them pause for a look, for a sigh, for a smile—such is the aim, difficult and evanescent, and reserved only for a very few to achieve. But sometimes, by the de-

serving and the fortunate, even that task is accomplished. And when it is accomplished—behold! all the truth of life is there: a moment of vision, a sigh, a smile—and the return to an eternal rest.

Here Conrad captures Pater's evanescent moment of flux. Unlike Pater's disciples in the 1890s, who found in the "Conclusion" an authoritative rationale for art for art's sake, Conrad, like Yeats, retains Pater's own emphasis on art for the moment's sake, for the sake of the truth of the moment of vision.

Virginia Woolf also sees art as cognitive primarily, and its main purpose is to express the artist's vision of reality, the artist's scheme of the world. Her focus is not art for art's sake but "life itself," for "without life," she says, "nothing else is worth while."[16] And to find life, she insists, the artist must "look within."

Because Woolf sees life, in typical post-Kantian fashion, as inward, life lived not in an external world but in the inner realm of consciousness, she insists, even more than Conrad, that the techniques of the novel must be transformed in order to render truth in its new aspects. She rejects Wells, Bennett, and Galsworthy, and calls them materialists because they rely on the old Aristotelian conventions and categories of plot, comedy, tragedy, probability, and verisimilitude, conventions designed to convey an outward-looking vision of reality based on the old metaphysics of substance.[17] "Life is not a series of giglamps symmetrically arranged," she says; rather, "life is a luminous halo, a semi-transparent envelope surrounding us from the beginning of consciousness to the end." "Is it not the task of the novelist," she asks, "to convey this varying, this unknown and uncircumscribed spirit, whatever aberration or complexity it may display, with as little mixture of the alien and external as possible?" In her call for new conventions, like those used by Joyce, that would capture life "close to the quick of the mind," she echoes Pater's aesthetics of expression: "Any

---

16. All quotes and summaries of "Modern Fiction" are taken from *Collected Essays*, 2:103–10.

17. In *Substance and Function* (3–9) Cassirer identifies the central role Aristotle played in fostering the older metaphysics of substance, which heavily influenced the shape and character of his own *Poetics*.

method is right," she insists, "every method is right, that expresses what we wish to express, if we are writers; that brings us closer to the novelist's intention if we are readers."[18] She is interested in neither the artist's personal emotions nor in the external world of fact, but in experience perceived through consciousness, or, to put it in Pater's less sophisticated terms, in the writer's "sense of fact."

I do not mean to imply here that Conrad was not part of the Modernist revolution in literary technique. Clearly, works like *Heart of Darkness* and *Lord Jim* experiment with techniques to gain access to the dark, inner recesses of human consciousness and to convey them in a way that does not foreclose on the ultimate inconclusiveness of experience. I claim here only that Woolf's "Modern Fiction" articulates more consciously than Conrad's Preface the need to forge new techniques to convey a new vision of human nature, and that in doing this she articulates the Modernist fulfillment of Pater's aesthetics.

Eliot's "Tradition and the Individual Talent," written the same year as Virginia Woolf's "Modern Fiction," carries the objectification of Pater's expressive theory to its furthest point. "Tradition and the Individual Talent" was written in reaction to the cult of originality, spontaneity, and personality that the influence of Romantic poetry had spawned in some of Eliot's immediate predecessors. In the essay Eliot specifically attacks Wordsworth's definition of poetry as "emotion recollected in tranquillity," a formula Eliot understatedly characterizes as "inexact," because for him poetry is "neither emotion, nor recollection, nor, without distortion of meaning, tranquillity."[19] In contrast to Romantic emphases, Eliot claims that the artist has no personality or personal emotions to express but only a medium and common emotions. The important emotions for Eliot are not the poet's, as with Wordsworth, but the emotions *in the poem*. The poet is present only as a catalyst: without him the creative fusion of elements does not take place, but no part of his personal self becomes a part of the newly

---

18. In *The Absent Father: Virginia Woolf and Walter Pater* (New Haven: Yale University Press, 1980), Perry Meisel demonstrates that Woolf's critical essays are modeled on Pater's and based on his "criterion of expressiveness in art" (40).

19. *The Sacred Wood*, p. 58.

created compound. Eliot's polemics, of course, represent an impossible and rather mechanical ideal, and he by no means practiced what he preached. His own poetry is deeply emotional and personal, but it is masked by his highly intellectualized "objective correlatives."

Despite the extremity of Eliot's polemics of impersonality, they did complete a shift Pater had begun, a shift from the expressiveness of the author's personal emotions to the expression of emotion by the poem and a concomitant interest in the crafting of the poem, or as Eliot put it, in the intensity not of the emotions and components in the poet's mind, but in the "intensity of the artistic process, the pressure, so to speak, under which the fusion takes place" in the work itself.[20]

One remaining consequence of the expressive orientation in literature remains to be discussed. The post-Kantian revolution in aesthetics that accompanied the revolution in epistemology and laid the philosophical foundations for an expressive theory also encouraged an attendant autobiographical impulse that has inspired literary genius from Wordsworth to the present. As a result of the shift of philosophical focus inward on the mind and of aesthetic focus on the emotions, the nineteenth century abounded in autobiographies that became major works of literary art. Wordsworth, Coleridge, De Quincey, Carlyle, Newman, and Mill all wrote major autobiographical works; and if we use the term *autobiographical* more loosely, we could include most nineteenth-century writers. All of Pater's major writings, whether fiction or criticism, have a heavily autobiographical interest; they are laden with his own intellectual and emotional preoccupations, whose progress can be traced from the early to the later works. Because he could never be comfortable exposing his personal concerns in an openly autobiographical work, he veiled them, often thinly, in his fiction and in his critical studies of various artists.

In masking his autobiographical concerns in his fiction and criticism, Pater again provided a model for his Modernist successors. While most of the major nineteenth-century autobiographies were non-fictional prose works, Wordsworth, Carlyle, and Pater being the major

---

20. *The Sacred Wood*, p. 55.

exceptions, in the twentieth century more or less disguised personae replace the more obviously autobiographical selves of nineteenth-century nonfiction, and the autobiographical impulse was incorporated into fictional works of art, most blatantly by Joyce; but many others, such as Butler and Lawrence, fictionalized their autobiographies or at least drew heavily on autobiographical materials for their art. Whitman's *Song of Myself* and Lowell's *Life Studies* are only two major landmarks of an autobiographical tradition in American poetry that persists today.

The shift in the autobiographical mode from nonfiction to fiction accompanied the shift in the expressive orientation from an emphasis on personal emotion and the mind of the artist to the more objective orientation with its emphasis on the emotions, the vision of experience, and the fusion of form and matter *in the work*: instead of being expressed as a personal rendering of one's own history, the autobiographic impulse was expressed "objectively" in an "impersonal" work of art. For all their polemics about impersonality, many major Modernists left us autobiographical transcripts in fictional disguise. Eliot's poetry as a whole constitutes one of the most eloquent and moving spiritual autobiographies of the past two centuries, comparable in the depth of its personal vision to the great nonfictional autobiographies of the nineteenth century. Yeats and others have also recorded their own spiritual journeys in their art. Even Beckett, as Deirdre Bair's biography has demonstrated, etches his own deeply personal, spiritual struggle in his art.[21]

In the "Scylla and Charybdis" episode of *Ulysses* Joyce enunciates an autobiographical theory of art in Stephen's parody of nineteenth-century biographical criticism, in which he demonstrates that Shakespeare re-created his own life in his art. Joyce's parody, then, acknowledges while it mocks an important autobiographical tendency that dominates the literature of the nineteenth and twentieth centuries, including Joyce's own work. Pater, for his part, was as consciously aware as Joyce of this autobiographical tradition. In a book he was reviewing he quoted a concise formulation that characterizes the central

---

21. *Samuel Beckett: A Biography* (New York: Harcourt Brace Jovanovich, 1978).

expressive thrust of this tradition: "An artist is one who reproduces the world in his own image and likeness" (*UE*, 122).[22] These words and the implicit metaphor of the Divine Creation could well have come from "Scylla and Charybdis," where Stephen clearly links the artist's task with the original act of Creation and echoes Pater's "Conclusion" when he asserts that the artist creates his work in his own image: "—As we, or mother Dana, weave and unweave our bodies, Stephen said, from day to day, their molecules shuttled to and fro, so does the artist weave and unweave his image."[23] But the same use of the metaphor of Divine Creation can be traced back to Coleridge's Romantic definition of the imagination as "a repetition in the finite mind of the eternal act of creation in the infinite I AM."

---

22. The book was William Samuel Lilly's *A Century of Revolution* (London: Chapman and Hall, 1889), a Catholic critique of the French Revolution.

23. *Ulysses*, p. 194.

11 / ASCESIS

SINCE POST-KANTIAN thought focused on function rather than substance, it gave a new importance to formal considerations. Of all Kant's aesthetic criteria in his *Critique of Judgment*, the tenet of "purposiveness without purpose," the notion of a formal, internal purposiveness without any external purpose, was perhaps the most pervasive in Modernist poetics. The work of art was perceived as autotelic and autonomous; it was not answerable to any standards or criteria outside itself. This emphasis of Modernist aesthetics existed more in theory than in practice, and it was espoused more often by theorists than by artists, most of whom were well aware of the ties between their art and the world of experience. Nevertheless, the principles of formalism were propounded relentlessly during the first half of the twentieth century. In a sense it was the natural offshoot of a philosophy that focused on the forms of perception, but the emphasis on autonomy was more polemical than actual; it was a necessary counterforce to the older aesthetics of decoration and decorum (art as "What oft was thought, but ne'er so well Exprest") based on metaphysics of substance.

The new preoccupation with form in Modernist art, whether it derived from an emphasis on the autonomous, internal design of a work of art or from an interest in the formal powers of perception themselves, naturally led to an obsession with craft and technique and the attendant virtue of ascesis. A highly disciplined craftsmanship was necessary to achieve formal perfection, but it was also necessary to be obsessed with craft in order to retool literary production to create the vehicles for conveying new modes of vision in a new age. As the shield of Achilles expressed the epic vision of Homer's world, so the new vision emerging in the early twentieth century would require Hephaestus to retool his shop to produce the new armaments required by the soul for the inward spiritual and psychological adventures of modern heroes. Only a total commitment to the crafting of new forms of expression could have achieved the stylistic revolution necessary to convey the new epistemology. Once when asked his opinions about the war, Joyce replied that he was only interested in style. This remark suggests not so much a detached formalism, as his own awareness of the kind of total commitment necessary to forge the instruments of vision for a new age; for Joyce realized, as did Pater, that style, conceived as the instrument of vision, encompassed everything.

In one of the most astute assessments of Pater's impact on his twentieth-century successors, Germain d'Hangest credits him with the cultivation of a scrupulous aesthetic conscience that has become a permanent element of the modern literary consciousness. According to d'Hangest, Pater impressed upon succeeding generations of writers a more exacting sense of aesthetic responsibility that included the necessity to strive for formal perfection and to chisel language as precisely as marble or precious stones.[1] Combined with the influence of nineteenth-century French novelists, particularly Flaubert, Pater's emphasis on the formal perfection and precision of prose style was so effective that by the early twentieth century Pound was exhorting his fellow poets that poetry must be at least as well written as prose. The combined influence of Flaubert, Pater, and Pound on prose and poetry in the twentieth century produced an obsession with craftsmanship that effected one of the most sweeping stylistic revolutions in the history of the modern English language, a revolution that completed the shift begun by Wordsworth from the rhetorical traditions that dominated the first several centuries of modern English style to the chiseled perfection of actual speech patterns that prevails as the stylistic ideal of many writers today.

---

1. "La Place de Walter Pater dans le mouvement esthétique," *Études Anglaises* 27 (1974): 169–70.

Pater embodies the qualities involved in the scrupulous artistic conscience noted by d'Hangest in a single word—ascesis. Using *ascesis* not so much in the restricted modern sense of a religious asceticism but more in the broader sense of the original Greek meaning of exercise or practice in the pursuit of any goal, be it military, athletic, or scholastic, Pater applied the term on a number of different levels, including philosophical, cultural, and moral, as well as aesthetic. Regardless of the level of application, it always implied for Pater the qualities of order, restraint, discipline, and control. Rooted deep in Pater's sensibility, the principle of ascesis is evident from his earliest writing, and it is invariably an attribute of his fictional heroes and the artists he admires. Florian Deleal, Marius, and Marius's friend the Christian soldier Cornelius all exhibit it as a character trait; and Pater found it in such diverse artists as Raphael, Montaigne, Charles Lamb, Prosper Mérimée, Newman,[2] and above all in Flaubert, who became the model for Pater's mature conception of ascesis. Although the principle emerged as an element in Pater's aesthetics as early as "Diaphaneitè" and "Coleridge's Writings," it began to evolve into a major polemic only in later works such as "The Marbles of Aegina," *Marius*, "Style," and *Plato and Platonism*.

Before examining the operation of ascesis in Pater's aesthetics, it would help to establish both the larger context and the pervasiveness of the principle in Pater's thought and sensibility by observing its operation on the philosophical and cultural levels of Pater's weltanschauung. At these levels its operation is most evident in Pater's analysis of Greek philosophy and culture, where he posits a dialectical tension between Ionic and Doric influences. The Ionic impulse Pater associates with the centrifugal forces in culture and history, forces that incline toward freedom, variety, movement, individualism, and separatism. In philosophy the Ionic is associated with the Asiatic influence of Heraclitus and the perpetual, formless flux of the primal matter of human experience. In the arts the Ionic temperament manifests itself in the sensuous, chryselephantine materials of early Greek craftsmanship, de-

---

2. David DeLaura demonstrates the presence of Newman in Pater's ascetic ideal of style in "Some Victorian Experiments in Closure," *Studies in the Literary Imagination* 8 (1975): 19–35, and in "Newman and the Victorian Cult of Style," *The Victorian Newsletter*, no. 51 (1977): 6–10.

light in color, material, changeful form, restless versatility for its own sake, and delight in the endless play of undirected imagination. Grace, freedom, happiness, liveliness, and variety are the virtues most esteemed by the Ionic sensibility, which focuses, as in early Greek crafts, more on the physical and the lower forms of life, rather than on the higher ethical forms of human nature. Hephaestus, the lame smith of the gods, is the archetypal Ionic deity.

The contrasting Doric impulse Pater associates with the centripetal forces in culture and history that incline toward rational control, order, sanity, simplicity, and unity. The abstract philosophic calm of Parmenides provides the Doric counterforce to the Heraclitean flux. Doric art, such as Phidian sculpture and Greek tragedy, is characterized by formal control, restraint, and simplicity. It focuses less on the sensual, physical, and lower forms of life than on ethics, the inner world of thought and passion, and the revelation of the human body and soul. The chief Doric virtues are order, harmony, sanity, self-discipline, and dignity. Apollo is the archetype of the Doric temper.

It was not as the apostle of sense that Pater advocated ascesis, for he associated it almost exclusively with the intellect. In Pater's broader application it becomes virtually synonymous with the Doric impulse in Greek culture. Notwithstanding his empirical emphasis on the primacy of sensation, Pater's profoundest sympathies lie with the Doric, not the Ionic. He perceives the Doric elements of Greek culture as more highly developed and refined than the Ionic, a preference both intellectual and emotional, as evident in the following passage from "The Marbles of Aegina," in which he extols the ascesis of Apollo, whom he calls the patron of "*reasonable* music, of a great intelligence at work in art, of beauty attained through the conscious realisation of ideas" (Pater's emphasis):

> . . . in art also the religion of Apollo was a sanction of, and an encouragement towards the true valuation of humanity, in its sanity, its proportion, its knowledge of itself. Following after this, Greek art attained, in its reproductions of human form, not merely to the profound expression of the highest indwelling spirit of human intelligence, but to the expression also of the great human passions, of the powerful movements as well as of the calm and peaceful order of

the soul, as finding in the affections of the body a language, the elements of which the artist might analyse, and then combine, order, and recompose. (*GS*, 255)

Into the bewildering, dazzling Ionic world of Greek handicraft, according to Pater's analysis, the Doric influence "introduced the intelligent and spiritual human presence, and gave it its true value" (*GS*, 256).

Despite his preference for Doric ascesis, Pater recognized that both the Ionic and the Doric tendencies operated simultaneously in dialectical tension with each other at all levels of experience, and that perfection was "attainable only through a certain combination of opposites" (*PP*, 24), an ideal opposition Yeats later founded his entire aesthetic philosophy upon. Pater explains in *Plato and Platonism*, for example, that all philosophy aims "to enforce a reasonable unity and order, to impress some larger likeness of reason, as one knows it in one's self, upon the chaotic infinitude of the impressions that reach us from every side" (35–36). As philosophy attempts to impose some kind of rational order on the universe around us and within us, so moral discipline likewise imposes order on human lives, and the arts impose a formal order on their sensuous materials (36). At all levels the governing dialectical principle is the same, the "eternal definition of the finite, upon . . . the infinite, the indefinite, formless brute matter, of our experience of the world" (60).

For Pater Pythagorean philosophy was an ideal formulation of this eternal dialectic between Doric and Ionic. The musical order and harmony of Pythagorean doctrine and the "religious brotherhood" (*PP*, 56) it fostered answered perfectly to Pater's notion of ascesis. Pythagoras himself is described by Pater as a forerunner of Plato who, emerging out of the sensual flux of Ionia, "has, like the philosophic kings of the Platonic Republic, already something of the monk, of monastic *ascêsis*, about him" (*PP*, 58; Pater's italics).

Ascesis for Pater, however, was not renunciation, but disciplined reconciliation—not a hermit in a desert or mountain cave, but a unified sensibility struggling to forge a balanced and harmonized ideal in life and art. Pater, as we have seen, was repelled by what he considered the "perverse asceticism" of Pascal's last years—"his medieval or oriental self-tortures, all the painful efforts at absolute detachment"

(*MS*, 79). In *Marius* Pater's protagonist is likewise repelled by Marcus Aurelius's stoic self-abasement, his contempt for the body, his renunciation of life, and his indifference to the atrocities of the Roman Colosseum. For Pater moderation—moderation after the manner of Montaigne—was an essential attribute of ascesis, and any extreme of renunciation was excluded as firmly as any extreme of indulgence.

Pater's paragon of ascesis was Plato, not because he exercised any rigorous abnegation or self-denial as a sort of religious ascetic, but because, like Pythagoras, he perfectly fused the Ionic and Doric elements of his own thought and sensibility. In Pater's view Plato combined within himself a "naturally rich, florid, complex, excitable" Ionian sensibility with the Doric impulse toward order and ascesis (*PP*, 110). Being a lover of temperance (*PP*, 136), Plato allowed the "austere monitors" of his Doric impulse to "correct," without suppressing, "the sensuous richness of his genius" (*PP*, 145).

In his analysis of Plato's aesthetics Pater finds that the dry Doric beauty advocated by Plato was produced, like his own personality, by an "originally rich and impassioned" (*PP*, 281) nature disciplined and tempered by reserve, restraint, and control. Plato's aesthetics, like his philosophy, emphasized simplicity, austerity, harmony, symmetry, musical proportion, and an organic subordination of parts to the whole. The agent of this Doric ascesis is primarily the intellect: "Art, like law," says Pater, quoting Plato, "[is] a creation of mind, in accordance with right reason" (*PP*, 275). Pater identifies this intellectual element, this centripetal controlling force, with "manliness in art," which he explains as "a full consciousness of what one does, of art itself in the work of art, tenacity of intuition and of consequent purpose, the spirit of construction as opposed to what is literally incoherent or . . . works at random" (*PP*, 280–81). In such art, according to Pater's Plato, form and meaning will fuse perfectly.

Although Pater recognizes that Plato's aesthetics are closely allied with his ethics (*PP*, 282), he characterizes this alliance in such an 1890s fashion as to make Plato into an aesthete. According to Pater, Plato "anticipates the modern notion that art as such has no end but its own perfection" (*PP*, 268). Pater's Plato is an advocate of art for art's sake who insists, as Oscar Wilde does, that life imitates art and not the reverse (as Plato actually insists in Book X of the *Republic*). But then Pater, who seems to prefer the arguments of Book III of the

Republic, reverses himself on the autonomy of art when he says that "it is life itself, action and character, [that Plato] proposes to colour" through art: "to get something of that irrepressible conscience of art, that spirit of control, into the general course of life, above all into its energetic or impassioned acts" (*PP*, 282). In other words, what art has to teach life is ascesis. "Art, as such, as Plato knows," Pater says somewhat paradoxically, "has no purpose but itself, its own perfection. The proper art of the Perfect City is in fact the art of discipline" (*PP*, 275–76). Pater says that what Plato really meant, when he makes him utter Gautier's famous phrase about "art for art's sake," is that the artist should stick to his own business and confine himself to his own special artistic gift. This is Pater's interpretation of Plato's advice to artists that they limit themselves to what they know; and for Pater it is the art of discipline, of the centripetal, formal power of Doric ascesis, that the artist knows and teaches.

The force of Pater's views on Plato was not lost on his successors. Later, in criticizing Pater, Eliot uses a similar argument—that the only valid meaning of "art for art's sake" must be for "the artist to stick to his job." "The right practice of 'art for art's sake,'" Eliot insists, "was the devotion of Flaubert or Henry James."[3] Eliot refused to accept the moral and ethical application of Pater's argument, but on aesthetic grounds, he found it very sound. As d'Hangest notes, one of Pater's most enduring bequests to twentieth-century writers is his emphasis on the quest for formal perfection in art and on a rigorous and ascetic devotion to that quest.

For Pater, as for Eliot and other modernists, Flaubert was the great "martyr of literary style" (*App.*, 27), and ascetic discipline in the craft of writing became ultimately associated with him as well as with Plato. Flaubert, in fact, replaced Goethe and Wordsworth as the guiding literary genius of Pater's imagination in his last years. With his essay on style and two reviews of Flaubert's correspondence, all published within a year in 1888 and 1889, Pater became one of the first major conduits of Flaubert's aesthetics into English letters.[4] In "Style" Pater quotes Flaubert's ascetic advice to a writer, "The only way not to

---

3. *Selected Essays*, pp. 392–93.

4. "Style" first appeared in *Fortnightly Review* in December 1888; the review of the first volume of Flaubert's letters (1830–1850) appeared in the *Pall Mall Gazette* in

be unhappy is to shut yourself up in art, and count everything else as nothing" (*App.*, 28).

Although Flaubert was a major presence in Pater's imagination during the last several years of his life, Flaubert only reinforced an existing ascetic impulse in Pater's own sensibility and inspired him to develop it as a major tenet of his aesthetics. As early as "Coleridge's Writings" Pater announces an ascetic ideal that informs his description of the artistic process as a successive refining away of all that is extraneous to the finished work, as a sculptor carves from a block of marble, a metaphor for composition that Pound often employed. "By exquisite analysis the artist," according to Pater, "attains clearness of idea, then by many stages of refining clearness of expression. He moves slowly over his work, calculating the tenderest tone, and restraining the subtlest curve, never letting his hand or fancy move at large, gradually refining flaccid spaces to the higher degree of expressiveness" ("CW," 122).

As with the Doric impulse in philosophy and culture generally, Pater associated the ascetic, formal impulse in art primarily with the intellect, not with sense and emotion. In the Coleridge essay he compares the refining process of the artist to that of a scientist constantly clearing the organs of observation and perfecting his analyses (108); and as science "begets an intellectual finesse" (131), so art affords "the spectacle of supreme intellectual dexterity" (122). Later in *Greek Studies* Pater refers to the operation of ascesis in the sensuous world of craftsmanship and design as the "rational control of matter everywhere" (221). There are the usual contradictions on this issue: ascesis manifests itself in the logical structure or rational design of art, but it is intuitive and organic as well; and Pater's characteristic confusion over what constitutes form and what constitutes matter and how they are related also infects his discussion of ascesis. Neveretheless, despite some contradiction and confusion, the preponderance of Pater's argument identifies ascesis with the intellectual and the formal in the artistic process.

In contrast to the intellectual quality of *mind* in art, Pater posits the

---

August 1888; and the review of the second volume of letters (1850–1854) appeared in *The Athenaeum* in August 1889.

quality of *soul*, and to this quality he assigns attributes usually named in accordance with a Romantic vocabulary that many of his Modernist successors rejected, attributes identified by such terms as inspiration, ineffable, immediate sympathetic contact, electric affinity, and infinity. A faculty of choosing and rejecting operated in the realm of soul as in the realm of mind, but in the realm of soul the faculty was intuitive and unconscious rather than conscious craftsmanship; and the unity it produced was a unity of atmosphere rather than of design, an atmosphere characterized perhaps by a certain color or perfume rather than a definite form. The early Yeats attempted a number of these atmospheric works in both prose and verse before he became aware of the new impulse abroad toward precise form. Although Pater saw the necessity for both mind and soul in art, his Modernist successors, such as Hulme, found the Romantic qualities of soul to be only so much "circumambient gas." So what Pater passed on to his Modernist descendants was primarily the intellectual discipline of ascesis.

Ascesis is also a central tenet in "Style," one of Pater's most influential essays. Here the emphasis on intellect remains, along with the metaphor of sculptural refinement. As Pater links ascesis in *Plato and Platonism* with conscious, purposeful construction, what he calls "manliness in art," so in "Style" he links it to what he calls the masculine scholarly conscience. "The literary artist is of necessity a scholar," claims Pater, "for the material in which he works is no more a creation of his own than the sculptor's marble" (*App.*, 12). The scholarly conscience must master the laws of language that the creative faculty may exploit them to the utmost. Such exploitation is not license, however; rather it involves restraint and renunciation. It is the freedom of the musician who has mastered his instrument only through rigorous discipline. The scholarly conscience is no pedant, but one who exhibits, in the freedom with which he moves within his medium, a mastery of the rules of that medium (*App.*, 12–14). The scholar in the artist is not so much interested in neologisms or archaisms as in "the finer edge of words still in use" (*App.*, 16). A style governed by such a conscience will be, like Flaubert's, "utterly unadorned," devoid of decoration, free of all "surplusage," which the writer will dread as a runner dreads it on his muscles. "For in truth," Pater concludes with a restatement of the process of refinement from

the Coleridge essay, "all art does but consist in the removal of surplusage, from the last finish of the gem-engraver blowing away the last
particle of invisible dust, back to the earliest divination of the finished
work to be, lying somewhere, according to Michelangelo's fancy, in
the rough-hewn block of stone" (*App.*, 19–20).

There are obvious theoretic difficulties with Pater's analogy of refining a literary work out of the potentially infinite resources of language, a preexistent semiotic system, to carving a gem or a statue out
of a preexistent, finite block of matter that has no prior semiotic value.
But if we can ignore these difficulties, we can find beneath them
an early formulation, based on the model of Flaubert, of the spare,
sinewy ideal that informs Modernist style, and of the difficulties associated with that style. Pater says:

> Self-restraint, a skilful economy of means, *ascêsis*, that too has a
> beauty of its own; and for the reader supposed [who also has a
> scholarly conscience] there will be an aesthetic satisfaction in that
> frugal closeness of style which makes the most of a word, in the ex-
> action from every sentence of a precise relief, in the just spacing out
> of word to thought, in the logically filled space connected always
> with the delightful sense of difficulty overcome. (*App.*, 17)

This aesthetic pleasure also applies to the structure of a work: "One
of the greatest pleasures of really good prose literature," Pater contends, "is in the critical tracing out of that conscious artistic structure,
and the pervading sense of it as we read." This "kind of constructive
intelligence," Pater claims, is "one of the forms of imagination" (*App.*,
24–25). Thus Pater anticipates both the stylistic rigor of Modernist
writing and the aesthetic pleasure that the reader of difficult Modernist works experiences participating in that rigor.

One of the primary aesthetic consequences of Paterian ascesis is
unity. Fostered by the masculine scholarly conscience, unity is the ultimate goal of the refining process of choosing and rejecting, and its
rigor matches that of choosing *le mot juste*. A rigorous ascesis, in
other words, is enforced at every level—"the phrase, the sentence, the
structural member, the entire composition, song, or essay." The "logical coherency" of a work of art should be evident, Pater says, "not
merely in the lines of composition as a whole, but in the choice of a

single word." This unity is not imposed mechanically but is organic; it involves, Pater says, "development or growth of design, in the process of execution, with many irregularities, surprises, and afterthoughts; the contingent as well as the necessary being subsumed under the unity of the whole." Under such unity, a work will be "true from first to last to that vision within," and the conclusion will be foreseen long before the work is finished (*App.*, 22–23).

By the time he wrote "Style" Pater had overcome his earlier compunctions about organicism that he had expressed in the Coleridge essay. Pater's organicism appears to be little more than a restatement of the Romantic version adapted somewhat to his own vocabulary and intellectual orientation, but what is unique about it is the rigor it acquires under his principle of ascesis. The architectural unity Pater envisions is that of "a single, almost visual, image, vigorously informing an entire, perhaps very intricate, composition" (*App.*, 23).

In "Shakespeare's English Kings," an essay written the year after "Style," he expresses this ascetic ideal of unity more fully. The essay focuses on *Richard II*, and it compares the play favorably to the ideal condition of music elaborated in the Giorgione essay, with its goal of presenting "one single effect to the 'imaginative reason.'" The form of *Richard II*, according to Pater, approaches the unity of a musical composition, "of a lyrical ballad, a lyric, a song, a single strain of music." Pater argues that if lyric poetry is to be considered the highest form of literary art because it preserves, "in spite of complex structure," a perfect "unity of impression," the unity of a "single passionate ejaculation," then "it follows that a play attains artistic perfection just in proportion as it approaches that unity of lyrical effect . . . all the various expression of the conflict of character and circumstance falling at last into the compass of a single melody, or musical theme." With lyric unity the centripetal forces overpower the centrifugal: "There must always be," says Pater, "a sense of the effort necessary to keep the various parts from flying asunder" (*App.*, 202–3). He eloquently concludes the essay with a panegyric to his ascetic ideal:

> As, historically, the earliest classic drama arose out of the chorus, from which this or that person, this or that episode, detached itself, so, into the unity of a choric song the perfect drama ever tends to return, its intellectual scope deepened, complicated, enlarged, but

still with an unmistakable singleness, or identity, in its impression on the mind. Just there, in that vivid single impression left on the mind when all is over, not in any mechanical limitation of time and place, is the secret of the "unities"—the true imaginative unity—of the drama. (*App.*, 203–4)

This ascetic ideal for lyric unity in drama, which Pater would substitute for the old Aristotelian unities, had a profound impact on the poetic drama of Yeats,[5] which in turn influenced Eliot's plays. Eliot also seems to have read Pater's "Shakespeare's English Kings," since he took a line from it, somewhat altered and disguised, for his "Prufrock." Moreover, the passage he took the line from also contains the informing conception of Prufrock as a transplanted Richard II.[6]

Although Pater seldom achieved his rigorously ascetic ideal in his own rather elaborate and ornate art, in *Plato and Platonism* he does give us, in one of the few really effective visual images in his writing, an excellent example of his Spartan taste: "Lenten or monastic colours, brown and black, white and grey," he says, "give their utmost value for the eye . . . to the scarlet flower, the lighted candle, the cloth of gold" (282). Economy and intensity of focus, then, are achieved by

---

5. See my "Paterian Aesthetics in Yeats's Drama," *Comparative Drama* 13 (1979: 33–48; reprinted in *Drama in the Twentieth Century*, ed. Clifford Davidson, C. J. Gianakaris, and John H. Stroupe (New York: AMS Press, 1984), pp. 125–40.

6. The relevant passage from "Shakespeare's English Kings" is:

No! Shakespeare's kings are not, nor are meant to be, great men: rather, little or quite ordinary humanity, thrust upon greatness, with those pathetic results, the natural self-pity of the weak heightened in them into irresistible appeal to others as the net result of their royal prerogative. (*App.*, 199)

The royal prerogative referred to here is the eloquent speech Shakespeare gave his kings. Compare this passage with the line from "Prufrock," "No! I am not Prince Hamlet, nor was meant to be," and the fact that Prufrock's plight is made so poignant only by virtue of his own eloquent self-pity, his heightened awareness of his own frailty in the face of the "overwhelming questions" that confront him. Two critics who have noted this borrowing of Eliot from Pater are Robert F. Fleissner, " 'Prufrock,' Pater, and Richard II: Retracing a Denial of Princeship," *American Literature* 38 (1966): 120–23, and Monsman in "Pater and His Younger Contemporaries," p. 9.

paring away all that does not serve to set the main subject in sharp relief.

Pater's rigorous ideal of ascesis was not always salutary in its effects; it fostered in Yeats, for example, the formal perfection of short intense works over longer, more ambitious ones. It did not preclude variety and complexity in art, however; and it did not prescribe a spare Spartan ideal such as a single scarlet flower against a monastic gray background, even though this may have been Pater's own taste. Ascesis can account for the style of Henry James as well as Hemingway, for Joyce as well as Yeats. Pater himself says that Flaubert's ideal of *le mot juste*, the absolute accordance of expression to idea, justifies while it safeguards many different kinds of style: "Say what you have to say," Pater insists, "in the simplest, the most direct and exact manner possible, with no surplusage:—there, is the justification of the sentence so fortunately born, 'entire, smooth, and round,' that it needs no punctuation, and also (that is the point!) of the most elaborate period, if it be right in its elaboration" (*App.*, 34–35). Pater practiced what he preached in this regard, for his own manuscript drafts are largely unpunctuated, yet his sense is almost always clear.[7] Joyce actually achieved this unpunctuated ideal masterfully in the "Penelope" episode of *Ulysses*; and many of his elaborate parodies in that book can also be reconciled with Paterian ascesis as being "right" in their elaboration. In these parodies the nature of the elaboration itself conveys its own significance; or, as a post-Modern critic might say, the discourse itself is its own story.

Pater even allows for the coexistence of different styles in the same work: "The blithe, crisp sentence, decisive as a child's expression of its needs, may alternate with the long-contending, victoriously intricate sentence." He continues with a description that captures the functional ascesis of his own best prose or of Henry James's intricate periods: "The sentence, born with the integrity of a single word, relieving the sort of sentence in which, if you look closely, you can see much contrivance, much adjustment, to bring a highly qualified matter into

---

7. By the time Pater's essays reached print, however, often they were atrociously punctuated, as in the passage cited about unpunctuated prose.

compass at one view" (*App.*, 23). Such a form of stylistic elaboration, however complex or intricate, would preserve the "vivid single impression left on the mind" that his ascesis demanded.

The ascetic precision of Pater's stylistic ideal attempts to rival the language of science and even assimilates some of its vocabulary, a process already under way generally in Victorian England. "The literary artist, therefore, will be well aware of physical science," Pater predicts, "science also attaining, in its turn, its true literary ideal" (*App.*, 16). Pater anticipates here the accommodation with the standards of precision and the vocabulary of science attempted by structuralist and poststructuralist literary criticism. He is also incorporating into his own aesthetic Flaubert's hope for a reunification of art and science. Pater once quoted from Flaubert's letters, "In proportion as it advances, art will be more and more scientific, even as science will become artistic. The two will rejoin each other at the summit, after separating at the base" (*UE*, 113). This reunion was also part of the Modernist program. Despite the polemics of writers like Yeats and a number of others, Modernism was not a wholesale rejection of the scientific world view. Flaubert's hope for the unity of art and science informed his own aesthetic, which in turn was assimilated, along with many of its affinities with the scientific sensibility, by many of the antiscientific polemicists. Unlike many of his contemporaries, Joyce was well aware of the importance of the scientific sensibility to the modern artist, and he embodies it in Leopold Bloom, who, symbolically at least, impregnates it into the artistic sensibility of Stephen Dedalus. Joyce thereby achieves the reconciliation prophesied by Flaubert.

Flaubert's ideal of *le mot juste*—"the one word for the one thing"— provided Pater with his model of scientific precision in literary art. This notion of precision is a much more suitable application of the scientific spirit to literature than the attempts of some contemporary criticism to ape the technical hardware of scientific jargon. Pater's temperament restrained him from pursuing the scientific rigor of Hegel's philosophy, a false rigor camouflaged by an obscure style and a technical vocabulary, according to Walter Kaufmann,[8] but one that

---

8. *Discovering the Mind: Goethe, Kant, and Hegel* (New York: McGraw-Hill, 1980), 1:210–11, 258, 267.

has nevertheless been absorbed into neo-Hegelian, post-Modern criticism.

Despite Pater's flirtation with scientific method, whether under the influence of his early positivism, Hegel, or Flaubert, he does not confuse art and science; and, more than any pseudoscientific jargon, Pater's own association of ascesis with intellectual rigor and structural logic appropriately adapts the scientific spirit to art and aesthetics. Pater refers to this scientific quality of literature as "the necessity of *mind* in style" (Pater's emphasis), by which he means "that architectural conception of work, which foresees the end in the beginning and never loses sight of it, and in every part is conscious of all the rest, till the last sentence does but, with undiminished vigour, unfold and justify the first" (*App.*, 21). This passage very accurately captures the conscious architecture of many Modernist works. Eliot's *Four Quartets* is an obvious example of such a conscious construction where on both the artistic and metaphysical levels the end is in the beginning and present throughout:

> And the end of all our exploring
> Will be to arrive where we started
> And know the place for the first time.

Eliot executes this architectural scheme, based in part on the pattern of Hegelian dialectic, by having the final metaphor of the poem, the tongues of pentecostal flame infolded into the petaled crown of a rose, unfold and justify "with undiminished vigour" the mysterious rose-garden scene that opens the poem.

As with other principles of his own aesthetics, Pater endows his protagonist in *Marius the Epicurean* with the monastic devotion of the artist to his craft. Under the inspiration of the literary fervor of his friend Flavian, Marius envisions his own nascent literary vocation as "a kind of sacred service to the mother-tongue." In Flavian's literary program, Marius construes a "theory of Euphuism" that awakens the "literary conscience" to "forgotten duties towards language." Flavian's program to revitalize with a judicious injection of colloquial idiom a language that had become "barbarously pedantic" and artificial was undoubtedly modeled on the Wordsworthian revolution in language; but it also anticipates the rejuvenation of common speech, what Pater calls asserting the "rights of the *proletariate* of speech," in Modernist literature (*ME* 1:94–97; Pater's emphasis).

Pater's own preciosity of language was hardly in the vanguard of this revolution, but the early euphuism of the "Conclusion" and the Mona Lisa passage was tempered in the direction of speech in later works such as *Plato and Platonism*, written primarily as lectures. This is yet another example of Pater announcing precepts of style that were left to his successors to implement.

Other "forgotten duties towards language" revived by the literary conscience awakened by Pater can be found throughout Modernist literature. For example, Pater's exhortation in *Marius* and later in "Style" (*App.*, 13–14) that it is the duty of the literary artist to establish and maintain the highest standards of language becomes part of the conscience of the "familiar compound ghost" Eliot creates in "Little Gidding" as his literary ancestor, a ghost who expresses their shared responsibility "to purify the dialect of the tribe." Another duty Pater identified in Flaubert and passed on to his successors was that of extending the limits of language (*UE*, 109–10), a duty executed in much of the formal and stylistic experimentation of Modernist writing, the most extreme of these attempts being *Finnegans Wake*. In general, behind Ezra Pound's exhortation to his contemporaries that poetry must be as well written as prose lie the model of Flaubert and Pater's ascetic ideal of style.

Conclusion /
From Principles to Praxis:
Joyce's *Portrait*

To TEST the validity of my claims that Pater formulated a substantial portion of the Modernist literary program and that Modernist aesthetics and techniques can be accounted for largely in terms of the two major philosophical traditions of the nineteenth century, this chapter will examine Joyce's *A Portrait of the Artist as a Young Man*, recognized by most as an indisputably Modernist work, from the perspective of the principles developed in the preceding chapters. If my claims are valid, this exercise should shed some new light on *Portrait* and suggest the degree of explanatory power inherent in the paradigm of Modernism I have constructed here from Pater's texts.

A traditional source study could point to various kinds of testimony about Pater's influence on Joyce: for example, to Joyce's ownership of copies of *The Renaissance* and volume 1 of *Marius the Epicurean* (both in later editions of 1911 and 1912),[1] to the long passages from *Marius* and *Imaginary Portraits* that Joyce copied into his notebooks,[2] to specific mentions of Pater or allusions to him in Joyce's

---

1. Richard Ellmann, *The Consciousness of Joyce* (New York: Oxford University Press, 1977), p. 123.

2. William York Tindall, Introduction to *Chamber Music*, by James Joyce (New York: Columbia University Press, 1954), p. 23 n.2.

writing,[3] or to Joyce's use of specifically Paterian ideas, attitudes, images, or stylistic techniques that could be found either in Pater's own texts or in those of his disciples, such as Wilde, George Moore, and Yeats. While the conclusions one could draw from such an inquiry would undoubtedly be interesting, they would suffer from the usual limitations of source studies, and I do not focus on this kind of evidence here. As a study in cultural confluence rather than literary influence, my inquiry will focus less on uniquely Paterian items in an inventory of Joyce's texts than on the allegiance of Pater and Joyce to a common intellectual paradigm.

Pater's career-long goals substantially exceeded his description of his own effort in *Marius* to characterize a "religious phase possible for the modern mind" (*Ltrs.*, 79). His writing as a whole explores how a "modern mind" might accommodate itself to intellectual culture generally, especially art, religion, and philosophy (Hegel's triad of absolute spirit). In this endeavor Pater succeeded admirably, for he provided his successors in the British aesthetic tradition, including many of the early Modernists, with a model for an aesthetic sensibility and an intellectual temper that addressed the needs of serious artists confronted with the revolutionary developments of post-Kantian thought, developments that had substantially altered the perception and understanding of experience.

The degree to which Pater fulfilled the role of precursor for Joyce can be suggested by a number of striking similarities in their intellectual and aesthetic tempers, similarities that, from my point of view, derive not so much from any specific influence Pater might have had on Joyce as from the general conceptual paradigm they shared. George Russell once complained, after Joyce had informed him that "he abhorred the Absolute above everything else," that Joyce "was infected with Pater's Relative."[4] Russell's remark reminds us that Joyce was as

---

3. See, for example, *The Critical Writings of James Joyce*, ed. Ellsworth Mason and Richard Ellmann (London: Faber and Faber, 1959), pp. 71, 78, 182, 202; James Joyce, *Ulysses* (New York: Random House, 1961), p. 422; and *Finnegans Wake* (New York: Viking, 1958), pp. 104–5 (and possibly 125, 398).

4. *The Workshop of Daedalus: James Joyce and the Raw Materials for* A Portrait of the Artist as a Young Man, ed. Robert Scholes and Richard M. Kain (Evanston: Northwestern University Press, 1965), p. 165.

enamored as Pater of the disinterested intellectual finesse of the relative spirit and of its power, as Pater put it, of "fixing delicate and fugitive details," of rendering a "more exact estimate of the subtlety and complexity of our life." The young Joyce also accepted Pater's ideal of transparence for style—"a style which did but obediently shift and shape itself to the mental motion" (*App.*, 206)—and he endorsed Pater's judgment that prose was the most appropriate verbal medium for the modern mind to capture its never-ending dialogue with itself, in all its intricate pathways of error, toward some tentative affirmation. Yeats, for example, reports the young Joyce as saying that "he had thrown over metrical form . . . that he might get a form so fluent that it would respond to the motions of the spirit."[5] The epiphany was one of the prose techniques Joyce developed to capture the fleeting moment in a complex, relativistic world.

Joyce not only embraced a relativistic universe, but like Pater he also was determined to make the best of it. Stephen's affirmations of experience in *Portrait*, Bloom's kissing of Molly's rump, and Molly's final series of *yeses* all suggest that in the intellectual temper of "Sunny Jim," as Joyce was called in his youth,[6] we have a reincarnation of the sunny skepticism of Montaigne that Pater portrayed in *Gaston de Latour*.

As with Pater, Joyce's skepticism and relativism did not foreclose on the possibilities of transcendent or at least quasi-mystical experience. They were both fascinated by Neoplatonists like Giordano Bruno, and Stephen's epiphanies on the strand in both *Portrait* and *Ulysses* share some of the mystical quality of Marius's experience in "The Will as Vision." Both Joyce's and Pater's renderings of mystical experiences, however, are carefully circumscribed: Marius quickly retreats to the relativistic world of the senses, and Stephen's visions, while borrowing their character from the ecstasies of the mystics, are

---

5. Richard Ellmann, *The Identity of Yeats* (New York: Oxford University Press, 1964), p. 86.

6. Richard Ellmann, *James Joyce* (New York: Oxford University Press, 1982), p. 26. Joyce once said to his brother Stanislaus, "Isn't my mind very optimistic? Doesn't it recur very consistently to optimism in spite of the trouble and worry I have?" (*The Dublin Diary of Stanislaus Joyce*, ed. G. H. Healy [Ithaca: Cornell University Press, 1962], p. 68; reprinted in *The Workshop of Daedalus*, p. 235).

clearly aesthetic and psychological rather than religious. At one point in *Stephen Hero* Joyce has Stephen deny that there is anything mystical at all in his writings and theories (81);[7] and like Marius, after he has had his vision Stephen remains immersed in the ordinary world. In short, both Pater and Joyce demythologize the mystical experiences of their protagonists and treat them more symbolically and psychologically than as actual transcendent experiences. Although Joyce liked to use the Nietzschean metaphor of the god-like artist repeating for eternity the original act of creation, he was well aware that the worlds he constructed with words were ultimately unmoored, floating, like the Blooms' bed, through the infinite void of the universe.

Joyce also shared Pater's interest in philosophy and his appetite for the most current ideas,[8] and neither used ideas as a systematic set of truths or beliefs but rather applied them in a strictly functionalist manner to organize and heighten our understanding of experience. Once when asked about Vico's theories of history, Joyce said, "I don't know whether Vico's theory is true; it doesn't matter. It's useful to me; that's what counts."[9] The views of Christianity held by Pater and Joyce also reflect their functionalist perspective. They both rejected the Christianity of their youth only to return to it later not as a religious system of belief but as a profound interpretation of human experience. Joyce borrowed extensively from Catholic doctrine and liturgy for many of the structural devices in his fiction. For Joyce as well as Pater, philosophy and religion served less to establish truth or belief than to temper the individual spirit and enhance its understanding of itself in its physical and mental environment.

In his passion for philosophical ideas Joyce satisfied better than Pater himself Pater's own criteria for the appropriate modern attitude toward such ideas—that they be treated with a certain amount of levity and unconcern and not taken too seriously. Joyce, in fact, was capable of a good deal more levity with ideas than Pater, who was always somber and sober about them despite his disclaimers and lack

---

7. Page references to *Stephen Hero* are to the Theodore Spenser edition (New York: New Directions, 1963).

8. *The Workshop of Daedalus*, pp. 198, 232.

9. *Portraits of the Artist in Exile: Recollections of James Joyce by Europeans*, ed. Willard Potts (Seattle: University of Washington Press, 1979), p. 207.

of commitment to them. Marius and Stephen both are characterized partly by the philosophers they entertain; but Pater's depiction
of Marius's engagement of Heraclitus or Aristippus, while detached,
lacks Joyce's irony in his depiction of how Stephen employs Aristotle
and Aquinas. Joyce's levity and irony is, as I noted at the outset, what
makes his texts particularly resistant to the traditional type of influence study.

The pose of a detached, world-weary aesthetic observer was another important quality of the intellectual tempers of Pater and Joyce.
Both were known for their reserve and aloofness. Pater's reserve and
aloofness, however, took the form of shyness; whereas Joyce's, at least
in his early Dublin days, took the form of arrogance—what Magee
and Gogarty called a "seedy hauteur."[10] Both Pater and Joyce endowed their protagonists with this detachment: as Marius remains
aloof from others, avoids all extremes of emotion, and eschews entanglement with earthly love in favor of a more idealized love of art, so
Stephen remains aloof from family, schoolmates, and girlfriends, feels
incapable of the passions of love or hate, and gravitates naturally toward cool, lucid indifference. In *Portrait* Joyce's narrator tells us that
Stephen "chronicled with patience what he saw, detaching himself
from it and testing its mortifying flavour in secret" (67).[11] In the end
Stephen, like Marius, rejects everything else for art. This indifference
toward the world around them was justified partly for both Joyce and
Pater by the notion of art as an ideal and privileged mode of experience that either enabled all other experience or subsumed all other
experience under it.

Thus while both Pater and Joyce present us with highly intellectualized sensibilities, neither is an absolutist in any sense; they both
embrace an intellectual world that is subjective, skeptical, and relative, and they restrict the operations of ideas to a finite world. Partly
because Pater had preceded him with an intellectual disposition similar to his own, Joyce could assume without much comment an intellectual position that several decades earlier Pater felt compelled to
argue.

---

10. *The Workshop of Daedalus*, pp. 197, 214.

11. Page references are to James Joyce, *A Portrait of the Artist as a Young Man*
(New York: Penguin, 1976).

As striking as these similarities of aesthetic sensibility and intellectual temper appear, we must turn to an analysis of *Portrait* itself to determine the full significance of the Modernist paradigm I have constructed from Pater's texts, for in addition to providing a model for the intellectual life that was acceptable to a modern mind, this paradigm also accounts for the aesthetic and structural principles that inform the novel.

What we witness in Joyce's novel is the transformation of a world view into radically new fictional structures and techniques. *Portrait* exhibits all the elements of the Paterian paradigm I have identified here—the tightly controlled subjective point of view, the distance and irony of a skeptical relativism, a functionalist perspective toward the products of the human intellect, the dialectic of sense and spirit in the pursuit of a unified sensibility, the privileging of aesthetic experience in that pursuit, an expressive orientation toward the creative process, and an awareness of the ascetic devotion necessary to forge new techniques appropriate to a new vision of experience. Even Joyce's use of the Daedalus myth, with the implied notion of Stephen as a reincarnation of Daedalus or Icarus, anticipates the more full-blown historical idealism of *Ulysses*, where notions of zeitgeist and metempsychosis operate more obviously.

If my analysis of Joyce's *Portrait* appears to say less about Pater than one would expect in a traditional influence study, I can only reply that the look and feel of the paradigmatic method I employ here differs significantly from that of ordinary source studies. In particular, the nature of the demonstration differs. My method makes no attempt to establish historical chains of influence between Pater and Joyce by proving that Joyce took this or that idea from Pater or his followers, or that his understanding of British and German philosophers derived primarily from Pater. While I find the major features of the Modernist paradigm in Pater's texts, once the paradigm has been constructed, there is little methodological justification for insisting on a specifically Paterian presence in Joyce's texts that cannot be demonstrated convincingly. Where Joyce might have picked up any specific idea is irrelevant to my argument. So when I refer frequently to Hegel in this chapter, I am not claiming that Joyce read Hegel or that he knew Hegel through Pater, but only that he was using ideas that have been associated prominently with Hegel, and, by implication, that Pater was a primary conduit for those ideas into the English aesthetic tradition.

The relationship of *Portrait* to the Modernist paradigm we find in Pater's texts can be established if we organize the analysis around three issues crucial to an interpretation of the novel: (1) Stephen's aesthetic theory; (2) the dialectical structure of the novel; and (3) the "expressive" orientation of *Portrait* and its aesthetics.

STEPHEN'S AESTHETIC THEORY

ALMOST WITHOUT exception, analyses of Stephen's aesthetics have focused on their relation to Aristotle and Aquinas, even though the most astute of them have been careful to point out how Stephen distorts their ideas.[12] When critics have looked beyond Aristotle and Aquinas, they have related Stephen's theories to fin-de-siècle aesthetics and have not looked much beyond the milieu created by Flaubert, Gautier, Pater, and Wilde, among others.[13]

This concern with Aristotle and Aquinas and with Joyce's more immediate aesthetic milieu has obscured for decades the prominent role played by the German idealists in the aesthetics of Stephen and Joyce. Most of Stephen's arguments in his discourse with Lynch emerge from the matrix of Romantic aesthetics, but the closest analogues to those arguments are not to be found in writers like Wilde and Gautier but in the original German sources for fin-de-siècle aesthetics. Stephen's invocation of Aristotle and Aquinas notwithstanding, his aesthetics, like Pater's, are derived from Kant and Hegel in both their general orientation and their specific details.

While Kant's theories appear to have reached Joyce through Coleridge, the nature of his exposure to Hegel is more complex and less conclusive. A few words can be said, however, about what was available to Joyce between 1898, the year he entered University College,

---

12. See, for example, William T. Noon, S.J., *Joyce and Aquinas* (New Haven: Yale University Press, 1957), pp. 45–56, and Maurice Beebe, "Joyce and Aquinas: The Theory of Aesthetics," in *Joyce's Portrait: Criticisms and Critiques*, ed. Thomas E. Connolly (New York: Appleton-Century-Crofts, 1962), pp. 272–89.

13. See, for example, Haskell M. Block, "The Critical Theory of James Joyce," *Journal of Aesthetics and Art Criticism* 8 (1950): 172–84, reprinted in *Joyce's Portrait*, ed. Connolly, pp. 231–49; and James H. Druff, Jr., "The Romantic Complaint: The Logical Movement of Stephen's Aesthetics in *A Portrait of the Artist as a Young Man*," *Studies in the Novel* 14 (1982): 180–88; and Dolf Sörensen, *James Joyce's Aesthetic Theory: Its Development and Application* (Amsterdam: Rodopi, 1977), p. 11.

and 1914, the year he finished *Portrait*. First of all, turn-of-the-century aesthetics were thoroughly inoculated with German philosophy, particularly Hegel's. Earlier in the century, British philosophy had begun to assimilate German philosophy. Stirling's *The Secret of Hegel* appeared in 1865 and William Wallace's *The Logic of Hegel* in 1874. Caird's books on Kant (1877) and Hegel (1883) appeared shortly thereafter. Bosanquet's influential translation of the Introduction to Hegel's *Philosophy of Fine Art* appeared in 1886 and his Hegelian *A History of Aesthetic* was published in 1892 and again in 1904. A French translation of Hegel's aesthetics was also available, Bénard's *Cours d'esthétique* (1840–52). By the 1870s the influential group of neo-Hegelians had formed at Oxford, including Wallace, Caird, Benjamin Jowett, T. H. Green, Richard Lewis Nettleship, F. H. Bradley, and Pater himself. Beyond the translations and commentary on Hegel, neo-Hegelianism was also widespread in Britain and Europe through the works of Nietzsche and Wagner. In short, Hegelian dialectics were everywhere during the formative years of Joyce's intellectual life.

The literary climate in Dublin around the turn of the century was also profoundly Hegelian. Pater had introduced Hegelian aesthetics into the British literary tradition by the 1860s, and in the generation before Joyce, which founded the Irish literary establishment, Hegelian aesthetics had received eloquent articulation in the works of Yeats and Wilde. Joyce was particularly fascinated by Yeats's early prose stories "The Tables of the Law" and "The Adoration of the Magi";[14] these stories, along with other essays and stories Yeats wrote around 1900, are heavily imbued with the Neoplatonic prophecy that the human soul is evolving into a realm of pure spirit, a prophecy that would have found authoritative sanction in Hegel's evolutionary idealism.[15]

---

14. Richard Ellmann, *Eminent Domain: Yeats among Wilde, Joyce, Pound, Eliot, and Auden* (New York: Oxford University Press, 1967), pp. 30, 34–35, 42. Joyce called "The Adoration of the Magi" "a story which one of the great Russians might have written" (*Critical Writings*, p. 71).

15. "The Tables of the Law," for example, evokes the heretical prophecy of Joachim of Flora that "the Kingdom of the Father was past, the Kingdom of the Son passing, and the Kingdom of the Spirit yet to come. The Kingdom of Spirit was to be a complete triumph of the Spirit, the *spiritualis intelligentia* he called it, over the dead letter" (*Mythologies* [London: Macmillan, 1959], p. 296). Hegel's notion of absolute spirit updates Joachim's prophecy and endows it with a foundation in logic.

That Joyce was familiar with Hegel's aesthetics from his undergraduate days has been established by Jacques Aubert's *Introduction a l'esthétique de James Joyce*,[16] the only treatment of Joyce's and Stephen's aesthetics that goes significantly beyond Aristotle, Aquinas, and the fin-de-siècle milieu. Aubert's detailed study of Joyce's early essays and notebooks attributes his knowledge of Hegel primarily to indirect sources such as Bosanquet's work and Butcher's commentary on Aristotle's *Poetics*. There are many passages, however, in the early essays and notebooks and in *Stephen Hero* and *Portrait* that are closer to Hegel's own arguments than to the interpolations of his commentators.

Joyce's Trieste library also contained a number of books either by figures prominent in the German aesthetic tradition or by figures influenced by them. His library had volumes by Lessing, Goethe, Schopenhauer, Nietzsche, Wagner, Renan, Pater, and Yeats.[17] Of course Joyce's reading was not limited to books he could afford to own in the early indigent years of his career. In any case, Aubert's study indicates that Joyce was familiar with German philosophy when he was a student in Dublin and that when he was in Paris during 1902 and 1903 he was reading more than Aristotle and Aquinas.

Joyce's preoccupation with the human spirit made the German Idealist tradition his most logical source for philosophic support, and his heavy dependence on dialectical structures, particularly in *Portrait*, *Ulysses*, and *Finnegans Wake*, is our warrant that directly or indirectly he drew extensively from the Idealists. We also have the testimony of Stanislaus Joyce for his brother's interest in the most current thought, and during Joyce's apprentice years up to the completion of *Portrait* aesthetic thinking was dominated by the Germans, particularly Hegel and his followers.

In Stephen's discourse on aesthetics with Lynch the importance of the epistemology and aesthetics of German idealism, especially Hegel's, is clearly evident once we look beneath the blind of Aristotle and Aquinas. Like the philosophy of German idealism, the central thrust of Stephen's aesthetics is epistemological, and like his Romantic predecessors, his focus is not on an abstract definition of beauty but on

---

16. Paris: Didier, 1973.
17. Ellmann, *The Consciousness of Joyce*, pp. 97–134.

the psychology of creation. Like Kant, Stephen concludes that "the first step in the direction of truth is to understand the frame and scope of the intellect itself" and that "the first step in the direction of beauty is to understand the frame and scope of the imagination, to comprehend the act itself of esthetic apprehension" (208). This same epistemological orientation informed Pater's aesthetics, for example, in his "Preface" to *The Renaissance* when he says "in aesthetic criticism the first step towards seeing one's object as it really is, is to know one's own impression as it really is" (*Ren.*, viii).

Stephen attributes this epistemological focus to Aristotle ("Aristotle's entire system of philosophy rests upon his book of psychology," he says [208]), but his focus reorients the outward-looking Aristotelian metaphysics of substance in terms of an inward-looking, post-Kantian metaphysics of function. Stephen himself recognizes the necessity for this reorientation in the case of Aquinas: "So far as this side of esthetic philosophy extends," he says, "Aquinas will carry me all along the line. When we come to the phenomena of artistic conception, artistic gestation and artistic reproduction I require a new terminology and a new personal experience" (209).

Precisely how Stephen moves from Aquinas to his "new" (by which he means German) terminology and experience is evident if we look at the center of Stephen's aesthetics constituted by what he calls the "necessary phases of artistic apprehension." These phases, according to Stephen, correspond to the "qualities of universal beauty" Aquinas identified as *integritas*, *consonantia*, and *claritas*, terms that Stephen translates as wholeness, harmony, and radiance. Despite the scholastic source of these terms, Stephen explains them in terms of Hegel's dialectical analysis of sense perception, with each quality corresponding to each of the three phases of dialectic. To illustrate his analysis Stephen tells Lynch to look at a basket. In the first stage of perception, according to Stephen, the mind

first of all separates the basket from the rest of the visible universe which is not the basket. The first phase of apprehension is a bounding line drawn about the object to be apprehended. An esthetic image is presented to us either in space or in time. What is audible is presented in time, what is visible is presented in space. But, temporal or spatial, the esthetic image is first luminously apprehended as selfbounded and selfcontained upon the immeasurable background of space or time which is not it. You apprehend it as *one* thing. You see it as one whole. You apprehend its wholeness. That is *integritas*. (212; Joyce's emphases)

In the second phase of apprehending a thing, Stephen says,

you pass from point to point, led by its formal lines; you apprehend it as balanced part against part within its limits; you feel the rhythm of its structure. In other words the synthesis of immediate perception is followed by the analysis of apprehension. Having first felt that it is *one* thing you feel now that it is a *thing*. You apprehend it as complex, multiple, divisible, separable, made up of its parts, the results of its parts and their sum, harmonious. That is *consonantia*. (212; Joyce's emphases)

Critics who have approached these passages from the perspective of Aristotle and Aquinas have not been able to explain a number of Stephen's points satisfactorily, including his epistemological orientation, his isolation of the thing perceived in space and time, and his distinction between apprehending it as *one* thing and apprehending it as a *thing*. If we look at these passages with reference to Hegel, however, all these points are accounted for. Indeed, most of Stephen's argument here resembles Hegel's in his section on sense perception in the *Phenomenology of Spirit*.[18]

In the *Phenomenology*, like Kant before him and Stephen after him, Hegel argues that "before we start to deal with . . . the actual cognition of what truly is, one must first of all come to an understanding about cognition" (46).[19] As Stephen would isolate the aesthetic object in space and time, Hegel also follows Lessing and Kant in say-

18. I make no specific claims here for direct access by Joyce to the *Phenomenology*, but if he did not have direct access either in the original German or in translation, his indirect source must have remained close to Hegel's original text.

19. Page references to Hegel's *Phenomenology of Spirit* are to the translation by A. V. Miller (New York: Oxford University Press, 1977).

ing that we must take any object of knowledge in "the twofold shape of its being, as 'Now' [i.e., in time] and as 'Here' [i.e., in space]" (59–60). For Hegel the total perception of an object takes place in three stages or "*distinct moments of apprehension*" (74; Hegel's emphasis). In the first stage Hegel says that we "become aware of the Thing as a *One*" and "preserve the self-identity and truth of the thing, its being a One" (72; Hegel's emphasis). This corresponds to Stephen's *integritas*, the apprehension of the basket as "*one* thing." The second moment for both Hegel and Stephen involves the analysis of the initially perceived oneness into its various properties. These properties for Hegel are not attributes of the thing but of perception; for example, he says that color, taste, and shape lie in perception and only "seem to be properties of the Thing" (72). The essence of a thing lies in the "*subsistence of the many diverse and independent properties*" (73; Hegel's emphasis), and this determinateness "constitutes the Thing's essential character" (75). This stage corresponds to Stephen's *consonantia*—seeing the basket as a *thing*.

Stephen's analysis inconsistently retains Aristotle's penchant for analyzing things in terms of constituent parts instead of in terms of qualities of perception, but otherwise Stephen follows Hegel's line of thought. In particular, common to both Hegel's and Stephen's analyses are the isolation of the thing in space and time and the distinction between the thing as One and the thing as constituted by its various properties or parts, with this distinction constituting the essential difference between the first and second stages of apprehension.

Stephen's third phase of *claritas* or radiance corresponds to the final stage of Hegel's dialectic of sense perception, which is constituted by a simultaneous recognition or synthesis of both the unique oneness of a thing and its differentiation or dismemberment into the multiplicity of universal properties that determine it. In this third stage the initial intuitive perception of oneness combines with analytic reflection to constitute what Hegel calls the concrete universal, that is, the object of sense understood. Stephen characterizes this third phase in terms of Hegelian necessity as the "only synthesis which is logically and esthetically permissible. You see that it is that thing which it is and no other thing" (213).

Stephen offers what appears to be an original insight into medieval philosophy when he says that the *claritas* of Aquinas is "the scholastic *quidditas*, the whatness of a thing" (213).[20] Stephen's *quidditas*, however, is more a quality of perception than of the thing itself. Consequently both the literal meaning of *quidditas* (i.e., whatness) and the concept it refers to is closer to Hegel's term *Dingheit*, or "thinghood," which appears prominently in a summary of the three stages of sense perception in the *Phenomenology* (73). For Hegel *Dingheit* is achieved in the third stage of dialectic, that of the concrete universal.

In Stephen's analysis this third moment of *quidditas* constitutes the essence of artistic apprehension, that is, the apprehension by the mind of the artist (as opposed to the reader or viewer of art). Apparently this is also what Stephen means by epiphany in *Stephen Hero*, where epiphany, *quidditas*, and *claritas* are equivalent (and therefore redundant) terms (213). In *Portrait* only *quidditas* and *claritas* remain as the names for the third phase of apprehension, which Stephen characterizes as follows:

> This supreme quality is felt by the artist when the esthetic image is first conceived in his imagination. The mind in that mysterious instant Shelley likened beautifully to a fading coal. The instant wherein that supreme quality of beauty, the clear radiance of the esthetic image, is apprehended luminously by the mind which has been arrested by its wholeness and fascinated by its harmony is the luminous silent stasis of esthetic pleasure. (213)

In this passage Stephen has adapted Hegel's concrete universal to aesthetic service and identified it through Shelley with the Romantic imagination, but its dialectic roots in Hegel—its fusion of wholeness with the harmony of diverse parts—remain intact.

Stephen, of course, greatly simplifies Hegel's dialectical analysis, and I have alluded here only to those elements in Hegel's analysis of sense perception that appear in Stephen's discourse. Despite his oversimplification and his inconsistent substitution of substantial parts for perceptual qualities, it is clear nevertheless that while Stephen may have taken his terms from Aquinas, the pattern of his analysis is Hegelian.

---

20. Noon, pp. 49–53; Beebe, "Joyce and Aquinas: The Theory of Aesthetics," in Connolly, pp. 284–88.

Stephen's linking of perception and the artistic imagination is not unique; it is characteristic of Romantic aesthetics generally. We have already seen how Hegelian phenomenology informs Pater's aesthetics. In fact, Stephen's analysis of *integritas, consonantia,* and *claritas* resembles the parable of the shell in *Plato and Platonism,* where Pater renders ordinary perception in terms of the three stages of Hegel's dialectic. We can also go back to Coleridge's definitions of the primary and secondary imagination (also derived from the Germans) where the creative secondary imagination is characterized as differing only in degree and mode of operation from the primary imagination, which he calls the "prime agent of all human perception."

After laying the epistemological foundations for his aesthetics, Stephen then builds a specifically literary edifice upon them—his lyric-epic-dramatic progression of the arts. Various attempts have been made to relate these three forms to Aristotle and Aquinas, but William Noon suggests the closest analogue when he cites Hegel's progession of symbolic-classic-romantic from the Introduction to *The Philosophy of Fine Art.*[21] Noon's suggestion, however, leads to an even closer analogue, for Stephen's analysis of lyric, epic, and dramatic art closely resembles Hegel's analysis of the literary arts in terms of these three traditional forms at the end of *The Philosophy of Fine Art.* Stephen does not follow Hegel's scheme exactly, and Hegel is not as rigid as Stephen about the necessary progression from one form to another.[22] Also, Stephen changes Hegel's order from epic-lyric-dramatic to lyric-epic-dramatic (a modification Wagner also employed),[23] and he reverses the qualities Hegel attributes to the epic and

---

21. Noon, p. 54. Noon also suggests Schelling's lyric-epic-dramatic schema, but Schelling's characterization of each mode differs significantly from that of Hegel and Stephen.

22. Hegel saw the later stages of civilization as more conducive to the lyric and the drama than the relatively less developed stages that produced the epic. He also saw the dramatic as presupposing both the epic and the lyric mode (250). Thus his progression is epic-lyric-dramatic. Page references to Hegel's *The Philosophy of Fine Art* are to volume 4 of the Osmaston translation.

23. In "Wagner, Joyce, and Revolution," forthcoming in the *James Joyce Quarterly,* Vicki Mahaffey argues for Wagner's *The Art-Work of the Future* as the direct source for Stephen's lyric-epic-dramatic progression; but I fail to find in Wagner's account the details from Stephen's discourse that can be found in Hegel's analysis of the three forms.

the dramatic. Stephen's analysis also focuses on the aesthetic image, whereas Hegel focuses on intellectual content (the Idea). These modifications, however, constitute the extent of Stephen's originality.

Hegel's criteria for classifying the three forms of literary art derive from his definition of art as the sensuous manifestation of the Idea. Art, according to Hegel, mediates between the world of sense and the world of thought; and poetry (by which he means the literary arts generally) combines the sensory appeal of the plastic arts with the life of the mind. He says that poetry maintains "a mediate position between the extremes of immediate objectivity [that is, the immediate objectivity of sense perception, as in the plastic arts] and the inner life of feeling and thought" (99). Each of the three literary forms in turn is determined by how its contents (from the realm of Idea) are expressed: in the epic they are expressed in terms of external events, in the lyric in terms of the inner consciousness of the poet/persona, and in drama in terms of the conflict between the consciousness of the protagonist and the events or consciousnesses external to him. Thus for Hegel the epic is the most objective form, the lyric the most internal or subjective, and the dramatic is a synthesis of the objective and the subjective.

Stephen likewise defines these three literary forms not as genres but in epistemological terms, or, more specifically, in terms of the dialectical relations between the aesthetic image, the artist, and others. "The image," Stephen says, "must be set between the mind or senses of the artist himself and the mind or senses of others." Given this, Stephen concludes that "art necessarily divides itself into three forms progressing from one to the next": "the lyrical form, the form wherein the artist presents his image in immediate relation to himself; the epical form, the form wherein he presents his image in mediate relation to himself and to others; the dramatic form, the form wherein he presents his image in immediate relation to others" (213–14).

Stephen's focus on the artist's image here simplifies and tightens his analysis considerably over Hegel's. Hegel's discussions of the epic, lyric, and dramatic modes refer to the artist and to the poetic or dramatic persona interchangeably and inconsistently; at times the content is related to the poet, at other times to the reciter of a poem or to the persona speaking in the poem or play. By viewing all three forms in terms of the artist's relation to the image he projects, Stephen avoids some of the pitfalls and complications attendant on Hegel's analysis.

Like Pater, Stephen has no sympathy with Hegel's absolutes, and he converts Hegel's emphasis on the absolute idea as the content of art to an emphasis on the artist's individual vision. Stephen speaks not of the ideational content of each form but of how the artist presents "his image." But despite Stephen's psychologizing of Hegel's absolute idea, his notion of the artist's image is still indebted to Hegelian analysis and its general orientation toward art. This image is presumably the artist's rendering of *quidditas*, that moment of inspiration when the total significance of a thing flashes before his imagination. But Stephen may also mean, as he says in *Ulysses*, that in art the artist re-creates his own image, he fathers himself, and like God he begets himself in his own offspring (194, 197, 208). In this case "his image" means *the image of himself*, or perhaps more precisely, the image of the contents of his own soul or inner being, what Pater called the "intimate impress of an indwelling soul" (*Ren.*, 63). Stephen's "image" then, is still essentially the Hegelian Idea, but reduced from the absolute to the finite and rendered in terms of individual psychology.

If we turn to the individual literary forms, we find that, while Stephen alters Hegel's scheme and exchanges the qualities of epic and dramatic, his analysis of each of the three forms is very close to Hegel's. Stephen says, "the lyrical form is in fact the simplest verbal vesture of an instant of emotion, a rhythmical cry such as ages ago cheered on the man who pulled at the oar or dragged stones up a slope. He who utters it is more conscious of the instant of emotion than of himself as feeling emotion" (214). Hegel sees the lyric mode as much more self-conscious than does Stephen, but otherwise very similar. For Hegel the lyric is "the direct outcry of the soul" (155);[24] its content takes the form of the conscious life of the poet, and it expresses the poet's moods, passions, feelings, and reflections. "The lyric poet," says Hegel, "deliberately expresses his own emotional life and his personal views of the world" (275). The lyric unfolds itself in self-expression and renders the individual inner life at the expense of external people, ob-

---

24. Whatever is not directly quoted from Hegel on the lyric mode is summarized from *The Philosophy of Fine Art*, 4:155–294.

jects, or events. External objects or events enter into the lyric mode only insofar as they express the inner life and bear the impress of the individual's inner vision. Hegel says that works of the lyric type "exclusively emphasize those characteristics of a given event which are consistent with the state of the inner life" (220). The lyric mode typically stops short of any practical impulse and seldom issues in definitive action or dramatic conflict. Hegel insists that the lyric poet himself "must be further presupposed as the focus and in fact realized content of lyrical poetry. . . . His exclusive expression and activity is . . . restricted to the fact that he endows his inner experience with an articulate speech such as portrays the spiritual significance of himself as subject in his self-expression" (214).

Beyond being a source for Stephen's definition of the lyric form, Hegel's analysis of the lyric provides a formula for the whole subjective narrative perspective of *Portrait*, for the eradication of the external world except as Stephen experiences it, and for the fact that the novel stops short of any definitive, dramatic action on his part—all of which will be discussed in subsequent sections of this chapter.

If we turn to Stephen's definition of the epic form, we find that its qualities also appear in Hegel. For Stephen the epic form proceeds out of the lyric: "The simplest epical form is seen emerging out of lyrical literature when the artist prolongs and broods upon himself as the centre of an epical event and this form progresses till the centre of emotional gravity is equidistant from the artist himself and from others. The narrative is no longer purely personal. The personality of the artist passes into the narration itself, flowing round and round the persons and the action like a vital sea" (214–15).

Stephen's description of the epic corresponds to what Hegel calls the dramatic mode, which combines the objectivity of the epic with the subjectivity of the lyric. Because it synthesizes the qualities of the other two, Hegel sees the dramatic as the highest phase of poetry. But otherwise his description of its qualities resembles Stephen's characterization of the epic form. For Hegel in the dramatic form the individual is not isolated but seen in relation to others and to the course of external events. The lives of others and the appearance of events have more objective reality than in the lyric mode; although they receive their significance from their relation to the subjective passions and volition of the individual protagonist, they are not totally absorbed into his consciousness. The protagonist in turn achieves his self-realization in terms of and by means of his conflict with others and with the course of events. The inner soul-life, in other words, is expressed through its realization in the external world.[25] This life "asserts itself, when, in its entire personality it is confronted with other personalities . . . and comes thereby into active contact with the world around it" (103–5). For both Stephen and Hegel, then, the image or content is rendered in terms of the interaction of a subjective consciousness with people and events external to that consciousness, and the artistic emphasis or focus falls neither on the individual consciousness nor on the external world but on the mediation or conflict between the two.

In Stephen's analysis the third and highest form of art is the dramatic, which emerges from the epic. His reasons, however, for preferring the dramatic differ from Hegel's, and he assigns to the dramatic form those qualities Hegel found in the epic. According to Stephen, in the dramatic form the artist "presents his image in immediate relation to others." In his famous characterization of the dramatic, Stephen says:

> The dramatic form is reached when the vitality which has flowed and eddied round each person fills every person with such vital force that he or she assumes a proper and intangible esthetic life. The personality of the artist, at first a cry or a cadence or a mood and then a fluid and lambent narrative, finally refines itself out of existence, impersonalises itself, so to speak. The esthetic image in the dramatic form is life purified in and reprojected from the human imagination. The mystery of esthetic like that of material creation is accomplished. The artist, like the God of the creation, remains within or behind or beyond or above his handiwork, invisible, refined out of existence, indifferent, paring his fingernails. (215)

Stephen's description of the dramatic form—which contains echoes of Pater's style as well as Pater's notion in the "Conclusion" of the dissolution of the self—corresponds to Hegel's epic mode. According to

---

25. Hegel's views on the dramatic mode are summarized from *The Philosophy of Fine Art*, 4:248–65.

Hegel, epic poetry renders its content "in the form of objective characters, exploits, and events" (293–94). He says that the epic poet, minstrel, or narrator must remain aloof and independent from the narrative contents and that he is "not permitted wholly to identify his own personality with their substance" (102–3). In the epic mode the subjective inner life of the poet must "fall into the background and become lost in his *subject*" (Hegel's emphasis) and the "creator himself vanish behind the world he unfolds to our vision." The content of the epic, which expresses his soul-life only indirectly, appears "to pass before us self-begotten, a work of independent birth" (116–17). But the subjective inner life of the poet can only disappear, according to Hegel, insofar as "the entire world of objects and relations are essentially absorbed by it and then permitted to stand forth freely from the veiled presence of the individual consciousness" (193). Or, as Stephen expresses essentially the same idea, life is "purified in and reprojected" from the artist's imagination. For Hegel, then, in the epic form "the poet projects himself into the *objective* world, which is set before us in the independent form and movement of its own reality" (219; Hegel's emphasis). In short, except for the fingernails, Hegel's conception of the epic form accounts for all the qualities of Stephen's dramatic ideal.

One question that has arisen in many discussions of Stephen's lyric-epic-dramatic paradigm is whether *Portrait* itself is lyric or dramatic. Interestingly enough, the answer depends on how you sort out the kind of ambiguity we find in Hegel's confusion of artist and persona, or in Stephen's terms, the artist and his image. If you focus on the relationship between Stephen as persona and the contents of the narrative, then *Portrait* conforms to Hegel's and Stephen's notion of the lyric as a subjective outcry of the individual soul that absorbs the external world into itself. If you focus on Joyce the artist, then it depends on how much distance you perceive between him and Stephen as his image. If you identify Joyce with Stephen, *Portrait* is lyric; but if you don't, and you perceive Joyce the artist as disappearing behind the contents of his narrative, then it is dramatic according to Stephen's definition (or epic according to Hegel's).

Stephen's epistemological orientation and his schematic progression of the literary arts are not the only German imports in his aesthetics. His distinction between static and kinetic art, his definition of rhythm, his characterization of beauty as "the most satisfying rela-tions of the sensible" (208), and his notion of aesthetic universality can be traced through Coleridge to their roots in Kant's analysis of aesthetic experience. To be sure, Kant was not alone in discussing these issues, some of which can be found in Plato and Aristotle, as well as in Aquinas, but Stephen's formulation of them has a distinctly Kantian character that cannot be found in the classical and scholastic sources he cites.

Stephen's discussion of tragic pity and terror is a good example of how he recasts a classical notion in a Kantian perspective. Stephen's analysis of pity and terror does not focus on the notion of catharsis but rather on the notion of arrest or stasis.[26] For Stephen tragic pity and terror are emotions that arrest the mind "in the presence of what-soever is grave and constant in human sufferings." Improper art (for example, pornographic or didactic art) is kinetic, according to Stephen, in that it excites either desire to possess something or loath-ing to avoid it. True aesthetic emotions, on the other hand, are static, and the "mind is arrested and raised above desire and loathing." Kinetic emotions are "purely physical," whereas "ideal pity" and "ideal terror" belong to a "mental world." If art excludes "good and evil which excite desire and loathing," it also must be distinguished from truth, which appeals only to the intellect: "Truth," says Stephen, "is beheld by the intellect which is appeased by the most satisfying relations of the intelligible: beauty is beheld by the imagination which is appeased by the most satisfying relations of the sensible" (204–8).

To properly illuminate Stephen's analysis of the static nature of the tragic emotions, we must turn to Kant rather than to Aristotle. For Kant purely aesthetic experience is addressed not to the objective in-tellect or cognition, but to the imagination and its subjective capacity for feeling pleasure or pain (37–38).[27] This aesthetic feeling differs

---

26. Aubert (144–45) says Joyce found all he needed on the issue of pity and terror in Butcher's commentary on the *Poetics*, Bosanquet's *A History of Aesthetic*, and Aris-totle's *De Anima* and *Metaphysics*. Stephen's basic definitions of pity and terror, how-ever, add nothing that could not have been synthesized from Butcher's commentary (pp. 255–70 of the Dover edition [New York: 1951]), while his Kantian emphasis on stasis is found in none of these sources.

27. Page references to Kant's *Critique of Judgment* are to the translation by J. H. Bernard (New York: Hafner, 1951).

from the merely pleasant, which simply gratifies the senses, and from the good, which satisfies by means of a cognitive judgment, in that the aesthetic experience of pleasure or pain is the result of a pure, disinterested, intuitive contemplation of the "relation of the representative powers to one another" (39–45, 56). By this Kant means that a judgment of pure beauty makes reference to neither the faculty of desire nor to any rational concept of the good; rather it is an entirely disinterested satisfaction induced by the internal purposiveness or formal relations within an aesthetic object, or as Kant says, the contemplation of the "agreement of the manifold with a unity" (63). This is Kant's famous formalist criterion of "purposiveness without purpose" (62), that is, the sense of purposiveness gained from contemplation of the internal design of an object without any external purpose.

Stephen renders Kant's formalist criterion in his definition of rhythm, which he says is what calls forth, prolongs, and dissolves the aesthetic stasis he is describing: "—Rhythm, said Stephen, is the first formal esthetic relation of part to part in any esthetic whole or of an esthetic whole to its part or parts or of any part to the esthetic whole of which it is a part" (206). This definition exaggerates to the point of parody Kant's notion of the disinterested contemplation of the "agreement of the manifold with a unity"; but, at the same time, it also maintains the central epistemological thrust of Stephen's argument, for the definition of rhythm, and thus also of stasis, corresponds to *claritas* or *quidditas*, the third phase of perception, in which the object is perceived as both a whole and a harmony of its parts.

I am not suggesting here that Joyce necessarily read Kant, for analyses of Kant's aesthetics were available to him, for example, in Bosanquet's *A History of Aesthetic*, which Joyce was familiar with, as Aubert has shown. Coleridge, however, also provided a very faithful Kantian analysis of aesthetic experience, particularly in his essay "On the Principles of Genial Criticism Concerning the Fine Arts,"[28] which repeats Kant's analysis of the beautiful as distinct from the merely agreeable and the good. Coleridge also renders the notion of "Multëity in Unity," which he says is "the most general definition of beauty," in

---

28. This essay first appeared in 1814 and was reprinted in 1837, 1855, and 1907. I have used the 1907 version that appears in *Biographia Literaria Edited with His Aesthetical Essays*, ed. J. Shawcross (Oxford: Oxford University Press, 1907), vol. 2. Subsequent page references to Coleridge's essay are to this edition.

terms very close to Stephen's definition of rhythm. One passage in particular captures the essence of his Kantian argument in language that anticipates Stephen's characterization of stasis and rhythm:

> *The sense of beauty subsists in simultaneous intuition of the relation of parts, each to each, and of all to a whole: exciting an immediate and absolute complacency, without intervenence, therefore, of any interest, sensual or intellectual.* The BEAUTIFUL is thus at once distinguished both from the AGREEABLE, which is beneath it, and from the GOOD, which is above it: for both these have an interest necessarily attached to them: both act on the WILL, and excite a desire for the actual existence of the image or idea contemplated: while the sense of beauty rests gratified in the mere contemplation or intuition. (239; Coleridge's emphases)

The language in this passage is very close to Stephen's. Joyce uses the word *stasis* for Coleridge's weaker term *complacency*, and he assigns the word *rhythm* to the relationship of the parts to the whole, but otherwise Stephen's ideas are pure Kant as transmitted through Coleridge.

Another issue in Stephen's aesthetics that can be traced to Kant through Coleridge is that of the universality of aesthetic judgments. Stephen says, "Though the same object may not seem beautiful to all people, all people who admire a beautiful object find in it certain relations which satisfy and coincide with the stages themselves of all esthetic apprehension. These relations of the sensible, visible to you through one form and to me through another, must be therefore the necessary qualities of beauty" (209). With his mention of the stages of aesthetic apprehension, Stephen has turned this notion of universality slightly toward his Hegelian epistemological progression, but essentially he had maintained Kant's notion of subjective universality and Kant's limitation of aesthetic experience to the "most satisfying relations of the sensible." For Kant, since aesthetic judgments are subjective, their grounds for universality can lie neither in the art object nor in concepts about what art should be. But if the judgment of beauty is to be more than a matter of individual taste, then it must *impute*, if not *postulate*, the "agreement of everyone." In other words, an aesthetic judgment "expects, not confirmation by concepts, but assent from others" (45–54). Coleridge renders this notion as "we *declare* an object beautiful, and feel an inward right to *expect* that others should coincide with us. But we feel no right to *demand* it" (242; Coleridge's emphases).

Kant's explanation of universality is the least satisfactory of all his aesthetic criteria, but what he appears to mean when he says the "conditions of universality" hold "for everyone who is determined to judge by means of understanding and sense in combination (i.e., for every man)" (54) is that universal assent can be expected because every human being possesses the same innate faculties for perceiving satisfying relations of the sensible, and these faculties, for Kant as for Hegel, are the primary faculties of perception. This is essentially what Stephen is saying, only much more clearly than Kant, when he says that "all people who admire a beautiful object find in it certain relations which satisfy and coincide with the stages themselves of all esthetic apprehension" (209).

Stephen's analysis of aesthetics, with its emphasis on logical necessity, on perception, and on the object of perception being perceived first as a unity, then analyzed into its component parts, and finally synthesized into a unified manifold should have suggested long ago the epistemology and aesthetics of Kant and Hegel; but Stephen's superficial use of Aristotle and Aquinas has diverted the attention of scholars as successfully as it diverts the attention of Lynch from the sources of both his modernity and the governing principles of his "applied Aquinas."

At one point in the discourse with Lynch, one of Stephen's frequent citations of Aquinas prompts Lynch to interrupt him: "—It amuses me vastly, he said, to hear you quoting him time after time like a jolly round friar. Are you laughing in your sleeve?" (209) This is a very good question, and it raises another good question: Is Joyce laughing in his sleeve?

Despite the German character of Stephen's aesthetics, the only Germans mentioned in *Portrait* are Lessing and Goethe. At one point in their conversation, Stephen and Lynch encounter a fat student named Donovan, who, apropos of Stephen's interest in aesthetics, says, "—Goethe and Lessing . . . have written a lot on that subject, the classical school and the romantic school and all that. The *Laocoon* interested me very much when I read it. Of course it is idealistic, German, ultraprofound" (211). Stephen does not reply, but when Donovan departs, Stephen embarks on his Romantic analysis of the "necessary phases of artistic apprehension" and the lyric-epic-dramatic progression that follows from it. It is in this part of his discourse that, like Hegel, he criticizes Lessing for concentrating on the inferior art of sculpture—inferior because it does not present the three forms of art clearly distinguished from one another. Donovan's remark, then, is the only hint Joyce gives us about the German nature of Stephen's aesthetics.

If Stephen was aware of his own debt to the Germans, Joyce, keeping the joke to himself, did not pass that awareness on to the reader. We are told at the beginning of chapter 5 that Stephen's mind sometimes "wearied of its search for the essence of beauty amid the spectral words of Aristotle or Aquinas" and that the "lore which he was believed to pass his days brooding upon . . . was only a garner of slender sentences from Aristotle's poetics and psychology and a *Synopsis Philosophiae Scholasticae ad mentem divi Thomae*" (176–77). Notice the careful wording of this last statement: it does not say the "lore he brooded upon" but the "lore which he was believed to pass his days brooding upon." In other words, the narrator does not give Stephen's secret away even to the reader.

At another point Stephen himself laments his parochial and outdated education: he feels "that the monkish learning, in terms of which he was striving to forge out an esthetic philosophy, was held no higher by the age he lived in than the subtle and curious jargons of heraldry and falconry" (180). And in his encounter with the dean of studies Stephen, who is only replying politely and with exaggerated modesty to the dean he sees as a servile mental laborer, says that he is using "one or two ideas of Aristotle and Aquinas" for his own immediate purposes but that he has no enduring commitment to them (187).

These various remarks by Stephen and about him are slyly inconclusive. We could perceive Joyce as portraying an aspiring young aesthete whose parochial education has ill-equipped him for his intellectual journey. This is the bumptious, sophomoric pretender Hugh Kenner sees. Or Joyce could be castigating Stephen's Jesuit education by allowing Stephen to surpass the limitations of his formal schooling in his discourse with Lynch, a discourse that actually employs the most current aesthetic thought of the time. It is hard to believe, however, that

Joyce was making fun of Stephen by using snippets of Aristotle and Aquinas to mask current European thought on aesthetics, especially when Joyce himself took pride in being au courant and looked to Europe for intellectual and social salvation. In other words, it appears that both Stephen and Joyce *were* laughing in their sleeves, and that Joyce has perpetrated an intellectual practical joke by drawing the red herrings of Aristotle and Aquinas across the path of scholarly inquiry, a joke that has successfully diverted his critics for the past seven decades.

STRUCTURAL DIALECTICS

STEPHEN'S AESTHETIC theory, however, is not the only manifestation of German thought in *Portrait*. The structure of the novel reflects the dialectics between sense and spirit fundamental to idealist philosophy, and the course of Stephen's development conforms to the evolution of the human spirit outlined by Hegel. Although the structure of *Portrait* does not follow Hegel in every respect, most of the deviations can be accounted for by Schiller's analysis of the aesthetic and by the general British tendency we find in Pater to psychologize the transcendentals of German thought and render them in terms of the finite experience of the individual.

Although a few critics have noticed dialectical patterns in *Portrait*,[29] none have elaborated on them, and most of the structural studies have taken their cue from Stephen's explicit concern with his Jesuit background, with Aristotle and Aquinas, and with heretical mystics like Giordano Bruno. Consequently most of the specifically structural studies of the novel employ a Christian paradigm, such as Sidney Feshbach's "ladder of perfection," Thomas Van Laan's *Spiritual Exercises* of St. Ignatius Loyola, or Robert Andreach's "fivefold division of the spiritual life" from Christian mysticism.[30] Typically these analyses

---

29. Hugh Kenner, *Dublin's Joyce* (1956; Gloucester, Mass.: Peter Smith, 1969), p. 129; Dorothy van Ghent, *The English Novel: Form and Function* (New York: Holt, Rinehart and Winston, 1953), pp. 270, 275. Without using the term, Ellmann also describes a dialectical structure in *Portrait* (*James Joyce*, pp. 297–99).

30. Sidney Feshbach, "A Slow and Dark Birth: A Study of the Organization of *A Portrait of the Artist as a Young Man*," *James Joyce Quarterly* 4 (1967): 289–300;

illuminate the novel up to a point but then leave much unexplained; or they must strain to make the evidence of the text fit the Christian paradigm. Andreach, for example, claims that *Portrait* "is built upon the stages of the fivefold division of the spiritual life" of Christian mysticism, but, he is forced to admit, "with a difference—the order of the stages is reversed and the individual stages are inverted."[31] Feshbach's excellent analysis combines Ellmann's emphasis on the gestation of the soul with his own application of the five levels of the Christian "ladder of perfection" from vegetative through animal, human, angelic to divine. Feshbach, however, has trouble explaining why in chapter 4 Stephen, who has supposedly evolved to the angelic stage at this point, dedicates himself to "the stagnation of vegetable life" (162).[32]

Ellmann's emphasis on the gestation of the soul remains the soundest structural paradigm for *Portrait*, but it can be elaborated in a way that is more comprehensive and illuminating than the Christian analyses. Although *Portrait*, along with *Stephen Hero*, the 1904 essay "A Portrait of the Artist," and Joyce's notebooks, has provided ample fodder to sustain decades of Christian analyses, like everything else in Joyce's writing, his use of motifs drawn from Catholicism was governed in the hierarchies of his mind by higher, secular, aesthetic principles. At the time Joyce was writing *Portrait*, the most comprehensive model available for the gestation of the human soul on every level was Hegel's. Hegel's elaborate analysis dealt with the soul from the simple act of individual perception to the evolution of a collective cultural *Geist* through history, and it had the advantage of offering a secular philosophical description of the human spirit to supplant the theological models of the Christian tradition. If we can accept Stephen's aesthetics as predominantly Hegelian, it should not be difficult to accept that Hegelian dialectics govern the structure of *Portrait*.

Thomas F. Van Laan, "The Meditative Structure of Joyce's *Portrait*," *James Joyce Quarterly* 1 (1964): 3–13; Robert J. Andreach, *Studies in Structure* (Bronx, N.Y.: Fordham University Press, 1964), pp. 40–71.

31. Andreach, p. 40.

32. Feshbach says somewhat obscurely that Stephen's choice of the vegetable life here "may correspond to the angelic *intellectus speculativus* in which the soul apprehends knowledge and discriminates between the true and false" (295).

In contrast to other structural paradigms that have been applied to *Portrait*, a Hegelian model can account for a number of things more consistently and more comprehensively: the intensely subjective focus of the narrative technique; the dialectical progression of the five chapters from Stephen's predominantly sensuous response in the first chapter to his predominantly intellectual response in the last chapter; the dialectical structures within each chapter and scene; the character of Stephen's major epiphany on the strand; the relations generally between sense and intellect throughout the novel; the necessity for Stephen's *non serviam* gesture—his rejection of family, country, and religion; the apparent inconclusiveness of Stephen's development in the final chapter; and finally, the privileged status of the aesthetic sensibility in Stephen's development.

Of particular importance to the structure of *Portrait* is Hegel's progression from the immediacy of intuitive, unreflective sensory perception through various stages of analytic, reflective mediation to the highest level of cognitive integration constituted by a self-conscious awareness of both the initial sense perception and the various processes by which the mind comprehends it. For Hegel this dialectical progression operates in all forms of cognition from a single individual perception, which Stephen uses as his model for *quidditas*, to the historical evolution of culture and an all-inclusive philosophical system. In the movement from individual perception to philosophic system, each completed dialectical circuit gives rise to successively larger circles. Hegel calls the highest levels of integration the realm of absolute spirit, and the kind of knowledge appropriate to this realm is represented by art, religion, and philosophy. At this level sensory experience is present, but it is completely saturated with mind or *Geist*. For Hegel art represents a balance between sense and spirit, but in his evolutionary scheme art was only a way station for the human spirit, whose ultimate destination is the realm of pure spirit represented by philosophy. In Hegel's scheme the human spirit passes from poetry, the highest of the arts, into the prose of religion and philosophy.

Although Joyce renders Hegelian ideas in terms of individual psychology—the growth of a young boy into a young man—this application of dialectics is encouraged by Hegel himself, who often used the development of a man from the embryo through the boy educating himself to the maturity of adulthood as an analogy for his whole system. Hegel also insisted that the individual mind passed through the same sequence of stages as the general mind, a process Pater represents explicitly in *Marius, Gaston,* and *Plato and Platonism.* Consequently, Hegel and Pater provided Joyce with a precedent for perceiving the macrocosmic development of the human spirit, or the conscience of a race, in terms of the growth of the individual.

Following Hegel's progression, *Portrait* traces the development of an individual soul from its earliest sensory impressions through various stages of integration of sense and spirit to its abstract reflections on art, religion, and philosophy. While the overall structure of *Portrait* reflects a completed dialectical movement in Stephen's experience, that movement is not finished by any means; for just as the overall dialectic contains many dialectic circles within it, so it too will be contained within subsequent movements in Stephen's life, as it is, for example, in *Ulysses.* Hugh Kenner has already noted that each chapter arrives at a synthesis which is dissolved in the next,[33] but the same could be said of each separate section; and the dialectical oppositions that dominate each section also reflect the major oppositions of the whole.[34] This kind of relationship between the parts and the whole is what Stephen suggests in his definition of rhythm. Each chapter and section of *Portrait* also deals with a separate phase of Stephen's development, and from beginning to end Stephen's soul undergoes a whole series of dialectical advances reflected in the structure of the novel.

The first scene of *Portrait,* comprising only one and a half pages, presents Stephen as an embryonic Hegelian spirit and establishes the primary dialectical forces in his life. The novel opens in the realm of almost pure sense experience as Joyce renders the world around the infant Stephen almost exclusively in terms of what he hears, sees, feels, smells, and tastes: his father tells him a story and sings him a song; he sees his father's hairy face and notes the smells of his mother and father as well as the oil sheet on his bed; he dances while his mother plays the piano, and he hears Dante and Uncle Charles clap for him; he notes Dante's two brushes and that the Vances live nearby. The operations of Stephen's intellect at this point are minimal: he con-

---

33. Kenner, p. 129.

34. Yeats's system in *A Vision* also uses this type of Hegelian model with circles operating within and begetting other circles.

nects lemon platt with the road the moo cow traveled; he repeats the song inaccurately; and he repeats phrases from his mother's and Dante's objections to his statement that he is going to marry the Protestant Eileen. While much goes on in this scene symbolically, Stephen is depicted as a toddler responding to experience primarily through sense, memory of sensory stimuli, and a few very elementary operations of reflection. This scene corresponds to the first stage of Hegelian dialectic, the state of the unreflecting, uncomprehending, raw immediacy of sensation.

The dialectical forces operating on Stephen's experience are arranged symbolically in this opening scene in such a way that the scene becomes a microcosm of the whole novel. Here all the opposing elements that form Stephen's sensibility and environment are introduced. Two sets of oppositions in particular orchestrate the dialectic for the rest of the novel—the contrast between father and mother and the contrasting colors of green and maroon on the velvet backs of Dante's brushes. Throughout the novel Simon Dedalus and the color green are linked together and symbolically associated with the sensory and the terrestrial in Stephen's life while his mother and the color maroon are associated with his spiritual existence.

Stephen's associations with his father involve several central motifs in *Portrait*. In the opening scene Stephen connects his father with his interest in sound that leads to his poetic vocation. His father tells him stories and sings him songs that he tries to repeat. Later we learn that Stephen also acquires his father's talent as a mimic (29, 75–76). Other associations with the father are not as positive—he has a hairy face, and he does not smell as nice as his mother. Later, in the Christmas dinner scene, Simon Dedalus is linked with the Parnell faction in the dialectic between politics and religion that terrorizes young Stephen and throws his allegiances into confusion. In the second chapter the negative associations with the father build as both the family's decline into squalor and Stephen's own degrading sexual fantasies merge in a vision provoked by the word *foetus* that Stephen sees carved in a desk in one of his father's old classrooms (89–90). Evoked by the word, his father's past, his family life, and his own adolescent sexuality (all related to his physical existence) oppress and humiliate Stephen. Later, from the more distanced perspective of his art, Stephen can recapture "the misrule and confusion of his father's house," but even then it remains associated with a very earthy image—"the stagnation of vegetable life" (162).

In contrast to his earthbound, stagnant father, Stephen's mother nourishes his spiritual side. In the opening scene she accompanies him on the piano as her brother Uncle Charles and Dante clap. Together the three of them provide him with encouragement, reassurance, and support. Stephen, however, has negative associations with his mother, as well as with his father. Along with Dante, the mother represents the oppressive authority of religion in his life (the eagles who will come to pull out his eyes). In Stephen's religious conscience the Virgin is also linked with his mother. Later, after Stephen rejects his religious upbringing, his spiritual aspirations manifest themselves secularly in his aesthetic ideals. His muse, for example, appearing as the temptress of his villanelle, replaces his mother and the Virgin as the maternal nourisher of his spirit.

The contrasting colors of green and maroon are closely linked to the opposition between father and mother, and they first appear in the image of the green rose in Stephen's confused rendering of the song on the opening page and then again almost immediately in the contrasting backs of Dante's brushes. Later Dante's green-backed brush becomes associated with Parnell, Irish politics, and nationalism, while the maroon-backed brush is linked to Michael Davitt and the Catholic Church's opposition to Parnell (16–17). The significance of these oppositions is further developed in the coloring and the verse which Fleming had put in Stephen's geography book (15–16). The first page of the book depicts the earth as "a big ball in the middle of clouds," and Fleming had colored the earth green and the clouds maroon "like the two brushes in Dante's press." Fleming's verse—

> Stephen Dedalus is my name,
> Ireland is my nation.
> Clongowes is my dwellingplace
> And heaven my expectation.

—sets up an opposition between Stephen's terrestrial dwelling place and his heavenly aspirations that reflects the contrast between the green earth and maroon clouds. The verse was written on the page facing the flyleaf where Stephen himself had written a list beginning with his own name and proceeding through successively larger geographic contexts, each including the preceding one, and ending with "The Universe." Stephen's list suggests the progressively larger contexts of Hegelian dialectics, and Fleming's opposition in both his coloring and his verse between the earth and the heavens turns out to be prophetic of the dialectical poles that will govern Stephen's life. For example, after experiencing his major epiphany in which his artistic vocation reveals itself to him, Stephen lies on "the earth that had borne him" and in a sunset contemplates "the heavenly bodies," which a moment later as he falls asleep transform themselves into another Dante's (the poet's) multifoliate rose "breaking in full crimson and unfolding and fading to palest rose" (172). The opposition, then, between green earth and maroon heavens sets up the fundamental dialectic between sensory experience and spiritual aspiration that becomes Stephen's fate. Under the color green we can cluster a number of associations that represent his sensuous existence—his father, his interest in sound, Ireland, the squalor of family life, and the squalor of his own sensuous lusts. Under the color maroon we can cluster his mother, Dante, religion, and his spiritual aspirations generally.

Later Stephen feels he must reject family, country, and religion in order to secure the necessary freedom to be an artist; but, at the same time, what he rejects has formed his artistic sensibility and constitutes the dialectic within which he must work out his destiny. Although the specific images that represent the dialectic forces in Stephen's life are drawn from Joyce's particular background, these images are grounded in the universal dialectics of sense and spirit, thus insuring that Stephen's struggle represents not only that of the artist but also that of all humanity. And the major features of that dialectic are all established in the brief scene that opens the novel.

Hugh Kenner has noted how "the action of each of the five chapters is really the same action."[35] If we define that action as dialectic, the same can be said of each episode within the chapters. In the second episode the father/mother–green/maroon dialectic of the preceding episode is supplanted by the hot and cold flashes Stephen feels as he comes down with a fever. Coldness is what Stephen associates with

---

35. Kenner, p. 129.

Clongowes, where he has been shoved into the urinal ditch by Wells. Opposed to his chilly associations with his school and schoolmates, who intimidate him, are Stephen's warm memories of the security of home and the even warmer fantasies of the coming Christmas holidays. This hot/cold—home/school dialectic is superseded in the next scene as Stephen's warm fantasies are quickly extinguished by the violent dialectics of the Christmas dinner argument, in which the conflict between politics and religion is mirrored in the divisions they cause in the Dedalus family. In the episode following Christmas dinner Stephen has returned to school and he is punished as an innocent victim and scapegoat for the unnamed sins of others, sins that caused the Jesuit teachers to crack down on "lazy idle schemers." Here the dialectic is a moral one in which Stephen opposes his individual sense of justice to the authority of the priests.

If we look closely at the movement in the first chapter, we see that Stephen proceeds from family to school to family and back to school. The movement, however, also exposes the young Stephen to successively larger spheres of involvement in life. From the narrow sphere of home and neighborhood in the opening scene, Stephen moves to a day at Clongowes where the focus is on Stephen's relationship with his schoolmates. His return home at Christmas is not a return to the cozy world he remembers; rather he is thrust into a larger, more violent realm of politics and religion. His subsequent return to school focuses less on his relations with his peers than on his Jesuit mentors, as he is propelled into a moral sphere where the just relationship between the needs of the individual and the needs of a social institution is unbalanced by the cloud of sin and the assumption of innate guilt. By the end of the chapter Stephen's natural boyhood allegiances to home, family, school, religion, politics, and teachers have been betrayed and frustrated. He has been confused and persecuted by all the objects of his attachments. Nevertheless Stephen's development can be gauged by his going forth into successively wider spheres of experience, each with its own dialectic and each overlapping the others. The first chapter, then, brings him through his early childhood and prepares him for the dialectics of puberty and adolescence, which dominate the next two chapters.

It is easy enough to find dialectic oppositions in each episode of the remaining chapters as Stephen's soul continues to be tempered by his experience. The core of the dialectical structure of *Portrait*, however, is constituted by the middle three chapters as a whole, where in the course of his adolescence Stephen proceeds on a more advanced level than in chapter 1 through another dialectical oscillation between sense and spirit. This central dialectic is resolved, temporarily at least, in the discovery of his artistic vocation. While a Hegelian dialectical progression still governs the general development of these central chapters, Schiller's more aesthetically oriented dialectics illuminate the specific patterns and details of these chapters better than the Hegelian model. As with Pater, Joyce's idealism leaned more toward Schiller's privileging of aesthetic experience in the reconciliation of sense and spirit than toward Hegel's more abstract realms of absolute spirit.

In the second and third chapters of *Portrait* Joyce has Stephen progress through two stages that are analogous to Schiller's distinction between the "sensuous drive" (*Stofftrieb*) and the "formal drive" (*Formtrieb*). The sensuous drive, to recall Schiller's *Aesthetic Education*, "proceeds from the physical existence of man, or his sensuous nature" and binds him to the laws of that nature: "It is indeed to this sensuous drive that the whole of man's phenomenal existence is ultimately tied . . . [and] with indestructible chains it binds the ever-soaring spirit to the world of sense" (78–81). In chapter 2 of *Portrait* Joyce renders Schiller's sense drive in terms of the declining fortunes of Stephen's family life and the debasing humiliations of his adolescent sexuality. The level of sensuality is on a more advanced plane of psychic integration than the relatively unreflective nature of the young Stephen in chapter 1, but it nevertheless begins another dialectical circle with Stephen's response to a sensuous environment. By the end of the second chapter Stephen's soul is clearly fettered by the domestic squalor of the Dedalus household, which engulfs and alienates him, and by the "jeweleyed harlots" of his adolescent imagination, who "sweep across and abase his intellect" (90, 115). This chapter concludes appropriately with Stephen acting out his fantasies in the arms of a prostitute.

Although this sensual stage of Stephen's adolescence alienates him from his family and himself, and although his spirit withers before the humiliation of his external environment and the degradation of his psychic life, this stage is nevertheless necessary to the dialectical evolution of his spirit, for the soul, in Nietzschean fashion, must descend into its own baseness and recognize it for what it is in order to overcome it. At this point Stephen himself sees "his own soul going forth to experience, unfolding itself sin by sin" (103).

In the next phase of Stephen's development the suffocating squalor of his family and personal life is negated when he reforms as a result of the retreat sermon. During the sermon, hell is described vividly in terms of the eternal punishment of each of the five senses, and Stephen mends his ways by denying his senses and bringing each of them "under a rigorous discipline" (150). It is not long, however, before Stephen finds his new spiritual purity as unsatisfying as indulging his lust. This movement from raw sense to pure spirit along with its attendant dissatisfactions can be explained readily by the dialectics of Schiller and Hegel.

Hegel considered both raw sense perception and analytic reflection to be abstract because in themselves they were incomplete. Schiller believed that human nature would be imperfect if either the sense impulse or the formal impulse predominated. Both Schiller and Hegel also held that the human spirit must pass through the aesthetic phase, in which sense and spirit are equally developed, in order to pass on to the higher phases of religion and philosophy. According to Schiller's Kantian analysis, to pass directly from the physical to the moral without passing through the aesthetic leads to a false application of reason that produces insatiable yearnings for the infinite and for absolute assurances beyond the natural world. Should one make this false passage from sense to reason, Schiller says, "The spirit in which he worships God is therefore fear, which degrades him, not reverence, which exalts him in his own estimation" (178–79).

As a result of the fear induced in him by the retreat sermon, Stephen makes this false passage from a predominant indulgence in his sensory environment, which he had found oppressive and demeaning even before the retreat sermon, to a predominance of spirit over sense without passing through an aesthetic phase. In Schiller's terms, a perverse application of reason, which here takes the form of Father Arnall's use of St. Ignatius's *Spiritual Exercises* and Pinamonti's tract "Hell Opened to Christians,"[36] leads Stephen to reject the sen-

---

36. For the relevance of the *Spiritual Exercises* and Pinamonti's tract, see Don Gifford's *Notes for Joyce: Dubliners and* A Portrait of the Artist as a Young Man (New York: Dutton, 1967), pp. 115–18.

suous world altogether. Although Joyce renders Schiller's formal or rational impulse in a peculiarly Irish Catholic form, thus transposing it from a logical to a theological foundation, this impulse nevertheless operates like Schiller's formal impulse in liberating Stephen from the laws of his sensuous nature, and Joyce's use of Ignatius and Pinamonti satisfies Schiller's conditions for the false application of reason.

After his bifurcation of experience into purely sensual and purely spiritual components, Stephen enters his aesthetic phase, which brings the two impulses previously at war within him into harmonious balance. In chapter 4 Stephen's resolve to purify his life of sensual indulgence gradually wanes, and after a vocation interview with the director of his school, Stephen rejects his religion, for all practical purposes, and rededicates himself to the world of sense. Instead of the arid spirituality of his religious phase, Stephen now "smiled to think that it was this disorder, the misrule and confusion of his father's house and the stagnation of vegetable life, which was to win the day in his soul" (162). This reimmersion in the physical world is not a regression to adolescent lust, however; rather it is a true synthesis of his sensuous and rational impulses. This synthesis emerges clearly in his epiphany of the girl on the strand, experienced at the moment his artistic vocation announces itself to him:

> A girl stood before him in midstream, alone and still, gazing out to sea. She seemed like one whom magic had changed into the likeness of a strange and beautiful sea-bird. Her long slender bare legs were delicate as a crane's and pure save where an emerald trail of seaweed had fashioned itself as a sign upon the flesh. Her thighs, fuller and softhued as ivory, were bared almost to the hips where the white fringes of her drawers were like featherings of soft white down. Her slateblue skirts were kilted boldly about her waist and dovetailed behind her. Her bosom was as a bird's soft and slight, slight and soft as the breast of some darkplumaged dove. But her long fair hair was girlish: and girlish, and touched with the wonder of mortal beauty, her face. (171)

This description of the girl, sensuous but not coarse or vulgar, is an idealized sensuality—neither the gross sensuality associated with the prostitute nor the pure spirituality of the Virgin, who became Stephen's patroness during his period of religious reform. She is like the Greek statues that for Hegel embodied the perfect fusion of sense and Idea.

Winckelmann had been largely responsible for the views on Greek sculpture held by the German idealists and their followers, and Joyce's description of the girl echoes Pater's essay on Winckelmann at the same time that it imitates Pater's own passages of purple prose. Pater had described Winckelmann's sensibility as having a childlike sensuousness that enabled him to finger pagan marbles "with no sense of shame or loss" (*Ren.*, 222). Likewise, Stephen gazes with the eyes of an artist on the wading girl, skirt hiked, in all her sensuous detail; and she returns his gaze "without shame or wantonness," that is, without the shame induced by religious conscience and without the wantonness arising from libidinous desires. Like Pater's aesthetic ideal, Joyce's ideal is a reconciled fusion of the heavenly and the profane, of the spirit and the flesh; like Greek sculpture it is an idealized form of the sensible world; and like Gaston's view of Ronsard's poetry, Stephen's epiphany turns the details of physical life into the artist's gold as the girl becomes "touched with the wonder of mortal beauty." As Schiller says that the realm of the aesthetic extends upward to reason as well as downward toward the world of sense (216–17), and as Hegel insists that "the sensuous is *spiritualized* in art," that "the life of *spirit* comes to dwell in it under sensuous guise" (1:53; Hegel's emphases), so Stephen's soul cries out "—Heavenly God! . . . in an outburst of profane joy" (171). Joyce, then, fulfills the aesthetic ideal of Pater, Schiller, and Hegel in his description of the wading girl by endowing his own notion of ideal beauty with sensuous form.

After achieving the aesthetic synthesis of sense and spirit at the end of chapter 4, Stephen appears to make little progress toward maturity in either his life or his art in chapter 5, a chapter that often has puzzled critics. Stephen's progress emerges more clearly, however, if we compare Stephen's relations with his family, peers, and teachers in this chapter with previous chapters, and if we perceive those relations in terms of the dialectical paradigms of Schiller and Hegel. In this light Stephen still does not emerge as a mature artist or a completed being in any sense, but we understand better why Joyce leaves him on the eve of his departure from Ireland for a yet wider sphere of experience in Europe.

The first episode of chapter 5, which renders a day in Stephen's life as a university student, repeats the second episode of chapter 1, which renders a day in Stephen's life at Clongowes. But this opening episode of the final chapter also reveals Stephen's relationship with his family, peers, and teachers, and so it also repeats on a new level most of the important relationships in Stephen's life. The episode opens amid the destitution of the Dedalus household. In the midst of a lousemarked box of pawn tickets and a battered alarm clock that does not keep correct time, Stephen has a breakfast of watery tea and fried bread-crusts. The condition of Stephen's body mirrors the squalor of his environment: he is so dirty that his mother must "scrub his neck and root into the folds of his ears and into the interstices at the wings of his nose." His father imperiously commands his brood with shrill, angry whistles and by lashing them with curses. His mother laments the scandalous changes that university life has wrought in her son. Stephen escapes this scene of domestic squalor through a trash-laden lane amid the screeches of mad nuns from a nearby asylum. Once out of his home environment, however, Stephen's soul, "loosed of her miseries," revels in a world of literary allusion, Elizabethan song, and speculations on Aristotle and Aquinas (174–77).

At the university Stephen is surrounded by students and teachers who fail to appeal either to Stephen's intellect or to his imagination. He cannot sympathize with the narrow-minded enthusiasms of his fellow students, and Stephen uses them mainly as sounding boards for his own thoughts and feelings. In a conversation with one of his Jesuit teachers Stephen finds him to be a weary, joyless, servile priest.

Stephen's relationships with his family, schoolmates, and teachers in this episode, then, contrast sharply with his previous experience. As a young boy in his first year at Clongowes, Stephen had looked to home and family for warmth and assurance only to be terrorized by political and religious dissension. Later he was engulfed and oppressed by the family's decline. As a young man, however, he expects nothing from home and family but poverty of body and spirit. Likewise, whereas at Clongowes and Belvedere Stephen was intimidated and persecuted by his schoolmates and teachers, at the university he holds himself aloof, beyond their reach, and he treats friends and teachers alike with condescension in his thoughts if not in his manners, which are usually deferential. In his own mind Stephen has risen above all the oppressive forces of his physical and mental environment that have threatened, in Schiller's terms, to fetter his aspiring spirit, or in Joyce's terms, to cast nets about his soul.

Thus we find Stephen escaping again from a sensuous world that oppresses him into an intellectual world of literary allusions and philosophical speculation. He had tried to escape the confines of the flesh once before as a consequence of the retreat sermon; but this time his motive is not fear, and he has passed through an aesthetic phase, symbolized by his epiphany of the girl on the strand, where he brought his sensuous and rational natures into harmony with each other.

The difference the aesthetic makes for Stephen becomes evident if we refer Stephen's position and activities as a university student to the paradigms of Schiller and Hegel, for this final chapter can be perceived fruitfully as a finite, psychological analogue both to Schiller's notion of the aesthetic condition and to Hegel's realm of absolute spirit. Indeed, Schiller's formulation of the aesthetic condition provides an eloquent rationale for Stephen's position and behavior. For Schiller the aesthetic condition paradoxically contains our sensuous and rational natures and simultaneously denies the laws or constraints they impose. His rationale is that the aesthetic is not the realm of action but the "ground of possibility" of all action. Since it constitutes the realm of the possible, it is not bound by the laws that govern only the actual. Beauty for Schiller is free from both passion and morality. Thus the initial denial of the laws of the actual physical and moral world in the aesthetic condition is prerequisite to their full implementation (150–61).

Schiller's analysis of the aesthetic accounts for Stephen's aloofness from family, friends, and teachers, and even from his own emotions, an aloofness Stephen maintains not only at the end but throughout the novel. At one point when persecuted by Heron, Stephen notes that he is actually incapable of the intense emotions of love and hate (82), and the momentary arousal of anger while he is composing his villanelle puts to rout his poetic inspiration, which returns only when the anger subsides (220–21). Schiller's aesthetic condition also accounts for Stephen's *non serviam* gesture, his compulsion to deny his entire environment—family, nationality, language, religion—and all the bonds and allegiances they entail.

All through the final chapter Stephen's mind repeatedly gravitates to the realm of aesthetics. This gravitation, combined with the final distancing of himself from the constraints of his physical and intellectual environment, suggests less that Stephen has or will become an artist than that he has achieved the freedom of the aesthetic condition, which is, according to Schiller, the necessary enabling condition for all truly meaningful human endeavor. Although Joyce has rendered Schiller's aesthetic condition in the finite terms of Stephen's individual psychology and circumstances, Stephen's position nevertheless conforms to the privileging of aesthetic experience that can be traced from Kant through Schiller, Hegel, Shelley, Pater, Wilde, and Yeats, to Joyce. That Stephen arrives by the end of *Portrait* at the necessary enabling condition of all meaningful experience explains why it is an appropriate concluding point for both a portrait of the artist as a young man and for the gestation period of a soul. It also explains why the conclusion of *Portrait*, which stops short of any significant action on Stephen's part, is more a beginning than an end.

If we turn from Schiller's aesthetic condition to Hegel's realm of absolute spirit, even more light can be shed on the final chapter. The realm of Hegel's absolute spirit, we recall, includes art, religion, and philosophy, and the mind in this realm exhibits an intensely self-conscious awareness of itself in the act of knowing. Here the world of sense perception remains only as it has been assimilated and purified by the rational spirit. In chapter 5 Stephen's mind seems to be inhabiting a realm very much like Hegel's absolute. He engages in all three activities that characterize this realm: he writes a poem, discusses religion with Cranly and aesthetics with Lynch. He also tells Lynch, "We are just now in a mental world" (206); and as many critics have noted, his own thoughts remain aloof and detached from the physical and mental environment around him. There are still some insistent intrusions upon Stephen's reveries by the unregenerate world of sense, such as the "hoydenish" flower girl who dispels his idealization of Davin's story of a young peasant woman; but as his discourse with Lynch and the composition of his villanelle show, in this stage Stephen typically assimilates the physical world into an idealized realm of aesthetic speculation and creativity. The resemblances, of course, between Stephen's mental activities and Hegel's realm of absolute spirit must be seen in the light of Pater's typically British adaptation of Hegelian absolutes to the finite experience of the individual. But if the perfection and completeness of Hegel's absolute idea are reduced to finite psychology, key qualities of the realm of absolute spirit are preserved, even if we view Stephen's meditations as a parody of Hegel.

These qualities include the pattern of movement from sense to spirit, the intensely reflective self-consciousness, and the rarefied mental atmosphere.

These Hegelian qualities of absolute spirit are part of what brands Stephen in this chapter as a rather typical turn-of-the-century aesthete;[37] for the aesthetics of the nineties and the pose of the aesthete derived ultimately from the German idealists. Stephen's villanelle in particular typifies poems of the nineties with its vague, world-weary rhythms and its temptress, who, like Pater's Mona Lisa, combines the corruption and worldliness of prostitutes with the ideality of the Virgin. After composing the poem Stephen imagines himself coupling with his idealized temptress in a reverie that echoes the "measureless consummation" Yeats characterizes as the ideal of nineties' poets like Lionel Johnson.[38] Reveries about temptresses and impossible consummations appear in typical nineties' poems like Johnson's "The Dark Angel" and Ernest Dowson's "Cynara." Stephen's reverie also echoes the ecstatic scene in Yeats's "Rosa Alchemica," where the entranced narrator dances with "an immortal august woman," who, like Stephen's temptress, is "more or less than human."[39]

Yeats perhaps may have acted as Joyce's local precedent for Stephen's aspiration to a realm of pure spirit as the destiny of human nature. The stories of Yeats that Joyce admired so much—"The Tables of the Law" and "The Adoration of the Magi"—embody Yeats's early belief that the arts were "about to take upon their shoulders the burdens that have fallen from the shoulders of priests, and to lead us back upon our journey by filling our thoughts with the essences of things, and not with things." In light of this belief, Yeats foresaw that "poetry will henceforth be a poetry of essences, separated one from another in little and intense poems. I think there will be much poetry of this kind," says Yeats, "because of an ever more arduous search for an almost disembodied ecstasy." According to Yeats, art like this would

---

37. For Stephen's aestheticism, see *The Workshop of Daedalus*, pp. 249–63; and Robert Scholes, "Stephen Dedalus, Poet or Aesthete?" *PMLA* 79 (1964): 484–89, reprinted in the Viking Critical Edition of *A Portrait of the Artist as a Young Man*, ed. Chester G. Anderson (New York: Viking, 1968), pp. 468–80.

38. *The Poems of W. B. Yeats*, p. 132.

39. *Mythologies*, pp. 289–90.

pass "upward into ever-growing subtlety . . . until at last . . . what seems literature becomes religion,"[40] just as in Hegel's realm of absolute spirit poetry passes into the prose of religion and philosophy. Although Joyce did not share Yeats's passion for the occult and the supernatural, Stephen's villanelle is just such a poem as Yeats describes. While Joyce was familiar, as his notebooks and numerous allusions in his fiction testify, with many of the same Neoplatonic sources Yeats drew from for his prophecy of a future realm of pure spirit, sources such as Joachim, Bruno, and the alchemists, both Yeats and Joyce would have found a powerful nonmystical reinforcement for the prophecy in Hegel's dialectical evolution of the human spirit into the realm of absolute spirit.

Like Yeats, Joyce ultimately declined to pursue Hegelian dialectic beyond art into the more rarefied realms of absolute spirit. Yeats's antidote to his nineties' aspirations for disembodied ecstasy was a return to the sensuous world in his poetry after 1900. While Joyce allows Stephen to pass over the border between poetry and the prose of thought into philosophic speculation, he does limit his application of Hegel, as Pater did, to the finite realm of individual psychology. In *Ulysses* Joyce provided an even stronger antidote for Stephen's intellectuality in the sensuous, down-to-earth personality of Leopold Bloom. This return to the senses in order to strike a balance between sense and spirit is a movement we find in many early Modernists besides Yeats and Joyce, and this movement conforms to the typically British adaptation of Hegel we find in Pater. Unlike Hegel, his British followers could not be content for very long in a realm of pure spirit, particularly if they were artists. Consequently they often preferred a more balanced fusion of sense and intellect in art, and like Pater they followed Hegel only so far as his Hellenic ideal, where the Idea is balanced equally with its sensuous form.

While the Hegelian absolute accounts for the mental atmosphere of *Portrait*'s last chapter, Hegelian dialectics also offer insight into Stephen's gesture of *non serviam*. In Hegel's thought, negation works a little differently than in Schiller's, and so the light it sheds on the conclusion of *Portrait* is somewhat different yet at the same time com-

---

40. *Essays and Introductions*, pp. 193–94, 266–67.

plementary to that shed by Schiller's notion of the aesthetic condition. For Hegel, at each stage of dialectic the previous stage is negated, not for the purpose of dismissing it entirely but as a prelude to assimilating that negated stage into the higher synthesis of the next level. As with Pater's Marius, all of Stephen's denials can be seen in this light, particularly if we identify Stephen with the young Joyce. Joyce rejected family, country, and religion through his self-imposed exile, but only to embrace them all again at a safer distance and a higher level of synthesis in his art. Likewise, Stephen's negations throughout the book can be seen as necessary to his development as an artist.

That Stephen completed Hegel's dialectical circle does not mean that at the end of *Portrait* he is a complete human being or artist. Joyce was too much of a skeptic to arrive at so pat a conclusion. Like most Modernists, Joyce could not share Hegel's evolutionary optimism; yet at the same time in *Portrait* he shares Hegel's and Pater's insistence that dialectic is a continuous, lifelong process and that its goal is not to arrive at some foreordained conclusion, but rather the goal is the entire process itself from beginning to end. This process in *Portrait* corresponds to the gestation or tempering of Stephen's soul, and by the end of the novel Stephen has completed only a small portion of what Pater calls the lifelong dialectic of the mind with itself, a dialectic in which the last infallible word "never gets spoken" (*PP*, 183,188,192). Stephen himself recognizes, after his epiphany on the strand, that he is only beginning, that his soul is only about to be born, and from here it goes "on and on and on and on" (172). After *Portrait* Stephen will proceed to another phase at a higher level of integration. We witness that phase in *Ulysses* where Bloom symbolically fertilizes Stephen's spirit yet another time.

For *Portrait* and for Modernist art generally, Hegel's dialectics and aesthetics, modified by Schiller's privileging of the aesthetic and restricted in its application by the British empirical temper to a finite psychological world, provide a powerful interpretive paradigm. This paradigm, eloquently articulated by Pater, does not necessarily supersede other paradigms, nor does it solve all the interpretive problems of *Portrait*. For example, if we perceive Stephen rising to successively higher levels of dialectical synthesis, we need not necessarily project that Stephen becomes the artist Joyce became. We can still agree with Hugh Kenner that in *Ulysses* Joyce rejects Stephen as too limited and incorporates him into a larger synthesis that includes Bloom as his dialectical opposite. The dialectical paradigm, in other words, cannot dictate the choice of one view of Stephen over the other any better than other paradigms have. Nevertheless, while the British Hegelian paradigm may not be able to settle all disputes over *Portrait*, at least it shifts their grounds to another level and in the process accounts for a number of the significant structural features of the novel.

PORTRAIT AND THE AESTHETICS OF EXPRESSION

HEGELIAN AESTHETICS led Joyce, as they did Pater, to formulate his own views of art in terms of an expressive orientation. Pater took Hegel's definition of art as the sensible manifestation of the absolute idea and converted it to a psychological rather than a transcendental notion by having the work of art express in sensible form not an absolute idea but the inner vision of the individual artist. In *Portrait* Joyce carries this development further by forging new techniques and forms to embody an expressive orientation in fiction as the subjective consciousness of a single character.[41]

Critics who read *Portrait* according to Stephen's ideal of dramatic art in which the author refines himself out of existence tend to empha-

---

41. In *Stephen Hero* Joyce had not psychologized his Hegelianism to the degree he did in *Portrait*, and he had retained the Hegelian notion of zeitgeist as constitutive of the artist's inner vision:

> . . . every age must look for its sanction to its poets and philosophers. The poet is the intense centre of the life of his age to which he stands in a relation than which none can be more vital. He alone is capable of absorbing in himself the life that surrounds him and of flinging it abroad again amid planetary music. . . . The age, though it bury itself fathoms deep in formulas and machinery, has need of these realities [of truth and beauty] which alone give and sustain life and it must await from those chosen centres of vivification the force to live, the security for life which can come to it only from them. Thus the spirit of man makes a continual affirmation. (*SH*, 80)

This continual affirmation of the spirit of man is what art accomplishes in the Hegelian scheme of things. While Joyce saw all his writing as an affirmation of the human spirit, the explicit notion of a universal zeitgeist was sacrificed in *Portrait* for the intensely subjective focus, a subjectivity that nevertheless retains its universality because founded on Hegelian principles.

size the objectivity of Joyce's technique and to ignore the subjective epistemological foundations of the novel. Harry Levin pointed out long ago that in writing *Portrait* Joyce "transferred the scene of action from the social to the psychological sphere," and the "claims to objectivity of a subjective novel . . . must be based on its rendering of intimate experience."[42] In other words, the objectivity of the novel is dependent, in dialectical fashion, on the precise rendering of Stephen's psychic interior, on the ability of Joyce to lose himself in the contents of his character's mind, or alternatively to completely express himself by saturating those contents with his own spirit. Joyce, like Pater, Flaubert, and Hegel before him, was very much aware that as an artist he could express only himself, that is, he could present only a vision of the world that had been purified and reprojected from his own imagination.

As with Pater's notion of subjectivity, however, the subjectivity of Joyce's technique is not a matter of mere solipsism, a purely individual subjectivity; rather it is a philosophical subjectivity compounded out of the empirical tradition of Berkeley and Hume and the tradition of German idealism, particularly as formulated by the dialectics of Hegel. This epistemological subjectivity pervaded turn-of-the-century aesthetics, and in England it could be traced through writers like Pater, Wilde, and Yeats to Joyce. In literature, as elsewhere, manifestations of this subjectivity were often mistaken for mere solipsism in contrast to literature based on traditional Aristotelian techniques, because those traditional techniques were founded on pre-Kantian philosophies of substance that looked out on a supposedly objective universe. This pre-Kantian world view, however, was no longer tenable for the modern mind, as Virginia Woolf recognized in her essay "Modern Fiction" when she exhorted writers to abandon Aristotle and imitate Joyce. Woolf's essay illustrates the response generally of early Modernist writers to the challenge issued to artists by the subjective premises of Hume and Hegel, a challenge that was formulated for them by Pater and that called for new techniques to render the internal external.

---

42. *James Joyce: A Critical Introduction* (New York: New Directions, 1941), pp. 48–49.

Critics who judge Stephen harshly because he seems to be so remote from real life have been looking for that life in the wrong place. Far from seeing the new techniques of *Portrait* as remote from life, Virginia Woolf, for example, saw them as much closer than the old techniques to life itself. Of course, Woolf—like Hume, Hegel, Pater, and Joyce—had redefined life as an interior mental universe and relocated it, in Woolf's terms, "close to the quick of the mind." If we judge Stephen harshly because we perceive more of his mind than of the world around him, then we are judging him according to standards contrary to the whole thrust of the aesthetics that inform the novel. If we perceive *Portrait* as converting Pater's aesthetics of expression into literary techniques, that is, as an artistic rendering or dramatization of an expressive orientation, then we can account equally for both the objectivity and the subjectivity of Joyce's techniques, for, like Stephen's dramatic ideal, Pater's theory of expression provides a very productive paradigm for interpreting *Portrait* but without ignoring the subjectivity of its focus and technique.

Like Pater's characterization of Diaphaneitè and Wordsworth, Joyce's artist combines an exquisitely sensitive capacity of reception with a formidable talent for projection whose function is to reveal the precise contours of the artist's vision by projecting it into an external concrete form. In *Stephen Hero*, in a passage Joyce did not preserve in *Portrait*, Stephen's ideal for art is expressed in terms that closely resemble Pater's diaphanous ideal:

> The artist, he imagined, standing in the position of mediator between the world of his experience and the world of his dreams—"a mediator, consequently gifted with twin faculties, a selective faculty and a reproductive faculty." To equate these faculties was the secret of artistic success: the artist who could disentangle the subtle soul of the image from its mesh of defining circumstances most exactly and "re-embody" it in artistic circumstances chosen as the most exact for it in its new office, he was the supreme artist. This perfect coincidence of the two artistic faculties Stephen called poetry. (*SH*, 77–78)

Although Joyce eliminated this passage when he rewrote *Stephen Hero* as *Portrait*, he did not alter the expressive orientation it espouses. Instead he condensed several lengthy discussions of aesthetics into the single discourse with Lynch, and he embodied the expressive orientation more appropriately in the form and techniques of the novel. Rather than merely stating the ideal of Pater's "Diaphaneitè"—"to be shown to the world as he really is"—and telling us that "as he comes nearer and nearer to perfection, the veil of an outer life not simply expressive of the inward becomes thinner and thinner" (MS, 249), Joyce shows dramatically that as Stephen matures the outside world around him gradually recedes, as in Hegel's characterization of the lyric mode, until at the end it is visible only as the external form that bears the intimate impress of his own soul.

Other evidence of Joyce's expressive orientation abounds in Portrait; but instead of being explicit, it is typically implicit in the structure, themes, and techniques of the novel. Another place where Joyce embeds the expressive orientation of his aesthetics is in the nature of Stephen's gradual evolution as an artist. In chapter 2 when the prepubescent Stephen fixates on the character of Mercedes from The Count of Monte Cristo as the object of his desire, Joyce characterizes his search for some manifestation of her in the real world in terms that express at the level of individual psychology Hegel's notion of art as the sensuous manifestation of the Idea. In his quest for Mercedes Stephen "wanted to meet in the real world the unsubstantial image which his soul so constantly beheld" (65). This desire to find the sensuous embodiment that answers to his inner vision becomes in Portrait one of the distinguishing traits of the aesthetic temperament. In a sense the entire novel is founded on Stephen's effort to find or realize his dream in concrete form. The dream vision takes different forms at different times, and Mercedes is only one of a network of female images that represent Stephen's aesthetic ideal. Others include the Virgin, the temptress of the villanelle, Rosie O'Grady, and the Emma of Stephen's imagination. Stephen's encounters with females in the real world, including his mother, Emma, and prostitutes, all reflect his inability to find his ideal in the flesh. The only instance in which the real and the ideal resonate with each other is the epiphany of the girl wading on the strand.

As Stephen matures this expressive ideal becomes more explicit. Near the end of chapter 4, as the vocation of the artist is about to announce itself to Stephen, he begins to realize that it is not so much "the reflection of the glowing sensible world through the prism of a language manycoloured and richly storied" that fascinates him but rather "the contemplation of an inner world of individual emotions mirrored perfectly in a lucid supple periodic prose" (166–67). This ideal did not constitute a complete rejection of the sensible world for Stephen but only a rejection of whatever in that world did not answer to the emotions of his own spirit. The task of the artist is, as he tells Lynch, "to express, to press out again, from the gross earth or what it brings forth, from sound and shape and colour which are the prison gates of our soul, an image of beauty we have come to understand" (206). This image may begin in the sensible world; however, it is not presented finally in its raw state but rather as it is transformed and purified in the virgin womb of the artist's imagination. The purification is accomplished in Hegelian fashion by commingling the life of the body with the "element of the spirit" (169).

At the end of the novel Stephen is not yet the artist he desires to become; he is still searching for his Mercedes, for the perfectly adequate concrete form to embody his own personal vision of beauty in the world. Distinguishing his quest from Yeats's nostalgia for the past, Stephen writes in his diary, "Michael Robartes remembers forgotten beauty and, when his arms wrap her round, he presses in his arms the loveliness which has long faded from the world. Not this. Not at all. I desire to press in my arms the loveliness which has not yet come into the world" (251). Joyce leaves Stephen on the eve of his departure from Ireland to seek this loveliness, this sensuous manifestation of his own inner vision of beauty, in lands more congenial to his questing spirit.

Like many other elements in Joyce's intellectual temper, the Hegelian character of Stephen's expressive ideal was anticipated by Pater. Pater's Leonardo sought and found his dream vision in the real world; and after Marius has his quasi-mystical vision in which he glimpses an ideal world, the narrator asks, "Must not all that remained of life be but a search for the equivalent of that Ideal, among so-called actual things—a gathering together of every trace or token of it, which his actual experience might present?" (*ME* 2:72). So Pater's Leonardo and Marius are counterparts to Stephen in his quest to "meet in the real world the unsubstantial image which his soul so constantly beheld." To be sure, there are significant differences between the inner visions of Marius and Stephen. Marius's vision was a transcendental intuition of a world harmonized by a powerful force or energy, while Stephen's was the more finite quest of the artist to find in the world about him the materials through which he could express his own spirit. If Stephen's failure to achieve his ideal by the end of *Portrait* is any indication, Joyce was also less sanguine than Pater about the chances of finding one's ideal. Pater once said, "To many at least of those who can detect the ideal through the disturbing circumstances which belong to all actual institutions in the world, it was already there" (*EG*, 34). Pater is referring here to the institution of the Catholic Church, in which Joyce found no ideal but rather considered it one of the nets that constrained the spirit. Despite these differences, however, both Pater and Joyce pursue the ideal in the Hegelian terms of expressing the human spirit through the gross matter of the earth, which then becomes transformed in the process into the beauty of art.

There is even a precedent in Pater for identifying Daedalus as the symbolic figure of the craftsman who could effect the transformation of gross matter into artistic beauty. In "The Beginnings of Greek Sculpture" (1880) Pater says, "The heroic age of Greek art is the age of the hero as smith," and "Daedalus is the mythical, or all but mythical, representative of all those arts which are combined in the making of lovelier idols than had heretofore been seen" (*GS*, 193, 237). Pater would have found Daedalus an altogether appropriate figure for his namesake Stephen to invoke as he seeks to create "loveliness which has not yet come into this world," and for Joyce himself to invoke in his epigraph to *Portrait* as one who sets his mind to work upon unknown arts ("ignotas animum dimittit in artes"). Pater perceived the daedal craft of the early Greek artisan in typical Hegelian fashion as "the endeavour to record what his soul conceived" of his experience in the world he inhabited (*GS*, 235), which is exactly what Joyce records of Stephen's experience in the Dublin of his own times. The Daedalus seen through Pater, then, is more than merely a figure of the artist cunningly devoted to his craft. Pater's Daedalus is also the symbol of the Hegelian artist, "a symbol," to use Joyce's memorable phrasing, "of the artist forging anew in his workshop out of the sluggish matter of the earth a new soaring impalpable imperishable being" (169).

The expressive orientation of Stephen's quest for a sensuous form that answers to his vision within is also evident in his interest in the psychology of creation, which justifies his invocation of Shelley's fading-coal metaphor to explain to Lynch his conception of *quidditas*. Most critics mistakenly have located Stephen's quality of *quidditas* in the work of art and not in the creative perception of the artist. For Stephen, as for Shelley, the momentary glow of the coal is not an attribute of the work or of the reader's response but of the artist's mind. Shelley's image of the fading coal suggests the unconscious nature of the instant of creative inspiration, inspiration which is "already on the decline" at the onset of composition: "The most glorious poetry that has ever been communicated to the world," says Shelley following Plotinus, "is probably a feeble shadow of the original conceptions of the poet."[43] Stephen does not emphasize the unconscious nature of inspiration; but rather he identifies it with the third stage of aesthetic apprehension—the synthesis he calls *radiance* that follows "logically and aesthetically" from the wholeness of *integritas* and the harmonious relations of parts that is *consonantia*. What was an unconscious, almost mystical, process for Shelley is demythologized by Stephen into a logico-aesthetic dialectic, but Stephen still retains Shelley's focus on the "original conceptions of the poet." In other words, Stephen maintains the Romantic interest in the psychology of creation and on the synthesis that takes place not in the work of art but in the artist's imagination.

Failure to acknowledge the expressive orientation of *Portrait* and of Stephen's aesthetics has led critics into difficulties over the interpretation of Stephen's villanelle. From the expressive viewpoint, arguments about the aesthetic merits of the villanelle are misguided.[44] The section containing the villanelle immediately follows the discourse on aesthetics with Lynch, and its composition does not function to either justify or vilify Stephen's artistic ambition; rather it serves, as Bernard

---

43. "A Defence of Poetry," in *The Selected Poetry and Prose of Percy Bysshe Shelley*, ed. Carlos Baker (New York: Modern Library, 1951), p. 517.

44. For example, see Scholes, "Stephen Dedalus, Poet or Aesthete?"; Wayne Booth, *The Rhetoric of Fiction*, pp. 328–30; and Charles Rossman, "Stephen Dedalus' Villanelle," *James Joyce Quarterly* 12 (1974): 281–93.

Benstock has pointed out,[45] as a concrete illustration of the creative process that Stephen discusses only abstractly with Lynch. As such an illustration Joyce's description of the villanelle's composition is a masterpiece, whether or not one likes the villanelle or even agrees with its characterization of the creative process. The focus of Joyce's description is on the multiple psychic origins of the poem. The proximate source is a dream, a wet dream apparently triggered by sexual fantasies about angels ("In a dream of vision he had known the ecstacy of seraphic life"). The dream draws its content from Stephen's view of Emma on the library steps the day before, from the religious icons of his Catholic upbringing, from his aspirations as an artist, and from his experience with prostitutes. His temptress, in other words, is a fusion of Emma, Virgin, whore, and muse.[46] Whatever the sources of the dream, it is clearly a moment of aesthetic stasis (the "enchantment of the heart" he told Lynch about) and an instance of the creative process Shelley characterizes by the fading-coal metaphor: "The instant flashed forth like a point of light," the narrator tells us, "and now from cloud on cloud of vague circumstance confused form was veiling softly its afterglow" (217). Clearly, even before the first words of the poem emerge, Stephen's inspiration is on the decline. Creation may be sparked by the initial flash, but composition takes place in the afterglow: "An afterglow deepened within his spirit, whence the white flame had passed, deepening to a rose and ardent light"; and once the composition had begun "the roselike glow sent forth its rays of rhyme" and image. Whatever the verbal merits of the completed villanelle, the disparity between the abstract liturgical imagery of the poem and the richly replete description of all the psychic elements that went into its composition illustrates the truth of Shelley's fading-coal metaphor and suggests perhaps why Joyce gave up verse, as he told Yeats, to pursue the art of prose as the most appropriate literary form to capture the complex intricacies of the modern mind.

As recognition of the Hegelian structure of *Portrait* does not resolve all interpretive cruxes, neither does an awareness of the expres-

---

45. "The Temptation of St. Stephen: A View of the Villanelle," *James Joyce Quarterly* 14 (1976): 37.

46. For these and other elements that enter into Stephen's villanelle, see Scholes, "Stephen Dedalus, Poet or Aesthete?"

sive aesthetics embodied in its techniques. One could still argue that Joyce's dramatization of Stephen's expressive orientation is ironic or that Joyce was parodying a Romantic mode of perception that had outlived its usefulness. Such an argument, however, would have to account for Joyce's own use in *Portrait* of techniques governed by Hegelian aesthetics of expression. Also, if Joyce wanted to parody a Romantic mode, why did he go to so much trouble to camouflage his Romantic sources with Aristotle and Aquinas?

In *Ulysses* Joyce uses other stylistic techniques that are not encompassed by an expressive orientation, but he also continues to employ dialectical structures and expressive techniques as well. For example, in the "Wandering Rocks" episode, as in *Ulysses* as a whole, the narrative styles span the entire spectrum of perceptual modes from the subjectivity of the individual consciousness to the objectivity of omniscient, disinterested observation. *Portrait*, on the other hand, exhibits none of the awareness we find in *Ulysses* of alternative modes of perception conditioned, not by the perceiving consciousness, but by the rhetorical style of the discourse itself. What we witness in *Ulysses* is Joyce's growing awareness of the limitations of the expressive paradigm he inherited from Pater and his philosophic sources. In an intellectual climate where, under the influence of thinkers like Saussure, language itself was beginning to displace the subjective consciousness as the locus of the creative process, a purely expressive theory of art could no longer satisfy a mind like Joyce's, voracious for the most current thought. *Portrait*, however, resulted from a confluence of intellectual currents that, while they prepared the way for the semiotic orientation of contemporary thought, still maintained Pater's focus on the functional nature of thought itself and on the individual consciousness—the artist's inner vision—as the creative center of thinking.

Bibliographical Appendix

Selected Studies of Pater's Relation to Major Twentieth-Century Writers and Critics

André, Robert. "Walter Pater et Marcel Proust." *La Nouvelle Revue Française* 11 (1963): 1082–89.

Arakawa, T. "T. S. Eliot's Interpretation of Arnold and Pater." *Studies in English Literature* (Tokyo) 13 (1933): 161–81.

Baker, Joseph E. "Ivory Tower as Laboratory: Pater & Proust." *Accent* 19 (1959): 204–16.

Bassett, Sharon. "The Uncanny Critic of Brasenose: Walter Pater and Modernisms." *Victorian Newsletter* 58 (1980): 10–14.

Beckson, Karl. "Yeats and The Rhymers' Club." *Yeats Studies* 1 (1971): 20–41.

Beckson, Karl, and John M. Munro. "Symons, Browning, and the Development of Modern Aesthetic." *Studies in English Literature, 1500–1900* 10 (1970): 687–99.

Beja, Morris. *Epiphany in the Modern Novel*. London: Peter Owen, 1971.

Beppu, Keiko. *The Educated Sensibility in Henry James and Walter Pater*. Tokyo: Shohakusha, 1979.

Bizot, Richard. "Pater and Yeats." *ELH* 43 (1976): 389–412.

Blissett, William. "Pater and Eliot." *University of Toronto Quarterly* 22 (1953): 261–68.

Bloom, Harold. Introduction to *Marius the Epicurean*, by Walter Pater. New York: New American Library, 1970.

——. Introduction to *Selected Writings of Walter Pater*. New York: New American Library, 1974.

————. "Late Victorian Poetry and Pater." In *Yeats*, pp. 23–37. New York: Oxford University Press, 1970.

Brown, Terence. "Walter Pater, Louis MacNeice and the Privileged Moment." *Hermathena* 114 (1972): 31–42.

Christ, Carol. "T. S. Eliot and the Victorians." *Modern Philology* 79 (1981): 157–65.

Cixous, Hélène. *The Exile of James Joyce*. Translated by Sally A. J. Purcell. New York: David Lewis, 1972.

Conlon, John J. "Eliot and Pater: Criticism in Transition." *English Literature in Transition* 25 (1982): 169–77.

Court, Franklin E. "The Matter of Pater's Influence on Bernard Berenson: Setting the Record Straight." *English Literature in Transition* 26 (1983): 16–22.

Cox, Catherine. "Pater's 'Apollo in Picardy' and Mann's *Death in Venice*." *Anglia* 86 (1968): 143–54.

D[avenport], A[rnold]. "Some Notes on 'The Waste Land.'" *Notes and Queries* 195 (1950): 365–69.

DeLaura, David J. "Echoes of Butler, Browning, Conrad, and Pater in the Poetry of T. S. Eliot." *English Language Notes* 3 (1966): 211–21.

————. "Pater and Eliot: The Origin of the 'Objective Correlative.'" *Modern Language Quarterly* 26 (1965): 426–31.

Dellamora, Richard. "Pater's Modernism: The Leonardo Essay." *University of Toronto Quarterly* 47 (1977–78): 135–50.

d'Hangest, Germain. "La place de Walter Pater dans le mouvement esthétique." *Études Anglaise* 27 (1974): 158–71.

Du Bos, Charles. *Le Dialogue avec André Gide*. Paris: Au sans Pareil, 1929.

Duffy, J. J. "Conrad and Pater: Suggestive Echoes." *Conradiana* 1.1 (1968): 45–47.

Eliot, T. S. "Arnold and Pater." In *Selected Essays*, pp. 382–93. New York: Harcourt, Brace & World, 1950.

Ellis, P. G. "The Development of T. S. Eliot's Historical Sense." *Review of English Studies* 23 (1972): 291–301.

Engelberg, Edward. *The Vast Design: Pattern in W. B. Yeats's Aesthetic*. Toronto: University of Toronto Press, 1964.

Fernandez, Ramon. "Note sur l'Esthétique de Proust." *La Nouvelle Revue Française* 31 (1928): 272–80.

Fishman, Solomon. *The Interpretation of Art: Essays on the Art Criticism of John Ruskin, Walter Pater, Clive Bell, Roger Fry, and Herbert Read.* Berkeley: University of California Press, 1963.

Fleissner, Robert F. "'Prufrock,' Pater, and Richard II: Retracing a Denial of Princeship." *American Literature* 38 (1966): 120–23.

———. "Prufrock's Ricardian Posture." *Research Studies* 47 (1979): 27–36.

Frank, Ellen Eve. *Literary Architecture: Essays Toward a Tradition: Walter Pater, Gerard Manley Hopkins, Marcel Proust, Henry James.* Berkeley: University of California Press, 1979.

Gilbert, Stuart. *James Joyce's Ulysses.* New York: Vintage, 1955.

Gordon, Jan B. "The Imaginary Portrait: Fin-de-Siècle Icon." *University of Windsor Review* 5.1 (1969): 81–104.

Hafley, James. "Walter Pater's *Marius* and the Technique of Modern Fiction." *Modern Fiction Studies* 3 (1957): 99–109.

Harris, Wendell V. "Pater as Prophet." *Criticism* 6 (1964): 349–60.

———. "The Road to and from Eliot's 'The Place of Pater.'" *Texas Studies in Language and Literature* 23 (1981): 183–96.

Hill, Charles G. "Walter Pater and the Gide–Du Bos Dialogue." *Revue de Littérature-Comparée* 41 (1967): 367–84.

Hirsch, Edward. "Yeats's Apocalyptic Horsemen." *Irish Renaissance Annual* 3 (1982): 71–92.

Hough, Graham. *The Last Romantics.* New York: Barnes and Noble, 1961.

Hulin, J. P. "Proust and Pater." *TLS* (18 July 1958): 409.

Iser, Wolfgang. *Walter Pater: Der Autonomie des Ästhetischen.* Tübingen: M. Niemeyer, 1960.

———. "Walter Pater und T. S. Eliot: Der Übergang zur Modernität." *Germanisch-romanische Monatsschrift,* Neue Folge 9 (1959): 391–408.

Killham, John. "'Ineluctable Modality' in Joyce's *Ulysses.*" *University of Toronto Quarterly* 34 (1965): 269–89.

MacNeice, Louis. *The Poetry of W. B. Yeats.* London: Oxford University Press, 1941.

Martin, Robert K. "The Paterian Mode in Forster's Fiction: *The Longest Journey* to *Pharos and Pharillon.*" In *E. M. Forster: Centenary Revaluations,* edited by Judith Scherer Herz and Robert K. Martin, pp. 99–112. London: Macmillan, 1982.

McDougal, Stuart Y. "The Presence of Pater in ' "Blandula, Tenella, Vagula." ' " *Paideuma* 4 (1975): 317–21.

McGrath, F. C. "Heroic Aestheticism: Yeats, Pater, and the Marriage of Ireland and England." *Irish University Review* 8 (1978): 183–90.

―――. "Paterian Aesthetics in Yeats's Drama." *Comparative Drama* 13 (1979): 33–48. Reprinted in *Drama in the Twentieth Century*, edited by Clifford Davidson, C. J. Gianakaris, and John H. Stroupe, pp. 122–37. New York: AMS Press, 1984.

―――. " 'Rosa Alchemica': Pater Scrutinized and Alchemized." *Yeats-Eliot Review* 5.2 (1978): 13–20.

―――. "W. B. Yeats's Double Vision of Walter Pater." In *Unaging Intellect: Essays on W. B. Yeats*, edited by Kamta C. Srivastava and Ujjal Dutta, pp. 72–84. Delhi: Doaba, 1983.

Meisel, Perry. *The Absent Father: Virginia Woolf and Walter Pater.* New Haven: Yale University Press, 1980.

Melnick, Daniel. "Yeats's Image of Culture." *Studies in the Literary Imagination* 14.1 (1981): 111–21.

Miller, Betty. "Proust and Pater." *TLS* (25 April 1958): 225.

Miller, J. Hillis. "Walter Pater: A Partial Portrait." *Daedalus* 105 (1976): 97–113.

Monsman, Gerald. "Pater and His Younger Contemporaries." *Victorian Newsletter*, no. 48 (1975): 1–9.

―――. *Walter Pater.* Boston: Twayne, 1977.

―――. *Walter Pater's Art of Autobiography.* New Haven: Yale University Press, 1980.

Morse, Samuel French. "Wallace Stevens, Bergson, Pater." *ELH* 31 (1964): 1–34.

―――. *Wallace Stevens: Poetry as Life.* New York: Pegasus, 1970.

Mourey, Gabriel. "Marcel Proust, John Ruskin et Walter Pater." *Le Monde Nouveau* 8 (1926): 702–14, 896–909.

Naremore, James. "Style as Meaning in *A Portrait of the Artist.*" *James Joyce Quarterly* 4 (1967): 331–42.

Nathan, Leonard E. *The Tragic Drama of William Butler Yeats: Figures in a Dance.* New York: Columbia University Press, 1965.

―――. "W. B. Yeats's Experiments with an Influence." *Victorian Studies* 6 (1962): 66–74.

Perlis, Alan D. "Beyond Epiphany: Pater's Aesthetic Hero in the Works of Joyce." *James Joyce Quarterly* 17 (1980): 272–79.

Praz, Mario. "Proust and Pater." *TLS* (6 June 1958): 313.

Read, Herbert. *The Tenth Muse: Essays in Criticism.* London: Routledge & Kegan Paul, 1957.

Scholes, Robert, and Richard Kain, eds. *The Workshop of Daedalus: James Joyce and the Materials for* A Portrait of the Artist as a Young Man, pp. 165, 255–58. Evanston: Northwestern University Press, 1965.

Schrickx, W. "On Giordano Bruno, Wilde and Yeats." *English Studies* (Amsterdam) 45 (Supplement 1964): 257–64.

Scotto, Robert M. " 'Visions' and 'Epiphanies': Fictional Technique in Pater's *Marius* and Joyce's *Portrait.*" *James Joyce Quarterly* 11 (1973): 41–50.

Sherman, Stuart P. "The Aesthetic Idealism of Henry James." *Nation* (NY) 104 (April 5, 1917): 393–99. Reprinted in *The Question of Henry James*, edited by F. W. Dupee, pp. 70–91. New York: Holt, 1945.

Smith, Grover. "T. S. Eliot's Lady of the Rocks." *Notes and Queries* 194 (1949): 123–25.

Sprigge, Sylvia. *Berenson: A Biography.* Boston: Houghton Mifflin, 1960.

Stone, Donald David. *Novelists in a Changing World: Meredith, James, and the Transformation of English Fiction in the 1880s.* Cambridge: Harvard University Press, 1972.

Sudrann, Jean. "Victorian Compromise and Modern Revolution." *ELH* 26 (1959): 425–44.

Temple, Ruth Z. "The Ivory Tower as Lighthouse." In *Edwardians and Late Victorians* (English Institute Essays, 1959), edited by Richard Ellmann, pp. 28–49. New York: Columbia University Press, 1960.

Tintner, Adeline R. "Another Germ for 'The Author of Beltraffio': James, Pater and Botticelli's Madonnas." *The Journal of Pre-Raphaelite Studies* 1.1 (1980): 14–20.

_____. "Henry James's Mona Lisas." *Essays in Literature* 8 (1981): 105–8.

_____. "Pater in *The Portrait of a Lady* and *The Golden Bowl*, Including Some Unpublished Henry James Letters." *The Henry James Review* 3 (1982): 80–95.

Webb, Igor. " 'Things in Themselves': Virginia Woolf's *The Waves*." *Modern Fiction Studies* 17 (1971): 570–73.

West, Paul. "Narrowed Humanism: Pater and Malraux." *Dalhousie Review* 37 (1957): 278–84.

Winner, Viola Hopkins. "The Artist and the Man in 'The Author of Beltraffio.' " *PMLA* 83 (1968): 102–8.

Yeats, W. B. Introduction to *The Oxford Book of Modern Verse: 1892–1935*. New York: Oxford University Press, 1936.

INDEX